The WORLD EATS HERE

The WORLD EATS HERE

AMAZING FOOD and the INSPIRING PEOPLE WHO MAKE IT at New York's QUEENS NIGHT MARKET

JOHN WANG AND STORM GARNER

PHOTOGRAPHY BY JOHN TAGGART

Illustrations by Beth Bugler

THE EXPERIMENT

NEW YORK

The Experiment, LLC
220 East 23rd Street, Suite 600
New York, NY 10010-4658
theexperimentpublishing.com

THE EXPERIMENT and its colophon are registered trademarks of The Experiment, LLC. Many of the designations used by manufacturers and sellers to distinguish their products are claimed as trademarks. Where those designations appear in this book and The Experiment was aware of a trademark claim, the designations have been capitalized.

The Experiment's books are available at special discounts when purchased in bulk for premiums and sales promotions as well as for fund-raising or educational use. For details, contact us at info@theexperimentpublishing.com.

Library of Congress Cataloging-in-Publication Data available upon request

ISBN 978-1-61519-663-0
Ebook ISBN 978-1-61519-664-7

Cover design, text design, and illustrations by Beth Bugler
Cover photographs by John Taggart (food), Storm Garner (crowd), and iStock.com/Alex Levine (lights, front and back)
Back cover photograph by John Taggart

Manufactured in Turkey

First printing April 2020
10 9 8 7 6 5 4 3 2 1

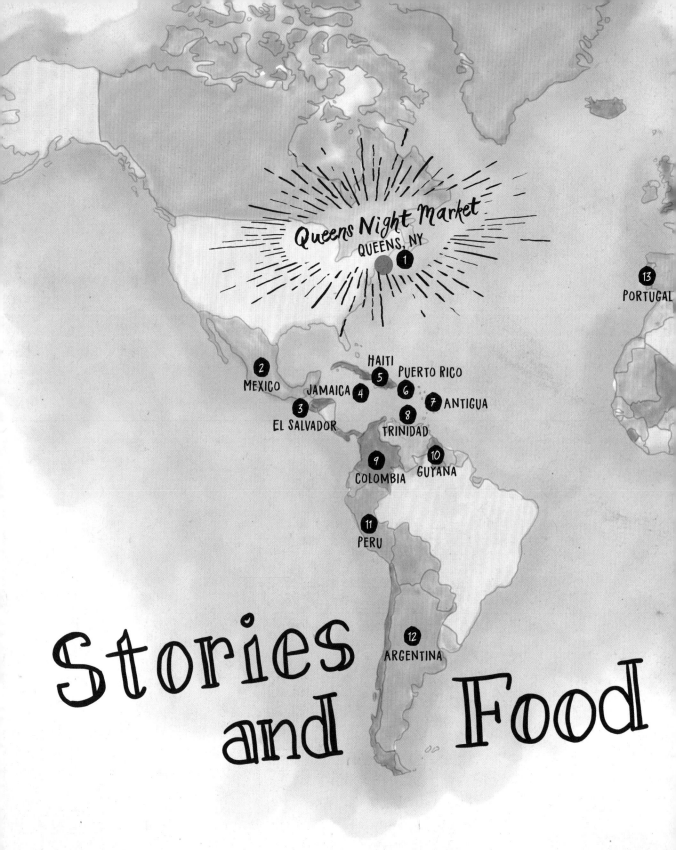

Queens Night Market
QUEENS, NY
1

13 PORTUGAL

HAITI
5
2 MEXICO
PUERTO RICO
JAMAICA
4
6
7 ANTIGUA
3
8
EL SALVADOR
TRINIDAD
9
10
COLOMBIA
GUYANA
11
PERU
12
ARGENTINA

Stories and Food

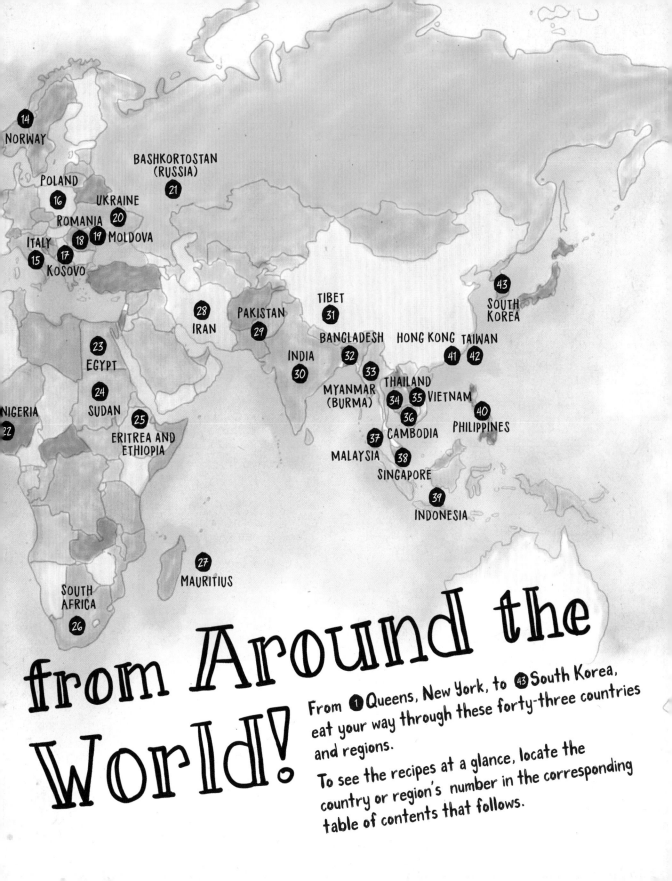

14 NORWAY

BASHKORTOSTAN (RUSSIA)
21

POLAND
16

UKRAINE
20

ROMANIA
18 19 MOLDOVA

ITALY
15

17

KOSOVO

28

PAKISTAN
29

IRAN

TIBET
31

BANGLADESH
32

HONG KONG
41

TAIWAN
42

SOUTH KOREA
43

23

EGYPT

INDIA
30

33

MYANMAR (BURMA)
34

THAILAND
35

VIETNAM

24

SUDAN

25

36

CAMBODIA

40

PHILIPPINES

NIGERIA
22

ERITREA AND ETHIOPIA

37

MALAYSIA

38

SINGAPORE

39

INDONESIA

27

MAURITIUS

SOUTH AFRICA
26

from Around the World!

From ❶ Queens, New York, to ㊸ South Korea, eat your way through these forty-three countries and regions.

To see the recipes at a glance, locate the country or region's number in the corresponding table of contents that follows.

Contents

The Americas and the Caribbean

Europe

RECIPES BY TYPE

FLATBREADS, TORTILLAS 'N' MORE—WRAPPED AND STUFFED

Huaraches with Refried Beans and Nopales 16

Tacos de Birria 20

Salvadoran Chicken Tamales 24

Arepas con huevos pericos (Arepas with Scrambled Eggs) 51

Arepas de queso (Cheese Arepas) 52

Lefse (Potato Flatbread) 78

Calzone di cipolla (Onion Calzone) 84

Ukrainian Blintzes with Creamy Mushrooms 106

Injera with Spicy Red Lentils 132

Pakistani Tandoori Chicken *Kati* Rolls 150

Dosas with Chicken Curry 154

RICE, NOODLES, AND PASTA

Diri ak djon djon (Black Mushroom Rice) 32

Puerto Rican Arroz con Pollo (Chicken and Rice) 36

Orecchiette with Broccoli Rabe 83

Kopytka (Polish Potato Gnocchi) 88

Chicken Biryani with Tomato Chutney and Cucumber Salad 138

Masala Noodles 158

Shan khao swe (Shan Noodles) 176

Laksa Noodles 202

Singaporean Nasi Lemak with Fried Chicken 208

Lugaw (Rice Porridge) 217

See yow wong chow meen (Soy Sauce Pan-Fried Noodles) 231

SOUPS AND STEWS

Antiguan Seafood Soup 40

Trinidadian Callaloo (Taro Leaf Stew) 45

Fårikål (Lamb and Cabbage Stew) 76

Ukrainian Borscht (Beet Soup) 108

Obe ata din din (Fried Stew) 118

Khoresh karafs (Beef Celery Stew) 142

Chotpoti (Chickpea and Potato Stew) 170

Ohno kaukswe (Coconut Chicken Noodle Soup) 182

Dinuguan (Pork Blood Stew) 224

PASTRIES AND SWEETS

Salvadoran Quesadillas 25

Guyanese Pine Tarts 58

Pastéis de nata (Portuguese Custard Tarts) 72

Almond Biscotti 82

Balkan Baklava 93

Kürtős kalács (Romanian Chimney Cakes) 98

Moldovan *Plăcintǎs* (Savory Cheese Pies) 102

Bashkir Farm Cheese Donuts 112

Persian Halva 145

Leche Flan 218

DRINKS

Champurrado (Mexican Hot Chocolate) 21

Antiguan Ginger Beer 42

Aguapanela con limón (Sugarcane Limeade) 52

Chicory Coffee 99

Sinh tố bơ (Avocado Smoothies) 190

Pandan Key Limeade 199

INTRODUCTION

John Wang
THE QUEENS
NIGHT MARKET

It's magic hour on a Saturday night: The summer heat melts away with the setting sun as a cross-section of the world gathers on a sliver of land tucked behind a science museum in Queens. Scents from Mauritius to Moldova to Mexico whet thousands of appetites. Family members come closer together, daring each other to taste morsels of far-flung origin. Children crowd the dance floor, replaced by grown-ups indulging in a little Cha-Cha Slide or improv tango as bedtime rolls around.

But the relaxed ease and palpable sense of joy belie the serious ambitions behind this weekly gathering: to create NYC's most diverse, welcoming, and affordable community space—and to celebrate the people, their food, and their stories that make up this incredible international city.

In a city chock-full of food fairs, food events, and food experiences, the Queens Night Market stands out among its peers. Now entering its sixth season, the Queens Night Market is NYC's most diverse food bazaar: It has drawn over a million patrons and averages nearly fifteen thousand visitors each Saturday night. But it's not trendy and fashionable, per se. It's obsessively democratic and accessible. A quick scan of the visitors reveals a uniquely representative distribution of ethnicity, age, and socioeconomic status. The food stalls themselves tend to be multigenerational family affairs, with the younger generation often taking direction from their forebears, as three generations laugh, cook, eat, and bond under the same blue 10' x 10' tent.

I was born and raised in Texas, but my love affair with night markets began during the childhood summers I spent visiting family in Taiwan. While I was there, I begged daily to explore the night markets. There's an ineffable electricity in the air when a city gathers in a welcoming space until the wee hours, oblivious to the class or cultural divides that might otherwise separate us socially. It was a feeling I wanted to replicate in NYC.

And that's how the Queens Night Market was born: out of my fondness for Taiwan's ubiquitous night markets, my distaste for the skyward cost of living in NYC, and my sheer adoration for the city's cultural and ethnic diversity. In spite of standard business school doctrine, I set out to prove that a business could cut across most socioeconomic and cultural barriers—not just in theory, but in practice. From the outset, the target demographic was *literally everyone.*

Living in a city that is increasingly unaffordable by the day, I was convinced that affordability was the single greatest equalizer. Besides, what's the point of living in a "foodie city" if few people can afford to enjoy the food? So I came up with a novel $5 price cap, with a few $6 exceptions, to help ensure that the audience would be a real mosaic of ethnicity, age, and income level.

I fully expected the headwinds to prevail, but it was exactly the kind of risky, sure-to-fail project that I had given up my corporate lawyer job to pursue. In some ways, my complete lack of experience was a blessing in disguise. The inexperience allowed me to dream without the strictures of standard practices and choruses of *it-can't-be-done*, and ultimately, to create something I would actually want to attend myself.

And it worked: To date, the event has launched *300 brand-new businesses in NYC* and represented *over 90 countries* through its food. NYC is home to more than 150 nationalities, with over 120 of them in Queens alone—and we aspire to represent all of them through our vendors one day.

Storm Garner

THE QUEENS NIGHT MARKET VENDOR STORIES ORAL HISTORY PROJECT

I met John in 2014, when he was toying with the idea of starting a night market in New York. Though I was too much of a mess to date him or anyone at the time, I fell in love with him as a friend and wanted to help actualize his dream. So using my writing and filmmaking skills, I made his first Kickstarter video, sent it to all my foodie and journalist friends, and connected him with a few people who I hoped could steer his vision toward realization.

It seems a bit risqué to admit here in a cookbook—but the truth is, as much as I love the food, I have always been more interested in the potential cultural resonance of the Queens Night Market. I believe there is some real social-healing magic to a casual, fun, accessible place—in a too-often segregated city—where the one thing I'm pretty sure everyone has in common is that we're all curious to learn about cultures different from our own.

So in 2018, once I'd determined that John would be a permanent part of my life anyway—

we got engaged, yada yada—I launched the Queens Night Market Vendor Stories Oral History Project, to document the life-stories of a wide array of the very people who make the Queens Night Market what it is—in the hopes of preserving, if not that deep magic itself, at least some hint of its essential ingredients.

In the words of Christine Jeanjaquet, Filipina owner of the gift shop The August Tree, and the very first Queens Night Market vendor I interviewed for my oral history project in December 2018: "It's too diverse to say there's a minority. And the feeling of that acceptance, that community—I felt that in the Queens Night Market. [. . .] The feeling of belonging, it's—it's a very, very, very nice place to be at."

My enrollment in the Columbia University oral history master's program connected me with Doug Boyd, the trailblazing director of the Nunn Center for Oral History, who will be working with me over the next few years to prepare the long-form, open-ended, video-recorded interviews for permanent archiving—fifty and counting as of December 2019. My goal is to make them as accessible as possible to people around the world for future educational uses: available online with video, transcripts, indexes, hyperlinked images, and multilingual translations, wherever possible.

Storm Garner interviewing Carlos Hon at BK Media Studios

Why? Because, at the very least, I believe these stories—of immigration and family histories, of culinary traditions and innovations, of day-to-day existence in NYC and memories in faraway homelands—have the power to make the world a little smaller and friendlier, and to inspire adventure, curiosity, entrepreneurship, and plain old human connection.

A technical note for the method-oriented: All of the interviews used to write the narratives in this book were conducted in 2019. Due to time constraints, for the most part, I have only been able to interview one person per Queens Night Market food-vending business so far: whoever was available and willing, whether or not they are the primary chef of the

Storm testing a gluten-free version of pastéis de nata: It worked . . . but not as good as the original!

business or the writer of the recipe submitted for the book. So now you hold in your hands not just portraits of talented cooks who've shared their cherished recipes, but also perspectives from the spouses, siblings, children, and friends who built and supported the platforms to showcase these talented cooks' creations.

It was far from easy to choose out of several hours of audio per interviewee just a few anecdotes, a few biographical tidbits, a few quotes for each story—which is, of course, far more complex than a page or two could possibly allow. The profiles in this book do not have clear beginnings, middles, and ends. No living person's story does. These narratives are far from complete, and that's the point: Above all, I hope they will make you curious to ask a few follow-up questions yourself, perhaps even in person at the Queens Night Market.

WHAT WE AND THIS BOOK ARE ALL ABOUT

Despite the three hundred food vendors from over ninety countries that have participated, we resist characterizing the Queens Night Market as a "food destination." It's not about foie gras, uni, truffle, and lobster—with the unique price caps, it really can't be. And it's certainly not about microemulsions, liquid nitrogen, molecular gastronomy, and deconstructed dishes. It's about so much more than food, food porn, or food trends. It's about the traditions and the stories accompanying the food that our vendors have chosen to share.

The Queens Night Market is built upon the specific personal histories, passions, and hard work of these vendors. We don't set out to debate what should be called "traditional" or "fusion," or what constitutes cultural appropriation. We simply insist, with few exceptions, that what each vendor sells has special relevance to their personal background and cultural heritage.

As a result, there's a sparkle in our vendors' eyes that comes from more than merely hoping to be the next celebrity chef or flash-in-the-pan viral sensation. It comes from a desire to recreate cherished culinary memories for thousands upon thousands of hungry and engaged visitors. By participating in the Queens Night Market, vendors, cooks,

and families set out not to prove a market opportunity (although that happens in the process very often), but to come together and share a piece of themselves—and, of course, to make some unbelievable food.

While a handful of Queens Night Market vendors graduated from top culinary schools, most still have careers outside the food industry. Our vendors tend to be first- and second-generation immigrants, sharing and prolonging the culinary traditions they hold dear. Our nearly singular focus on diversity and accessibility—in a city that speaks over eight hundred languages—makes the Queens Night Market a true melting pot.

This book doesn't pretend to represent all the voices and legacies of this remarkable city—it documents and highlights just a small sampling of the traditions that make up the culinary and cultural landscape of Queens and NYC.

The World Eats Here brings together eighty-eight of the best recipes from the Queens Night Market, along with the amazing stories of more than fifty vendors and chefs who've shared them with us.

A recipe may be a family secret passed down through generations, an homage to a disappearing custom, the recreation of a distant fond memory, or a little-known national treasure waiting for a spark to explode it onto the international stage. The dish may evoke a family tradition, trace a family's path from emigration to immigration, serve as the focal point of entrepreneurial ambition, illuminate an esoteric cultural quirk, memorialize a cultural celebration, or pay tribute to parents or grandparents. In many cases, the recipes in the book are being written down and documented for the first time. Many vendors are quick to note that ingredient measurements are often adjusted to taste or according to their mood, and you should feel free to do the same!

There is a mind-boggling array of delicious food served at the Queens Night Market—but for this book, we wanted to share recipes that do not require special equipment, and whose ingredients can be found in international supermarkets or ethnic grocery stores. The shopping experience is part of the fun, and adds to the cultural takeaway of following these recipes and stories—it's like going on a treasure hunt!

We hope you will learn to recreate the earthy umami of Haitian *diri ak djon djon*, the textural mélange of Burmese fermented tea leaf salad, the spongy clamminess of Eritrean injera, or the nearly overwhelming sweetness of Persian halva. And, as you enjoy the food, we hope you'll take a moment to get to know the masterminds behind them—because, while this is a cookbook filled with amazing recipes curated by John, it's also an anthology of compelling human portraits and unique, powerful voices from New York that were collected, transcribed, and edited by Storm.

Not all the vendors in this book will continue with the event. To some, the Queens Night Market is an entry point; to others, an interim milestone; and to others still, an end point. Someday, the actors will move on from our Saturday night festivities. Their stories, we hope, will endure. This book simply seeks to document a moment in time—a group portrait of some of the food and people who have made the Queens Night Market so special.

The Americas and the Caribbean

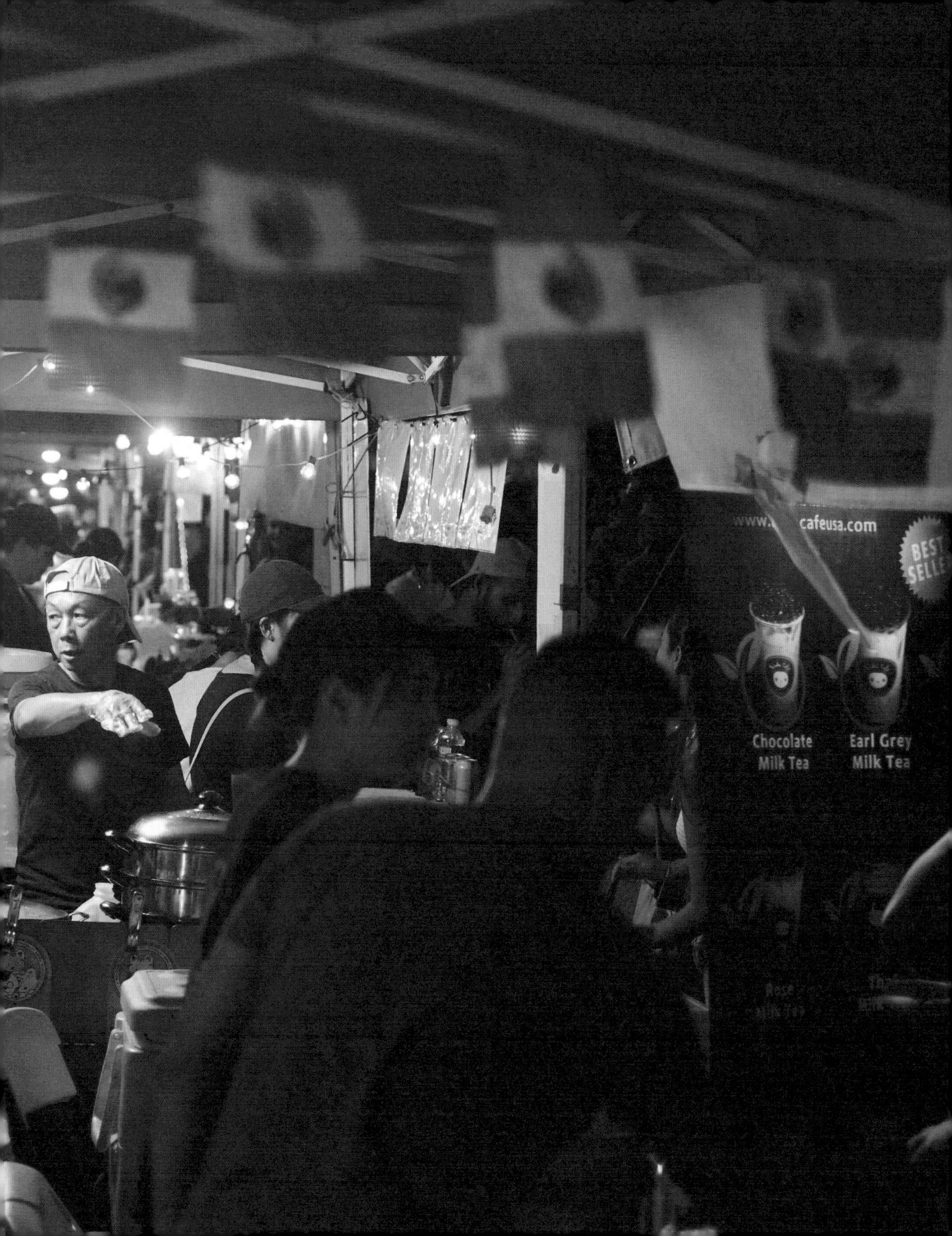
Chocolate Milk Tea
Earl Grey Milk Tea

Andrew Steinberg

BERG'S PASTRAMI
(1) NEW YORK

Growing up in Queens, New York, in the '80s and '90s, as the sixth child of an African American social worker and an Ashkenazi Jewish anthropologist-turned-film-industry-grip, Andrew Steinberg got to celebrate both Christmas *and* Chanukah every winter, with his nana's Southern soul food, and latkes with his late father's special apple-pear sauce. He remembers as a kid hearing about Mariah Carey's struggles with her biracial identity but always felt grateful for his.

"I feel like being multiethnic was the best thing. It was great! I could hang out with the Jews; I could be accepted by the African American crowd; I was accepted by the Caribbean American crowd. I don't feel like people shunned me; I just felt like I was *more* accepted. But growing up in Flushing, I think we look at ethnicity a little differently, because there's at least fifteen ethnicities in every class. Like you're friends with whoever you're friends with."

Having paid his way through college by working in restaurants already, he knew what to do when he couldn't find a teaching job during the 2008 recession after graduating with a degree in physical education: He just delved right back into the restaurant industry with gusto. Eventually, he felt he'd learned enough to start his own catering business: Chef Steinberg Catering aims to represent food from the entire

> "GROWING UP IN FLUSHING, I THINK WE LOOK AT ETHNICITY A LITTLE DIFFERENTLY, BECAUSE THERE'S AT LEAST FIFTEEN ETHNICITIES IN EVERY CLASS. LIKE YOU'RE FRIENDS WITH WHOEVER YOU'RE FRIENDS WITH."

Jewish diaspora. "I feel like in New York you have the Jewish deli, selling their matzo ball soup and their cured meats, and then you have your bagel store, and then you have your Israeli kebab place, you have your Sephardi and Bukharian restaurants. . . . So anything a Jew has ever eaten, I try to represent that on my catering menu."

Pastrami was always a bit of a fixation at family gatherings—the mere smell conjuring up whole afternoons of holiday fun with cousins—so Andrew was especially keen on mastering pastrami as part of his catering endeavor. Through extensive research and careful study of the Katz's Deli technique especially, Andrew managed to make a pastrami so good that he was soon urged to "just sell that" by friends and clients—and that was all it took: Berg's Pastrami was born as a pop-up at the Queens Night Market in the spring of 2019.

PASTRAMI SANDWICH

Andrew vividly recalls the aroma of his grandfather's pastrami, slowly smoking on the family grill. He actually didn't get to taste his grandfather's pastrami until his teenage years, when he learned that the adults had cleverly been stuffing the kids with hot dogs and burgers so they could save the pastrami all for themselves.

Andrew insists that the most important skill in making pastrami is patience. Considering he waited thirteen years to taste pastrami for the first time, and that his pastrami takes eight days to make, he seems to have patience in spades. His pastrami is worth the wait.

Toasting the spices for the rub before grinding is optional, but tasty. Serve the sandwich with a side of pickles, or just eat the pastrami by itself.

Makes 4 to 6 sandwiches

CURING

1¼ cups (360 g) kosher salt

½ cup (100 g) granulated sugar

1 tablespoon plus 1 teaspoon pink curing salt (Prague powder)*

5 pounds (2.25 kg) brisket flat (the point of the brisket can also be used for fattier pastrami)

SPICE RUB

1 cinnamon stick

¼ whole nutmeg, freshly grated

1 tablespoon mustard seeds

1 tablespoon black peppercorns

1 tablespoon coriander seeds

1½ teaspoons fennel seeds

1½ teaspoons red pepper flakes

1½ teaspoons allspice berries

4 whole cloves

Mustard

8 to 12 slices caraway rye bread

* Pink curing salt is approximately 5 percent sodium nitrate, which gives the final product a pink hue. Please keep it clearly labeled in your cupboard because ingesting large amounts can be toxic. If you choose not to add this, your pastrami will still taste delicious, but it will just have more of a grey color as opposed to reddish pink.

1. To cure the brisket, pour 1 gallon (3.75 L) water into a large pot and add the kosher salt, sugar, and pink curing salt. Heat over medium heat and stir until the salt and sugar are dissolved. Remove from the heat and let cool.

2. Place the brisket in a food-safe container, then cover with the cooled curing liquid. Refrigerate for 7 days.

3. Thoroughly rinse the brisket with cold water. Pat dry with a paper towel, then leave in the refrigerator uncovered for 8 hours.

4. To make the spice rub, combine all the ingredients in a dry pan and cook on medium-low heat, stirring occasionally, until fragrant, about 2 minutes. Allow the toasted spices to cool and then grind them with a spice grinder or mortar and pestle. Completely cover the brisket with the rub.

5. To smoke the brisket, set an electric smoker to 225°F (105°C), or set up a two-zone smoker on a charcoal grill, with one zone at around 225°F (105°C).** Smoke for 6 hours, or until the internal temperature of the meat has reached 195°F (90°C).***

6. Remove the brisket from the smoker and allow it to come to room temperature. Cover with plastic wrap and let rest in the refrigerator overnight.

7. Unwrap the brisket and steam over a lightly boiling water for 2 hours.

8. Slice the pastrami against the grain to your preferred thickness. Spread mustard on the bread slices and pile on the pastrami as desired.

Two-zone indirect heating

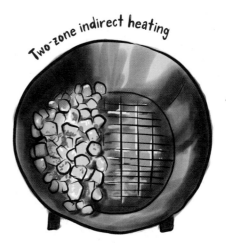

** To create a two-zone grill, place the coals and wood chunks on one side of the grill and cook with indirect heat on the other side.

*** Applewood or hickory wood is preferred for smoking.

Jeffrey Hernandez

LA CARNADA

② MEXICO

A New York–born child of immigrants from Mexico, Jeffrey grew up in Brooklyn in the '90s watching his mother, Margarita Hernandez, become a popular New York street-food phenom, selling her Mexico City–style huaraches next to a soccer field. When he was just thirteen, his father was murdered and his American passport stolen while he was on vacation visiting family. Chaos ensued. He ended up staying in Mexico City for years, even living on the streets for a while, and returning to New York hardened and hurt by the experience. Now a construction worker by day, Jeffrey credits his newfound love of reading—novels, nonfiction, anything—for giving him the hope and inspiration to finally turn around the tragedy that tore his family apart. Mastering his mother's huarache recipe and popularizing it in her honor at the Queens Night Market is a step in that direction.

"**M**y mother was selling huaraches in Red Hook for years and years. Then she started getting a lot of notoriety; people started hearing about it.

Newspapers came, television reporters came— just so much publicity on the spot that the city got involved, and they started seeing all these violations of, let's say, waste management: We'd just throw our garbage into the regular garbage cans around.

So they didn't like that, and little by little they started boosting up the prices for the permits, asking for more permits, asking for food handlers' licenses, and so many other things. They eventually told us to get trucks, and my mother was like, *OK, we'll do that,* but then after she saw that it wasn't going to be possible, she was like, *No, it's not worth it, I'm not gonna be in a truck in ninety-degree weather just for a little bit of money.* After that, she just stopped selling.

So we got kicked out, basically.

Dad would come play soccer; he had a soccer team. She was cooking for him, she took her press, she made some tortillas handmade, and people just started asking her, like, *Hey, would you sell me some food?* At first, she was like, *No, it's just for us; I'm not selling food,* but then one day she saw she had extra food and was like, *OK.* So after that, the next week, they came again, *Hey, could you sell me some food?* And she took some extra food again, and from there, it started getting bigger—she bought a bigger grill—and bigger, until she finally put up her spot.

When she started I was like nine, eight—around there. I remember sleeping over there, like under a table. She would just put the tablecloth lower, and I would go up under it, and she had a little portable TV. She would keep me entertained like that. After a few years I started helping her. I was in charge of sodas, and just the prepping for the food, but I never actually made the huaraches.

My father passed away a bit after. We went on vacation and he got killed in Mexico. We were still running the business, so we came back, and she asked for my help. I was a little bit older, like eighteen, and I was just in another mind-set, and I was just like, *No, I'm not going to help you. I have other things to do.*

And I've always had that in the back of my head: She stopped mostly because she had no support—from me or from anybody—and she didn't sell for a few years after that.

She was the main vendor at Red Hook Park. She was like *the one.* So I wanted to bring that back. I was doing bad things in

my teenage years. . . . I didn't have the mind-set that I have now. So I started changing, around three years ago—all for the good. I just wanted to bond with her, more and more. I kept looking for things. . . . But it was hard, because we never had that relationship. So I figured this would be great: some extra money and having her as a partner. And it worked out. We're closer now.

I had told her that I believed that we could make something big again, and that her food was great, and that I just wanted to test myself—to see how I could manage a business, 'cause I was reading a lot of business and self-help books. I asked her if she could help me, and if she wanted to do something big, and this time I would support her with everything. She asked me a few times if I was really going to do it, 'cause she still had her doubts about me. . . . So she didn't know if I was serious. And once I showed her the email from the Queens Night Market saying we were accepted, she got into *go mode.* She was excited. So that made me get excited—and we just kept going."

HUARACHES
WITH REFRIED BEANS AND NOPALES

A huarache (literally "sandal" in Spanish) is masa dough formed into the shape of a sandal, loaded with any number of toppings. In the US, refried beans are usually used as a topping, whereas in Mexico, the masa is stuffed with refried beans before being fried. Jeffrey carries on the latter tradition and tops them with nopales for this iteration. For the sake of convenience, this recipe results in huaraches about a half or third the size you would find in Mexican street markets.

· ·
Makes 2 servings
· ·

REFRIED BEANS

½ pound (225 g) dried pink beans

1 tablespoon salt

6 tablespoons corn oil

NOPALES

1 large fresh cactus leaf, clean and de-thorned*

½ white onion, sliced into half-moons

3 tablespoons corn oil

1 tablespoon garlic powder

1 tablespoon salt

1 tablespoon ground black pepper

HUARACHES

¾ cup (90 g) masa harina (such as Maseca)

8 tablespoons corn oil

Meat and/or veggie topping, such as 7 ounces (200 g) chopped cooked steak, chicken, chorizo, zucchini

Shredded iceberg lettuce

Pico de gallo

Crema Mexicana or sour cream

Grated queso fresco (Mexican-style fresh cheese)

Salsa verde or other salsa

* Cactus leaf can be found in most Latin grocery stores. If unavailable, canned nopales also work.

1. To make the refried beans, pour the beans and salt into a pot and add enough water to cover the beans by about 2 inches (5 cm). Bring to a boil and simmer over medium-low heat until the beans are tender, about 2 to 3 hours. Add more water, if necessary. Drain.

2. Heat the oil in a deep skillet over medium-low heat. Add the beans to the skillet and mash them as they fry to desired consistency. Continue frying until the beans turn dark brown, about 20 to 30 minutes. Remove from the heat and set aside.

3. To make the nopales, slice the cactus leaf into long, thin strips about ¾-inch (2 cm) wide. Add all the ingredients to a bowl and mix well. Cook in a skillet on medium heat, stirring occasionally, until most of the liquid has evaporated. The nopales should be soft and darkened. Remove from the heat and set aside.

4. To make the huaraches, mix the masa harina with ½ cup plus 2 tablespoons (150 ml) water in a bowl until it forms a smooth dough that no longer sticks to your hand, about 5 minutes. The dough is ready when you press the edges and it doesn't crack. Divide the dough into 2 equal balls. It helps to keep the hands wet while mixing the masa.

5. Place 1 ball in your palm, flatten with the other hand, and use your fingers to make a pocket for the refried beans. Be careful not to press too hard and break through the other side.

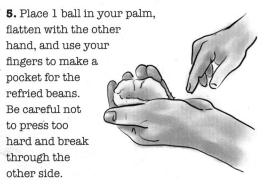

6. Place about 1 heaping tablespoon of the refried beans in the pocket and fully enclose (you will have some refried beans left over).

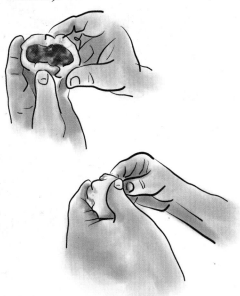

Gently roll the dough into a cigar shape about 6 inches (15 cm) long with your hands.

7. Place the dough between two 12-inch (30 cm) square sheets of plastic wrap and flatten using a tortilla press, a heavy flat object (such as a book), or your hands, forming an oval shape about ¼-inch (6 mm) thick. Repeat steps 5 through 7 with the second ball of dough.

8. Heat 2 tablespoons of the oil in a skillet over medium heat. Carefully peel the top sheet of plastic off of one huarache, then flip and peel off the bottom sheet. Immediately place it in the hot skillet and cook until the outer edges start turning brown, 2 or 3 minutes. Add another 2 tablespoons oil to the top of the huarache, flip, and cook for 2 or 3 minutes, until the bottom edges begin to brown. Flip 2 more times, cooking about 45 seconds on each side. When the huarache is crispy and golden, remove from the pan. Repeat with the second huarache.

9. Top the huaraches with your desired toppings and the nopales, lettuce, pico de gallo, crema, queso, and salsa, and serve.

Maximina Alvarado

EL TROMPO

MEXICO ②

Growing up in the Iztapalapa borough of Mexico City, Maximina wanted to be a flight attendant—that is, until she realized she was afraid of planes.

Maximina comes from a family of business owners, and few people seem as excited and optimistic about entrepreneurship as she genuinely is. She's even been known to give pep talks to discouraged subway vendors:

Follow your dreams, keep pushing. . . . ¡Adelante!

Me ha tocado ver dos o tres amistades que tengo que venden en los trenes. Son luchadores. Hay otros que asustan, que escondan o piensan que lo están haciendo mal. Yo pienso que ellas pues sigan adelante y si no tienen el apoyo de nadie pues ellas mismas.

"I have two or three friends who sell in the trains. They are fighters. There are other people

"QUEENS NIGHT MARKET HAS TAKEN A GREAT SIGNIFICANCE FOR ME BECAUSE IT IS A PLACE TO MEET OTHER PEOPLE AND CULTURES FROM OTHER COUNTRIES."

who get scared and hide or think that they are doing poorly. I remind them not to give up, and even if they don't have support from anyone, they have themselves."

Maximina has been living in Queens for over ten years and loves it because the residents and the energy are always just *corriendo*—running. She revels in how many small businesses make up the fabric of this vibrant borough. She owns El Trompo with her husband, Modesto, and her four kids chip in where they can. The family will sometimes sit around the TV watching MasterChef, each donning gloves, and working on a new batch of salsa.

She takes pride in working hard and persevering and is extremely economical with her time, making the most of every moment. Whether she's focused on her business or enjoying a day off at Governor's Island with her family—she's always "corriendo."

Before starting at the Queens Night Market, she and Modesto ran a tiny eatery just one block away from the event. After two years of insistence, her daughter finally convinced her to apply to be

Maximina's husband, Modesto

a vendor. When they were accepted and started selling at the market, they would shutter their shop on Saturday nights, with a handwritten note taped to the door saying you could find them down the street, with an arrow pointing toward the Queens Night Market.

"Queens Night Market has taken a great significance for me because it is a place to meet other people and cultures from other countries. You can interact with them and know their gastronomy and crafts that maybe we did not know. It is also the opportunity for them to know a little about Mexico."

Early in her residency at the Queens Night Market, Maximina used to make each tortilla by hand, reveling in the process of pressing each ball of nixtamalized corn to order. Then one night a friend stopped by and told her she needed to get faster. When Maximina looked up, she realized a line of dozens of hungry customers had formed, waiting for a taste of Mexico. It was one of the first times she stopped "running" and just took in the awe of the moment. It was also the last time she made each tortilla to order by hand.

TACOS DE BIRRIA

Maximina began cooking birria when she first arrived in NYC and was acclimating to the new country, culture, and customs. Birria was something familiar, and making it kept her grounded and in touch with her roots in Mexico. It is traditionally made in an underground oven, with the meat wrapped in the leaves of an agave plant, but in the US it is often made on the stove in kitchens. This recipe for birria tacos is savory, rich, warming, and considered by many to be a cure for hangovers. Birria refers to the cooking process, the meat, and the resulting consommé.

Makes 4 to 6 servings

½ pound (250 g) beef shank*

½ pound (250 g) beef backbones or neckbones*

2 tablespoons dried oregano

2 black peppercorns

1 clove

1 teaspoon salt

¼ teaspoon ground black pepper

2 tablespoons corn oil

2 dried guajillo chiles, soaked

1 dried pasilla chile, soaked

2 large tomatoes, quartered

2 garlic cloves, peeled

2 pounds (900 g) corn tortillas

1 white onion, diced

Chopped cilantro

Lime wedges

Hot sauce

* For a gamier flavor, beef can be replaced (or mixed) with lamb or goat leg and ribs.

1. Place the beef in a pot with the oregano, peppercorns, clove, salt, and pepper, and add enough water to submerge the meat. Cover and cook on medium heat for 1¼ hours, or until the meat is fork-tender.

2. Remove from the heat. Pull apart the meat with a fork and set aside. Transfer all the liquid from the pot into a blender.

3. Heat the oil in a skillet over medium heat and pan-fry the chiles for a few minutes, until they just begin to brown, then transfer to the blender. Add the tomatoes and garlic to the skillet and cook for about 5 minutes, until the garlic is browned and the tomato skin is peeling off. Remove from the heat and peel the tomatoes.

4. Add the garlic and tomatoes to the blender in batches, if necessary, and purée into a uniform sauce.

5. Transfer to a large pot and add the meat. Simmer over medium heat until the liquid is reduced by half, about 20 minutes.

6. Warm the tortillas in a skillet or on a grill. Fill with the meat and garnish with the onion, cilantro, lime, and hot sauce. Serve the consommé together with the tacos or by itself later garnished with cilantro, onions, and lime.

CHAMPURRADO
Mexican Hot Chocolate

. . . .

Makes 8 servings

. . . .

¼ pound (115 g) piloncillo or panela
   (unrefined cane sugar) or ½ cup
   (100 g) granulated sugar

1 cinnamon stick

6 to 8 ounces (170 to 225 g)
   Mexican drinking
   chocolate, such as
   Ibarra or
   Abuelita
   brands

2 cups (480 ml)
   whole milk

¾ cup (90 g)
   cornmeal

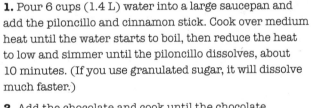

1. Pour 6 cups (1.4 L) water into a large saucepan and add the piloncillo and cinnamon stick. Cook over medium heat until the water starts to boil, then reduce the heat to low and simmer until the piloncillo dissolves, about 10 minutes. (If you use granulated sugar, it will dissolve much faster.)

2. Add the chocolate and cook until the chocolate completely melts, about 5 minutes, stirring occasionally.

3. In a separate bowl, whisk together the milk and cornmeal until thoroughly integrated, creamy, and without lumps. Slowly add the cornmeal mixture to the saucepan, stirring constantly, and ensuring there are no lumps.

4. Turn the heat to medium-high and return to a boil. Reduce the heat to low and simmer, stirring constantly. The liquid will begin to thicken in 6 to 8 minutes. Heat for an additional 5 minutes to cook the cornmeal further, but do not boil for longer than 15 minutes in total, because the beverage will become too thick.

5. Serve in cups or mugs, but be careful as the thick beverage retains a lot of heat! Store leftovers in the refrigerator and drink chilled or reheat to serve hot.

Maria Ortez

LOS ALMENDROS

③ EL SALVADOR

Maria came alone to the United States in 1980 from San Miguel, El Salvador, at age eighteen to help her family. Sitting next to Maria, who still has a hard time expressing herself in English, her grown daughter, Jocelyn, recounts, "Grandpa sent her over because they were killing people back then. A lot of people were migrating here at the time because of the situation—the gangs, civil war, and everything. So her parents wanted to protect her and help her have a better future. One of her uncles was already here in Fort Lee, New Jersey, so she came to stay with him. She brought her younger siblings later."

Maria has lived in Fort Lee ever since, though she goes back to visit El Salvador often. She took on work as a housekeeper when she first arrived in New Jersey but soon missed her home cuisine that she'd taken such care to learn from her own mother and grandmother back in San Miguel. Her father had owned a dairy farm just outside the city, which she would enjoy visiting as a child on weekends. They supplied milk and cheeses—*queso de mantequilla* and *cuajada* especially—to the region.

> ## "SHE'S BRINGING THINGS FROM THE PAST TO PEOPLE IN THE PRESENT."
> ### —MARIA'S DAUGHTER JOCELYN

There were no Salvadoran restaurants in the early 1980s in Fort Lee, so Maria would share her food with whomever she could—her clients, her friends. "Everyone was loving her food and they were like, *Oh, you should start selling on your own*, so then that's what she started doing. She has always made pupusas and tamales—then people asked for sandwiches, for stuffed hen (*gallina rellena*) instead of a turkey for the holidays—pastries, sweet bread" . . . the list goes on and on.

Maria has made pupusas and tamales at street fairs and for private catering clients for decades now. When she's at it, dexterously forming the pupusa shapes in her hand and chatting with the customers, it's like she's on fire: Her joy is palpable and contagious.

"It brings her a lot of memories, and she loves doing it," says Jocelyn. "She's bringing things from the past to people in the present: I don't know the things that she knows, you know? And I can't cook the way that she cooks. So she feels amazed being able to bring something from her homeland that is so strong and that brings pleasure and happiness to people who experience it.

For example, in the town where we live, we have a lot of Asians, and we have a lot of Koreans coming to us saying, *Oh my god, your pupusas are delicious!* So for my mother to see that her food from a small country in Central America, coming to the other side of the continent, being transmitted to people from the other side of the world, bringing different cultures together? . . . For her to see that really amazes her."

SALVADORAN CHICKEN TAMALES

As in many Latin and Caribbean cultures, tamales are a holiday staple in El Salvador. You'll often find tamales accompanying gallina rellena (stuffed hen) on special occasions. Tamales can also be enjoyed for breakfast. These tamales are wrapped and boiled in banana leaves, whereas tamales using sweet corn are usually wrapped in corn husks. This recipe is Maria's, but every Salvadoran family varies the spices and fillings to their own tastes.

Makes 5 servings (about 10 tamales)

- 1 medium white or yellow onion, roughly chopped
- 1 green bell pepper, seeded and roughly chopped
- 1 plum tomato
- 4 garlic cloves
- 8 cups (1.9 L) chicken broth (homemade from a whole chicken or store-bought), at room temperature
- 4 cups (460 g) masa harina (such as Maseca)
- 2 teaspoons ground cumin
- 2 teaspoons Spanish paprika
- 2 teaspoons salt
- 2 teaspoons ground black pepper
- 1 tablespoon olive oil

- ¼ chicken from broth, shredded, or one large chicken breast, boiled and shredded
- 1 chicken bouillon cube
- About 10 banana leaves (*hojas de plátano*),* cut to about the size of a paper towel
- ½ of 5.5-ounce (156 g) jar pitted green olives, optional
- ½ of 15.5-ounce (439 g) can chickpeas, drained and rinsed

* These can be purchased frozen from Latin grocery stores.

1. Place the onion, bell pepper, tomato, and garlic in a food processor and pulse for a few minutes until finely minced. Strain the liquid through a sieve into a large pot (nonstick, if possible), setting aside the solids.

2. Add the broth, masa harina, and 1 teaspoon each of the cumin, paprika, salt, and pepper to the pot and mix by hand or with a whisk until smooth, making sure there are no lumps. Bring to a boil over medium heat, stirring constantly, then remove from the heat.

3. Heat the oil in a separate pot over medium heat. Add the chicken, strained vegetables, bouillon cube, and the remaining teaspoon each of cumin, paprika, salt, and pepper and stir until the vegetables are cooked through, about 15 minutes. Remove from the heat.

4. Lay out a piece of aluminum foil that is slightly larger than a banana leaf. Place a banana leaf over the foil. Using a serving spoon, add a scoop or two of the boiled masa to the leaf and spread into a layer about ½-inch (13 mm) thick, leaving about ½- to 1-inch (12.5 mm to 2.5 cm) margins on the top and bottom edges, and 3- to 4-inch (7.5 to 10 cm) margins on the sides. Add one or two heaping tablespoons of the chicken filling and some chickpeas and olives to the center of the masa.

5. Fold over one edge of the foil so that the banana leaf wraps around and encloses the masa. Make sure the foil is tight against the banana leaf. Flatten the sides of the foil and tuck them tightly under the tamal, which should be the shape of a burrito. Place in a large pot and repeat steps 4 and 5 until you have used up the filling.

6. Add enough water to the pot to just cover the tamales. Boil for about 1 hour and remove the tamales from the water to cool and harden for at least 1 hour.

7. Enjoy lukewarm or by reheating in boiling water or microwaving. Tamales can be stored in the fridge for 2 to 3 days or in the freezer for up to 1 month.

SALVADORAN QUESADILLAS

These Salvadoran quesadillas are not to be confused with their eponymous Mexican counterparts. These are baked sweet breads made with cheese and akin to pound cake in texture, density, and sweetness. They're moist, flavorful, and hearty and usually served in the morning, perfectly complementing coffee or hot chocolate.

Makes 8 servings

2 cups (480 ml) whole milk

2 cups (315 g) rice flour (such as Goya rice flour)

1 cup (200 g) granulated sugar

½ cup (1 stick/115 g) butter, melted

2 eggs

2 tablespoons *cuajada* cheese or ricotta cheese

Pinch of salt

1. Preheat the oven to 425°F (220°C). Butter a 9-inch (23 cm) round or square baking pan.

2. Beat all the ingredients together with a hand mixer in a large bowl until there are no lumps.

3. Pour the batter into the prepared pan. Bake for about 1 hour, or until a toothpick inserted into the center comes out clean. Remove from the oven and let rest in the pan until cool enough to handle.

4. Flip the pan upside down onto large serving plate or cutting board. Remove the pan. Cut the quesadilla into wedges or squares. Serve warm.

Alberto Richardson

TREAT YOURSELF JERK CHICKEN

JAMAICA

After a quarter century working for New York's Metropolitan Transportation Authority (MTA), Alberto and his two business partners—his wife, Ria Richardson, and his cousin Karetha Henry—started Treat Yourself Jerk Chicken in 2019 to sell their Jamaican jerk chicken on the weekends. The smoker is always a central attraction at the Queens Night Market, the deliciously seasoned smoke wafting up against the sunset and streetlights. It's so popular, in fact, the Treat Yourself team is now working on a system to create dependably consistent and authentic outdoor-smoker-grilled jerk in even larger quantities.

"I wish I had a picture of this grill my father built going back twenty years now when I first moved to Yonkers, that he actually designed from scratch. We came to the house, there was a fifty-five-gallon drum. He cut it in two; he put the hinges on; he welded legs to it—'cause he's a welder (a teacher by trade, but he teaches welding)—and that was my first drum.

We cooked so many things on it: We barbecued; we did ribs, chicken, vegetables, you name it. We used to give a lot of family events—really big in Jamaican culture. So food was always a big part of that. We would do corn; we would do fish. So many foods we'd do on that one drum. Unfortunately, I don't have that drum anymore. I mean the bottom rotted out—my father actually put sheet metal to kinda keep it going but eventually it just gave out and I gave it to the scrap yard. But that's really a piece of history that my father created, you know?

A little bit about me: Born and raised in Kingston, Jamaica; migrated to this country in the early '80s. My mother actually migrated first, which is typical back then. The father, the head of the household, was there working, doing whatever he could to provide for the family. A short while after my mother migrated here—she sent for me first, as I was the youngest. I had to get acclimated to how things were in the States, as we Jamaicans would call it, 'foreign.' Also, a new school, new words. Back home, we speak what's called Patois, and variations sometimes referred to as the Queen's English, right—so, you know, having to learn a different form of dialect. . . .

As my beautiful wife, Ria, used to say—we've been married twenty years—she says, *Listen, out of all your brothers, you're the only one that has such a thick accent. You've been here your whole life. You left at an early age. You left before all of them. Even your friends, who came to this country later than you, they speak differently from you. You're the only one with that accent!*

I don't know—the culture's just so embedded in me. I kinda just embraced it."

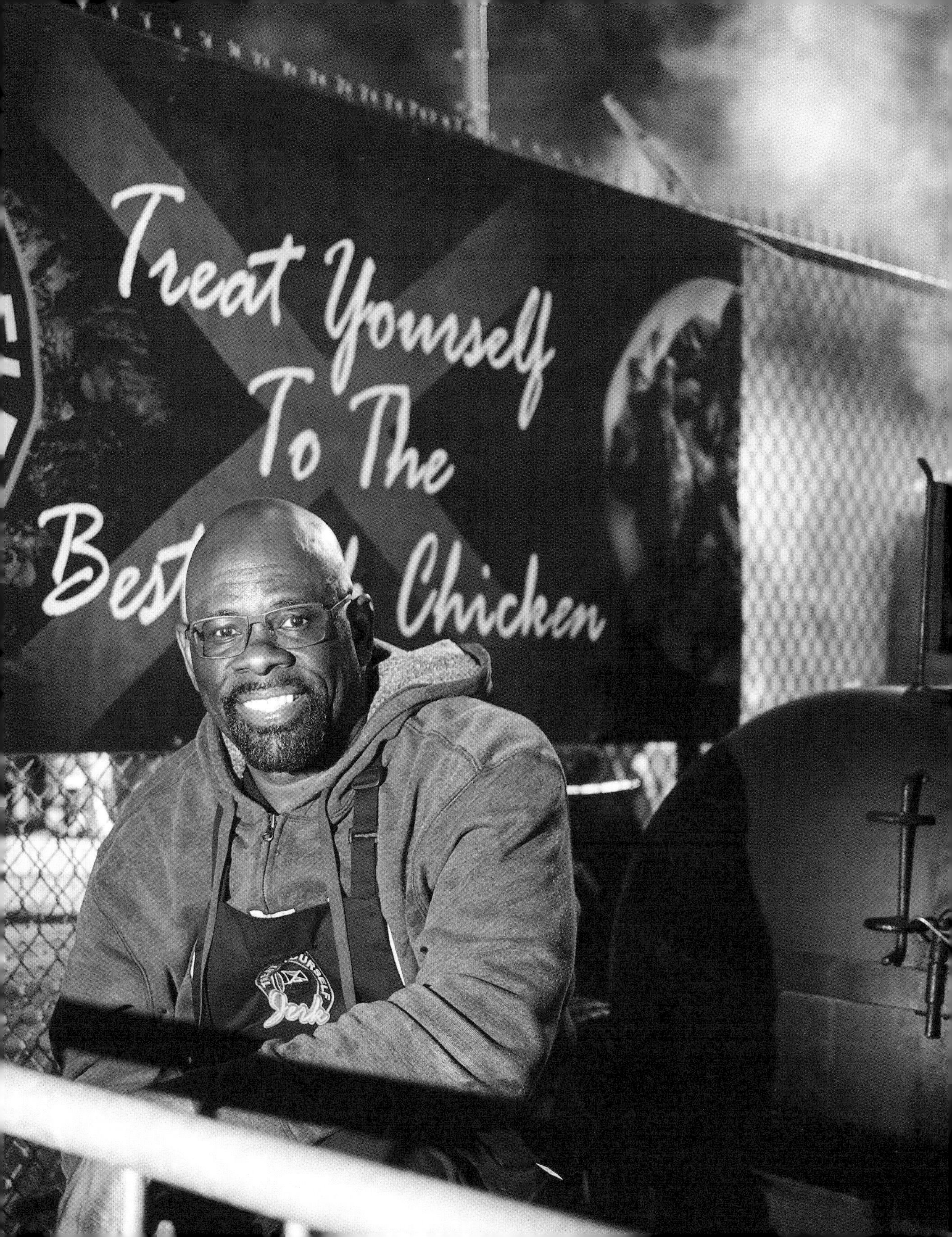
Treat Yourself
To The
Chicken
Jerk

JERK CHICKEN

Jamaicans often make jerk chicken while "running a boat," which refers to a gathering of friends making food for each other. Traditionally, jerk chicken is smoked with pimento wood—from the tree that produces allspice—and covered with a sheet of zinc (used for roofing) to trap the smoke. Alberto prefers using charcoal because he adores the smell, but he still uses pimento wood in his smoker chamber to give it that nostalgic spiced smoke flavor. Serve with bread or rice and peas.

Makes 6 servings

- 6 chicken leg quarters with skin, about 1 pound (450 g) each
- ⅔ cup (160 ml) distilled white vinegar
- 2 tablespoons adobo seasoning
- 1 tablespoon garlic powder
- 1 tablespoon ground black pepper
- 1½ teaspoons sweet paprika
- ⅔ cup (170 g) wet jerk seasoning, such as Walkerswood
- 1 or 2 Scotch bonnet chiles, finely minced, optional
- One 12-ounce (355 ml) can light beer

1. Clean the chicken leg quarters by removing any excess pieces of fat, but leaving some visible, and removing any bloody or organ bits. Place in a large bowl and just submerge with water. Add the vinegar to the water and let sit for 10 minutes, then drain and rinse.

2. Poke holes over the entire chicken quarter with a fork or knife. This is known as "juking it up" in Jamaica.

3. Combine the adobo seasoning, garlic powder, pepper, and paprika in a bowl. Massage into each leg quarter. Massage the jerk seasoning and Scotch bonnet, if using, into the leg quarters.

4. Place the seasoned chicken in an airtight container or sealable plastic bag and refrigerate for 24 to 48 hours.

5. Light a charcoal grill and heat (or create a temperature zone; see page 13) to between 275 and 300°F (135 and 150°C).

6. Wipe excess seasoning off the chicken and place the leg quarters on the grates, skin up. Close the grill and cook for 20 minutes uninterrupted. Open the grill and flip the chicken so the skin side is down. Cook for about 40 minutes more, or until the juices run a light golden-brown color. Check periodically to ensure the chicken is not burning, but leave the grill closed as much as possible and turn as infrequently as possible. *

7. Remove the fully cooked chicken from the grill and let cool, uncovered, for 10 minutes.

8. Chop the quarters into three or four pieces with a butcher's knife and serve.

"A lot of my memories from the Caribbean are from early. But the culture's so rich that if you spent some time with me, you'd become a little Jamaican, an adopted Jamaican . . ."

* The temperature of the grill should not exceed 350°F (180°C). If the temperature inside the grill rises above that or flames are visibly flaring, poke a small hole in a beer can and spray beer over the coals and chicken to control the temperature and burning coal. The heat, rather than the flames, should be cooking the chicken. The beer spray also helps keep the chicken moist and imparts a subtle flavor to the chicken.

Gardi Armand

TANIA'S KITCHEN

HAITI

"People think by default you speak French if you grew up in Haiti. That's not true. The native language is Creole—you don't automatically speak French. To speak French, you need a little bit better education. So my parents decided to send me to French schools."

Gardi was born in 1977 in New York City—in Harlem Hospital, where his mother worked as a nurse—and attended a French private school on the Upper East Side until age six, when he moved back to Port-au-Prince, Haiti, to live with his businessman father and paternal grandmother in a house with a garden and cook, attending a French school there, too. "Living in Haiti for so many years, that's where I picked up all my Haitian habits and learned the Creole language very well," even though he never studied it formally.

Years later as a college student at Hofstra University in New York City, Gardi was deep in DJ mode, blasting some of his favorite Haitian music from his dorm room, when a young woman named Tania, a fellow Haitian, stopped by to ask who the artist was. He told her and then closed the door, eager to get back to practicing his DJ skills. A few days later, she came by to ask about another song Gardi was playing in his room, and this time they got to talking. They discovered that her cousin was one of Gardi's best friends from French school in New York and in Port-au-Prince: Small world! Gardi and Tania have been inseparable ever since—and now have four kids together.

Despite a successful career in IT culminating in eleven years at a hedge fund, Gardi was growing tired of the nine-to-five grind. Though the idea started out as a joke with his wife, he bought a Rita's Italian Ice franchise in 2013, selling Italian ice at festivals, street fairs, and whatever events he could book. As he built up

his clientele and familiarized himself with the industry, Gardi noticed that there was a demand for hot food—and that the Haitian food he knew and loved was nowhere to be seen. It got him thinking: His mother was a great cook, with decades of experience cooking in quantities; though she'd worked as a registered nurse since before Gardi was born, she had always catered for friends' events on the side. Tania and her mother—also both Haitian—were excellent home cooks as well.

"This was a no brainer. So I told my mom, *Listen, you've been doing this for the longest as a oh-I'll-do-this-for-you-as-a-friendly-thing. Why don't we turn it into a business?*" Gardi promised to take care of the numbers and marketing if his mother, with Tania's and her mother's help, would oversee the cooking. He announced to all his Italian ice catering contacts that he was now selling hot authentic Haitian cuisine and booked his first big event in 2016 as Tania's Kitchen, showing up with staff and two *chaudière* pots. Since then he's been able to expand his equipment list considerably and even hopes to open a restaurant for his mother to preside over once she finally retires from nursing, but the chaudière, Gardi says, is at the heart of Haitian cooking.

"Everything is cooked in a what we call a chaudière—a big metal, heavy pot. I'm sure most of Haitian households still have a big old pot, thirty to forty years old, that they still use. There are newer pots available now, but my mom still owns the old-fashioned ones. So my logo is that same big pot. That's what I want to be known for: If anyone sees the red pot, they know it's Tania's Kitchen."

"EVERYTHING IS COOKED IN A WHAT WE CALL A CHAUDIÈRE—A BIG METAL, HEAVY POT. I'M SURE MOST OF HAITIAN HOUSEHOLDS STILL HAVE A BIG OLD POT, THIRTY TO FORTY YEARS OLD, THAT THEY STILL USE."

DIRI AK DJON DJON
Black Mushroom Rice

The source of the inky color in diri ak djon djon is an edible black mushroom native to northern Haiti. While you can substitute other dried mushrooms (such as portobello), it's worth seeking out djon djon or even ordering them online for the full experience. Diri ak djon djon is a dish typically served on Sundays or special occasions, especially at weddings and Christmas. It's not common to add meat, but chefs will sometimes include peas and shrimp (added at the same time as the water and seasonings). Gardi loves to serve diri ak djon djon alongside pork griot (fried pork).

Makes 4 to 6 servings

2 cups (75 g) dried Haitian black mushrooms*

5 tablespoons canola oil

1 medium yellow onion, chopped

4 garlic cloves, crushed

3 teaspoons all-purpose seasoning

1 teaspoon salt, plus more to taste

1 whole Scotch bonnet chile, studded with 3 cloves

3 parsley sprigs

3 thyme sprigs, tied together with the parsley sprigs

2 cups (350 g) long-grain rice (such as basmati)

1. Place the mushrooms in a pot with 2 cups (480 ml) water and simmer on low heat for at least 1 hour.

2. Remove from the heat and let cool for a few minutes. Transfer the mushrooms and black water to a blender and blend on high until the water is pitch black. Strain through a fine-mesh sieve, keeping just the liquid.

3. Heat the oil in a heavy pot on medium-high heat. Add the onion and garlic and sauté until softened. Add 3 cups (720 ml) water, the black mushroom water, all-purpose seasoning, salt, pepper, Scotch bonnet, parsley, and thyme and bring to a boil.

4. Add the rice and stir for 2 to 3 minutes to evenly distribute it. Cover and cook on medium-high heat until most of the water has been absorbed, 20 to 30 minutes. Reduce the heat to the lowest setting and let cook for another 10 to 15 minutes to steam and allow all remaining liquid to be absorbed.

5. Add more seasonings to taste, if desired, remove the parsley and thyme sprigs, and serve.

* Available in Caribbean/West Indian grocery stores

AKRA
Malanga Fritters

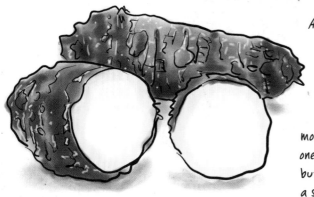

Akra is usually served at functions and large gatherings in Haiti. It's not usually made casually at home because grating the malanga can be labor intensive, although Gardi and Tania make it on Saturday movie nights at home. As with most fried finger foods, it's hard to eat just one. There isn't any traditional dip for akra, but try complementing it with Haitian *pikliz*, a spicy, vinegary cabbage slaw.

Makes about 24 fritters

4 to 5 large malangas

3 tablespoons onion powder

8 to 9 garlic cloves, minced, or 1 teaspoon garlic powder

1 teaspoon salt, plus more to taste

1 Scotch bonnet chile, minced

1 teaspoon sazón seasoning, with saffron preferred, optional

Vegetable or canola oil, for frying

1. Peel the malangas and grate them into a bowl.

2. Add the onion powder, garlic, salt, Scotch bonnet, and sazón seasoning to taste, if using, and mix well together. Refrigerate for at least 1 hour.

3. Pour about 5 to 6 inches (13 to 15 cm) oil into a deep pot and heat over medium heat to about 350°F (180°C).

4. Use a tablespoon or knife to scoop the mixture into thumb-sized fritters. Add to the pan in batches and fry until golden brown on all sides, about 6 minutes total, flipping them if necessary. Be careful not to overcrowd the pan; leave room for each fritter to float while frying.

5. Drain on paper towels. Serve immediately.

Frances Roman

COCOTASO

PUERTO RICO

Frances was born and grew up in Brooklyn, living first in the Marlboro Projects and later in Ozone Park, a more suburban-feeling neighborhood in Queens. At home there was always a big pot of something on the stove, and dinner was at seven. Her extended matriarchal Puerto Rican family always ate together, and if you weren't there on time for dinner, you were lucky if you found leftovers later. While the meal was being prepped, the kids would sneak up to steal bites of food, and Grandma would jokingly threaten to give them a *cocotaso*—a bop on the head—with her stirring spoon!

The prepping of dinners was always a big, warm family experience for Frances—until she came out to her family at fifteen years old. Her high school principal caught her kissing a girl in the hallway. "My mom didn't take it too well, so like most parents, she rejected me, and uh, yeah—it got really, really crazy for me."

Frances moved out, living variously at "friends' homes, the A train, anywhere," while holding down a full-time job at a pharmacy and completing high school at night and during the summers. Then her girlfriend's family moved to Florida, and Frances followed, feeling she had nowhere else to go. There, she did "a little bit of college, a lot of cooking" and returned to New York in 2010 as a State Farm Insurance agent.

"I wanted to change everything. I felt like I needed to prove that I was more than whatever stigma my mom had in her mind. . . . So I came back to New York, and was like, *Hey—I'm educated, I'm a professional.* I wanted her to see that whatever idea she had of lesbians is fake."

It was awkward at first, moving back home after so many years, especially when introducing partners, but Frances was determined, and she and her mother were soon debating cooking techniques again.

"Now she acknowledges my wife as my wife. She was at my wedding. . . . And my mom's now super excited to be on this journey with us, though it took her forever to get there. Food brought us together."

And now Frances's mother, Eli (pronounced "Ellie"), is an integral part of the Cocotaso team. Frances's wife, Victoria, and daughter help out, too—and the gay pride rainbow flag flies high over their tent at the Queens Night Market.

Frances; her wife, Victoria; and their daughter, Alana

ARROZ CON POLLO
Chicken and Rice

Arroz con pollo is classic, one-pot comfort food. Frances's grandmother would make this dish at least once a week to feed the army of aunts, uncles, and cousins residing under one roof.

This recipe is time tested and passed down unchanged from Frances's great-grandmother. Getting the perfect texture of rice and right integration of flavors in every bite can take some practice, but it's well worth it. Serve with a side of avocado, tostones, or maduros.

Makes 5 to 6 servings

ADOBO SEASONING

1½ tablespoons kosher salt

2 teaspoons garlic powder

2 teaspoons onion powder

1 teaspoon ground black pepper

1 teaspoon ground cumin

1 teaspoon ground coriander

SAZÓN SEASONING

1 tablespoon ground coriander

1 tablespoon dried oregano

1 tablespoon garlic powder

1 tablespoon onion powder

1 tablespoon dried cilantro

1 tablespoon annatto powder (ground achiote seed)

1 tablespoon ground cumin

2 teaspoons salt

1 teaspoon ground black pepper

SOFRITO

1 medium sweet onion, diced

1 green bell pepper, seeded and diced

3 garlic cloves, chopped

¼ cup (5 g) cilantro leaves, chopped

¼ cup (35 g) roasted red peppers (jarred is fine), diced

12 Spanish olives, pitted and chopped

1 whole chicken, skinned and cut into 8 pieces, or 8 skinless chicken thighs

3 tablespoons olive oil

One 15-ounce (425 g) can gandules (pigeon peas)

2½ cups (485 g) medium-grain rice, rinsed

1. To make the adobo and sazón seasonings, combine the ingredients in airtight containers for storage.

2. To prepare the chicken, coat it with 2 teaspoons of the adobo in a large bowl.

3. Heat a caldero or heavy pot with a lid over medium-high heat. Pour in 1 tablespoon of the oil and add the chicken. Cook on each side for 4 to 5 minutes, until browned. Remove the chicken and set aside.

4. To make the sofrito, pour in the remaining 2 tablespoons oil and add the onion, bell pepper, garlic, cilantro, roasted peppers, and olives to the pot. Sauté until tender, about 5 minutes.

5. To make the arroz con pollo, add the gandules and their liquid and the sazón seasoning to the sofrito and cook for 2 to 3 minutes, until it begins to boil. Add the chicken and cook for 2 minutes to heat through. Add the rice and stir to distribute it evenly. Add about 3½ cups (840 ml) water or enough to cover the rice and chicken by about ½ inch (13 mm). Bring to a boil and cook until the water reduces enough that the rice is just becoming visible. Cover with a lid, reduce the heat to low, and simmer for 25 to 30 minutes, until the rice is tender. Remove from the heat and serve.

When asked how Puerto Ricans use sofrito, adobo, and sazón, Frances responded,

"We put this shit on everything."

RELLENOS DE PAPA
Stuffed Potato Croquettes

You'll find *rellenos de papa* at virtually every *cuchifrito* (fry shop) in Puerto Rico, and if you ask Frances, they're one of the greatest gifts to the culinary world. They are literally meat and potatoes—mashed potatoes enveloping seasoned ground beef—deep-fried to perfection. Serve with *pique* (Puerto Rican hot sauce). This recipe has passed unchanged from Frances's great-grandmother down to Frances's daughter.

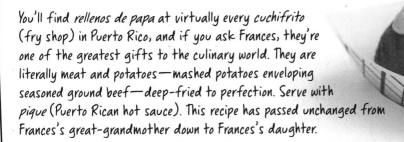

Makes 10 to 12 rellenos

PAPAS

2 pounds (1 kg) Yukon Gold potatoes, peeled and halved

1 cup (240 ml) achiote oil*

¼ cup (15 g) cilantro, chopped

PICADILLO

2 tablespoons olive oil

1 medium green bell pepper, seeded and diced

1 medium red bell pepper, seeded and diced

2 tablespoons chopped Spanish olives

2 garlic cloves, minced

Pinch of dried oregano

½ cup (130 g) tomato paste

1 tablespoon sazón seasoning (page 36)

Salt and ground black pepper

1 pound (450 g) ground beef, preferably chuck or 80 percent lean

Flour, for dusting

Vegetable oil, for frying

1. To make the papas, boil the potatoes in about 8 cups (1.9 L) salted water for 20 to 30 minutes, until the potatoes fall off the fork when you poke them. Drain, mash, and add the achiote oil and cilantro. Mix and let rest until cool enough to handle.

2. Meanwhile, to make the picadillo, heat the oil in a large skillet over medium-high heat. Add the bell peppers, olives, minced garlic, and oregano and cook until tender, about 5 minutes.

3. Stir in the tomato paste and season with the sazón and salt and pepper to taste. Add the beef and brown until fully cooked, then turn off the heat.

4. To make the rellenos, cover your palms well with flour and spread a golf ball-sized portion of the papas on the palm of your nondominant hand. Press the center with your fingers to form a hole. Fill with about 1 teaspoon of the picadillo and close it up, using additional papas if necessary. Repeat this step until you have used all the dough.

5. Pour about 2 to 3 inches (5 to 8 cm) oil into a deep pot and heat over medium-high heat to about 375°F (190°C). Fry 4 or 5 rellenos at a time for 2 to 3 minutes, until the undersides are golden brown. Flip and fry for additional 2 to 3 minutes to ensure all sides are evenly golden brown.

6. Serve hot. Eat with your hands!

* Achiote oil is used in Puerto Rico to add color and flavor to dishes. To make it, heat 1 cup (240 ml) vegetable or olive oil and 2 tablespoons annatto seeds in a small saucepan over medium heat just until the seeds begin to steadily pop to the top and the oil turns a bright orange color (10 to 15 minutes). Remove from the heat and let stand for a minute. Strain the oil. Store in a half-pint (240 ml) mason jar.

Laura Joseph

LA'MAOLI

ANTIGUA

Cricket is the most popular team sport in the 108-square-mile Caribbean island of Antigua, where Laura was born and raised with the sounds of the ocean in her ears, minutes from the nearest beach in the idyllic fishing village of Urlings, far from tourist activities.

When a big cricket game was coming up, her family's home would suddenly transform into a flurry of activity in preparation for serving whole meals to fans at the stadium in St. John's—the capital city of Antigua and Barbuda, a half hour's drive away.

Unlike Americans at baseball games, Antiguans like to eat whole meals while they watch cricket. In preparation for the games the next morning, Laura and her family "would be up all night making food—and all day selling and vending." Seafood soup was a perennial favorite on the menu.

"We ate it a lot. It's more a hand food 'cause there's shells and stuff involved, so it's a fun food to eat, served with bread and a beer or something. We would eat it all the time. Even as kids." Kids in Antigua learn how to eat crustaceans, mollusks, and whole fish at a young age. One piece of common wisdom they follow

while still on the learning curve is *Don't talk while eating fish; you'll choke or swallow a bone!*

A street-food staple, seafood soup is also served at restaurants: "I think *seafood soup* is the correct name, but when you google it with all the ingredients in it, it comes up as bouillabaisse. And when you order it in the restaurants in Antigua, they also call it bouillabaisse—I think for restaurant purposes, for tourists. Only like *local-local* you'll hear it called seafood soup."

Since moving to the US for college—she now works primarily in the medical field—Laura, along with her family, has figured out how to keep the tastes of home on hand, even in NYC, where seafood costs more and just doesn't compare quality-wise to what they can find back in Antigua.

ANTIGUAN SEAFOOD SOUP

"We go back and forth, and we bring back the seafood with us. You're allowed fifty pounds. . . . But customs officers actually stop us, they ask, *What are you carrying? Seafood!* And it's always pretty OK. It's not livestock, like a cow, or a sheep, a goat; those are the things they look for. But fish, and conch, and lobsters: It's fine, we've been doing this for years." They parboil the seafood so it doesn't spoil, then freeze it, pack it with cold packs in checked luggage, fly over, and stash it in their New York freezers, where it keeps for up to three months.

Laura started La'Maoli in 2019 with the help of her family to bring her favorite Antiguan foods to the Queens Night Market, where the team often has a lot of explaining to do to about her homeland. The Antiguan tourism office should pay her for all the pointers she gives out! But her favorite tips are inspirational messages to young women like her who are starting their own businesses: "No matter who you are or where you're from, always follow your dreams. And when you do, please remember that just because you're struggling, it doesn't mean you're failing: All success comes through sustained efforts."

One-pot dishes are basically an art form in Antiguan cuisine, including such staples as seasoned rice, pepper pot, and *fungi*. Many of these recipes find their roots in the native Arawakan culture. This seafood soup is a one-pot dish that highlights the bounty of fresh and delicious seafood that blesses the small country of Antigua and Barbuda in the West Indies. The recipe can easily be tailored to your preferences, adding and subtracting ingredients to suit your tastes; sometimes whole fish (such as red snapper) and crab are added. According to Laura, "Some people cook some starch into it, like potatoes, just to give it some body. But I like it clean, just served with bread." Or consider enjoying it with boiled yams, or boiled green bananas, and a cold beer.

Makes 6 servings

- 5 pounds (2.25 kg) conch, removed from the shell
- 5 pounds (2.25 kg) octopus
- Salt
- 2 lemons, halved
- 1 or 2 small lobsters (or lobster shells without the head, cut into 3 pieces)
- 24 mussels with shells
- 12 clams with shells
- ½ cup (120 ml) olive oil
- 5 white onions, chopped
- 4 celery stalks, chopped
- 1 green bell pepper, finely chopped
- 1 red bell pepper, finely chopped
- 4 garlic cloves, peeled and minced
- 1 bunch chives, chopped
- One 28-ounce (794 g) can whole peeled tomatoes, chopped
- 4 fish bouillon cubes
- 12 to 15 large shrimp, unshelled and deveined
- 1 bunch fresh thyme
- 2 cups (480 ml) white cooking wine
- 1 Scotch bonnet chile
- ¼ cup (65 g) cornstarch or flour, thoroughly dissolved in 1 cup (240 ml) water

1. Cut up the conch and octopus to a reasonable size for boiling. Boil the conch and octopus in two separate pots, each with a dash of salt and 2 lemon halves in enough water to completely submerge the seafood. Cook until tender, up to 1 hour.

2. Meanwhile, simmer the lobster in 10 cups (2.4 L) lightly salted water for 25 to 30 minutes, then wash and scrub all the shells of the mussels and clams to remove any seaweed or dirt and set aside. Remove the lobster and save the broth.

3. When the conch and octopus are done, remove from the pots, reserving 2 cups (480 ml) of the conch broth, and cut the conch and octopus into bite-size pieces when cool enough to handle.

4. Heat the oil in a large soup pot over low heat and add the onions, celery, bell peppers, garlic, chives, tomatoes, and bouillon cubes. Cook for about 15 minutes, or until softened and fully cooked.

5. Add the shrimp to the pan and cook for 3 minutes, or until just cooked through, and then remove to prevent overcooking. Add the clams and mussels to the pot, cover, and cook for 5 minutes. Add the thyme, reserved lobster broth and conch broth, conch, octopus, lobster, shrimp, wine, and Scotch bonnet. Simmer for 10 minutes, until the seafood is tender and easily pierced by a fork.

6. Add some of the cornstarch slurry and stir until thickened, adding more after a few minutes, if desired. Simmer for 5 minutes, remove the thyme and Scotch bonnet, and serve.

ANTIGUAN GINGER BEER

Antiguans drink ginger beer at any time of day, and especially for Christmas and Sunday dinners. In addition to being tasty and refreshing, ginger beer is purported to have many health benefits, helpful with digestive ailments, nausea, and inflammation.

. . . .
Serves 6 to 8
. . . .

1 gallon (3.75 L) bottled or distilled water

1 pound (450 g) unpeeled fresh ginger

2 cups (400 g) white rice

3 cups (600 g) granulated sugar

¼ cup (60 ml) clear vanilla extract

1. Pour the water into a large pot with a lid and bring to a boil over high heat.

2. Wash and grate the ginger on the finest side of a grater, or blend into a purée.

3. Remove the pot from the heat and transfer the ginger and rice to the boiling-hot water. Stir and leave covered overnight or for several days, depending on your preferred spiciness. (The longer it soaks and ferments, the spicier it becomes.)

4. Pour the ginger mix through a funnel and a fine-mesh strainer or sieve into a 3-gallon (11 L) jug or container to remove the ginger and rice. Squeeze as much juice out of the ginger pieces as possible and then discard them.

5. Add the sugar and vanilla, adjusting to taste. (Antiguans like it hot and sweet!) Stir until the sugar is dissolved.

6. Chill or add ice and enjoy.

Sean Ramlal
CARIBBEAN STREET EATS
TRINIDAD

Guayaguayare is just a small fishing village at the tip of Trinidad, but about a mile offshore sits the first oil well in the country, now run by BP. Sean's father, originally from Guyana, worked out on the rig for BP—two weeks on, two weeks off—throughout Sean's childhood. Sean's grandmother was the village baker, making bread in her outdoor oven, and in his family "everyone was a cook," except Sean, since he was the youngest of four siblings and always well fed by others. On Sundays, Sean's mother would get up at dawn to start preparing the post-church family meal, which always included some kind of callaloo.

Young Sean would watch and occasionally help out by prepping a few ingredients, but that was the extent of his involvement—until one Sunday, his mother had been running late and hadn't had time to start the callaloo before church. Thirteen-year-old Sean stayed home alone from church that Sunday. As a budding teenager, he could just as well have played his guitar or slept in, but something compelled him to go play in the kitchen and try his own hand at the callaloo he'd seen made so many times before. When his parents and older siblings came home

"I MOVED TO THE US FOR MICHAEL JACKSON."

from church, they found a small feast all set out on the table prepared by their youngest—and possibly also a mess in the kitchen.

Since that day, Sean started considering himself a cook, too, and made a point of learning the family's favorite recipes. But at seventeen, in 1984, Sean was tiring of island life. "I moved to the US for Michael Jackson," he likes to joke.

In New York City, he found romance instead, when his cousins there introduced him to the beautiful Savatree Singh, from Guyana, just a few months after his arrival in the US. They fell madly in love, married young, and now have five children, who all play a role in their family food business, Caribbean Street Eats. They have been working the NYC market and street fair scene since 1997, specializing in shark sandwiches and tropical fruit juices flavored with spices and angostura bitters—a favorite Trinidadian export.

TRINIDADIAN CALLALOO
Taro Leaf Stew

Makes 8 to 12 servings

12 dasheen (taro) leaves, preferably young*

3 crabs, quartered

Lemon or lime juice

Salt

Ground black pepper

¼ cup (60 ml) liquid green seasoning**

1 tablespoon vegetable oil

2 cups (280 g) cubed, peeled calabaza*** or other winter squash, such as butternut or acorn

1 medium yellow onion, chopped

1 medium carrot, chopped

3 green or orange pimentos (Trinidad Seasoning peppers), chopped, optional

3 garlic cloves

1 Scotch bonnet chile (or habanero for less heat)

4 fresh thyme sprigs or 1 tablespoon dried thyme

8 large or 12 medium okra, chopped

4 cups (960 ml) fresh coconut milk or two 13.5-ounce (400 ml) cans or one 1.76-ounce pack dried coconut powder, dissolved in 4 cups (960 ml) water

2 vegetable or chicken bouillon cubes

1 tablespoon Golden Ray or other salted butter, optional

* Dasheen (or taro) leaves can be found in South Asian and West Indian grocery stores. Spinach can be substituted in a pinch.

** Green seasoning is a Caribbean staple available at West Indian grocery stores. It's a blended mixture of fresh herbs and vinegar and used to season fish, poultry, meat, and other dishes.

*** Calabaza, sometimes called West Indian "pumpkin," can be found in Caribbean and Asian grocery stores, often sold in wedges or already cubed.

In Trinidad, callaloo is often served as part of Sunday lunch. The soup is creamy from the fresh coconut milk, earthy from the dasheen leaves, with subtle notes from the crab and herbs. Serve over rice, with ground provisions, such as taro or yams, or just by itself. Callaloo makes great leftovers; refrigerate or freeze and reheat it on the stove or in the microwave.

1. Wash the dasheen leaves and remove and discard the pointed tips. Chop finely, including the stems.

2. Wash the crabs with lemon juice, rinse, remove the gills, and season with salt, pepper, and green seasoning.

3. Heat the oil in a deep pot over medium heat and sauté the calabaza, onion, carrot, pimentos, garlic, Scotch bonnet, and thyme for about 2 minutes, just so the flavors begin to marry. Add the dasheen leaves, okra, coconut milk, and bouillon cubes. Cover and cook over medium heat for about 45 minutes, stirring occasionally to prevent the ingredients from sticking to the pot, until everything is tender and ready for easy blending.

4. Remove the Scotch bonnet and the thyme sprigs (if using fresh) and use an immersion blender on the low setting to purée. Be careful not to over-liquefy. (A regular blender can also be used, pulsing on low and returning to the pot.)

5. Add the crab to the pot and cook for 10 minutes, until cooked through.

6. Add the butter and season with salt and pepper to taste. Remove from the heat and serve.

DOUBLES
Curried Chickpea Sandwich

Doubles are the most popular street food in Trinidad, available any time of day, and often during breakfast hours. As a child, Sean looked forward to eating doubles after grocery shopping with his mother. A doubles is two *baras* (spiced flatbreads) enclosing *chana* (chickpea) curry, topped with condiments and wrapped in parchment paper. They're saucy and messy and deeply satisfying.

. . . .
Makes 10 servings
. . . .

BARAS

2 cups (250 g) all-purpose flour

¾ teaspoon baking powder

¾ teaspoon instant yeast

¼ teaspoon granulated sugar

¼ teaspoon ground turmeric

¼ teaspoon salt

1¼ tablespoons vegetable oil, plus more for rolling and frying

¾ cup (180 ml) warm water

CHANA CURRY

1 pound (450 g) dried chana (chickpeas), soaked overnight and drained (or follow package instructions)*

1 teaspoon baking soda

2 tablespoons liquid green seasoning (see note on page 45)

2 garlic cloves, minced

1 teaspoon geera (roasted ground cumin)**

½ teaspoon salt, plus more to taste

Vegetable oil

1 medium yellow onion, diced

¼ teaspoon curry powder

¼ teaspoon ground turmeric

6 to 8 recao (culantro or saw-leaf herb) leaves or cilantro sprigs, chopped

Condiments of your choice, such as tamarind chutney, pepper sauce, cucumber chutney, and chadon beni sauce

* Dried chickpeas are ideal. If you are short on time, use two 15-ounce (425 g) cans of chickpeas, boiled for 15 minutes with the baking soda.

** Geera can be found at Indian and West Indian grocery stores.

1. To make the baras, whisk together the dry ingredients in a large bowl until well combined. Drizzle in 2¼ teaspoons of the oil and combine. Using the dough hook of a stand mixer (or by hand), start adding the water and kneading gently until a sticky dough has formed. You may add up to ½ cup (120 ml) more warm water if needed. Add the remaining 2¼ teaspoons oil and continue kneading for 1 to 2 minutes to integrate the oil. The dough should still be sticky to the touch. (Be careful not to knead too hard, as baras should be light and airy.)

2. Cover the dough with a damp kitchen towel or plastic wrap. Set aside until doubled in size. (While the dough is ready after it has doubled, depending on various factors such as humidity, the dough may react better if allowed to rest longer, up to several hours.)

3. Lightly punch down the dough to release some air and tear into 20 equal pieces, each about the size of a golf ball. Lightly roll between oiled hands to form uniform balls. Set a small bowl of oil nearby to keep hands oiled.

4. Pour about 2 inches (5 cm) oil in a small pot and heat over medium heat to 350°F (180°C).

5. Place one ball of dough into the center of your nondominant (oiled) hand or on an oiled flat surface. Use your dominant hand to press the dough in a circular motion until it's as thin as you can get it, about 3 to 4 inches (7.5 to 10 cm) in diameter. Peel the dough off your hand and place in the hot oil and flip two or three times quickly for a few seconds. Each bara takes about 4 to 6 seconds to cook, so only cook one at a time. They will puff slightly and cook through. Place the baras in a paper-towel-lined bowl to drain and keep covered with a kitchen towel. Steam created will allow them to further soften for layering.

6. To make the chana curry, pour the chana into a pot along with the baking soda and 4 cups (960 ml) water and bring to a boil over high heat. Skim any foam from the top. Add the green seasoning, garlic, ¾ teaspoon of the geera, and the salt and cook, uncovered, until the chana is easily mashed with the back of a spoon, 25 to 30 minutes. Drain and set aside.

7. In a separate wide, deep pan set over medium-low heat, pour enough oil to coat the bottom of the pan. Add the onion, curry powder, and turmeric. Stir frequently, until the mixture becomes grainy, at least 5 minutes.

8. Raise the heat to medium, add the chana, and cook for a few minutes, stirring frequently, until completely coated. Add 2 cups (480 ml) warm water and bring to a simmer.

9. Use a potato masher or the back of a large spoon to mash the chana as the water simmers. Continue until most of the chana is mashed, with some noticeable pieces visible. Add the remaining ¼ teaspoon of the geera and additional salt to taste. Sprinkle in the recao and mix well. Turn off the heat when the thickness is to your liking.

10. To assemble the doubles, spoon a couple tablespoons of chana over one bara, add your desired condiments, and then top with another bara. Wrap each doubles with parchment paper to make a pouch and serve. Eat with your hands and feel free to make a little mess.

Danny Atehortua

AREPALICIOUS

COLOMBIA

Danny has worked in the NYC ferries system for two decades, first for the Statue of Liberty ferry and most recently at the NYC Department of Transportation, overseeing the maintenance of the Staten Island Ferry. Though he and his wife, Shirley, were already pretty busy with day jobs and raising their kids, Danny had always been such a fan of Shirley's cooking that in 2015 he started selling it to the public on weekends in markets. When a former employer of Shirley's—a restaurateur couple—came to visit the Arepalicious tent at the Queens Night Market in 2018, they were so impressed, they invested in the first Arepalicious brick-and-mortar restaurant, which has quickly become a neighborhood favorite in Ozone Park, Queens.

" I was born in Colombia in 1980. I came to the United States in 1992, when I was twelve. So the beginning of junior high. My father was here before us. He came, like, five years earlier. Then, because of everything that was going on in Colombia

Danny and Shirley at their restaurant in Ozone Park, Queens

at that time, with Pablo Escobar and all that stuff, he worked the papers out, so we came and moved to the United States.

After three or four years, I met my wife, Shirley, in high school. And we've been together ever since. It's gonna be twenty-four years that we know each other. She loves to cook. And I like what she cooks! In Colombia they have a product that is the arepa. And she was always making it. It's like a Sunday thing. It's not for everyday; when everybody's together, they make it. And it was very good.

In Colombia, she's from the city, from Bogotá: It's colder, so they eat the arepa with cheese, because of the weather. Where I'm from, Medellín, it's hotter—so our arepa is plain. It's just white corn and a little salt, and that's it, nothing else. 'Cause the workers from that time, the coffee farmers, they can take the arepa with them and it's not gonna get spoiled. In colder weather, you know, it's easier for them to keep everything, even if it has more ingredients.

So she started making it, and family and friends started taking orders. So Shirley would make arepas to sell to our friends every weekend, and she went from making one type to twenty types.

In Colombia, it's not like here—you go outside and you don't know your neighbor.

Over there, you know everybody. Like you can start walking down the block and everybody say hi to you—*Oh! Hi, hi, hi!* You sit outside, they come. Now, here, everybody's independent. Like, even where I live, the people from the first floor, I might see them once a month. You know what I mean? *Hi!* and just continue walking.

Over there, you know everybody. Everybody knows you, and whatever you need, you can go to the neighbor: *Oh, can I get . . . ? Oh, sure! Here.* So they're like that. You feel like everybody's your cousin. You can sit down and speak to someone: It's like you've known him for twenty years. But no, no, I've just met him! I mean, it's like that.

In Medellín, they call it the city of forever spring because it's always seventy-five to eighty degrees, so it's like spring weather. But in the 1980s, we had problems with the Mafia, so it wasn't safe. I mean, any moment, a bomb could blow up. Or there were killings of a lot of cops. I mean it was in the middle of the conflict, when I used to live there. And I lived in a bad neighborhood. So a lot of the people that worked for them used to be from the neighborhood, too. My father one time was driving and he passed a bridge. A minute later, they blow out the bridge 'cause they wanted to kill some cops that were going that way. So that was a little bit of a scary moment. The Mafia ran the city. So it was a fight between the government and them.

The city now, though, the city itself—it's four hundred times better now. Now, going to Medellín is like going to New York. You have your good neighborhoods; you have your bad neighborhoods. Something happens to you, it all depends where you are.

When I was little, we visited Colombia all the time—'cause my parents paid for it! Since I got married, I go maybe every five, seven years. Now my kids, they grow up, they went, they like it—so they might go more often than me. They like the culture."

"IN COLOMBIA, IT'S NOT LIKE HERE . . . OVER THERE, YOU KNOW EVERYBODY. LIKE YOU CAN START WALKING DOWN THE BLOCK AND EVERYBODY SAY HI TO YOU— OH! HI, HI, HI! YOU SIT OUTSIDE, THEY COME."

AREPAS CON HUEVOS PERICOS
Arepas with Scrambled Eggs

Makes 3 servings

AREPAS

2 pounds (900 g) dried white hominy corn (*maíz trillado blanco*)*

1 tablespoon salt

Butter, for grilling

HUEVOS PERICOS

6 eggs

¼ cup (60 ml) whole milk

1 teaspoon salt

¼ teaspoon ground black pepper

⅛ teaspoon garlic powder

1 tablespoon salted butter

3 plum tomatoes, diced

⅓ cup (30 g) chopped scallions

* This recipe starts from scratch, including making the cornmeal. Maserepa, which is precooked cornmeal, is readily available for purchase for readers without grinders or who just want to skip a few steps.

Colombian children begin eating arepas as soon as they're old enough for solid foods. Arepas can be topped with just about anything, from butter to cheese and proteins. While *arepas con huevos pericos* is a traditional breakfast dish found in many Colombian cafeterias, this specific dish immediately transports Danny back to the breakfast table at home with his grandmother. According to Danny, yellow cornmeal yields softer and sweeter arepas, but where he grew up in Colombia, it was also more expensive, so white corn arepas ruled the roost.

1. To make the arepas, rinse the hominy corn until the water runs clear. Transfer to a large pot and just cover with water (about a gallon/3.75 L). Cook over medium-high heat until the corn is soft, about 45 minutes. Transfer to a large strainer and rinse with cold water.

2. Run the corn one time through a corn or pasta grinder on the lowest setting. Mix in the salt by hand.

3. Flatten the dough by hand to about ¼-inch (6 mm) thickness and form about 20 disks, 5 inches (13 cm) in diameter.

4. Heat some butter on a griddle or flat pan over medium-high heat. Grill the arepas for about 3 minutes on each side, until they begin to brown. Transfer to a plate and cover to keep warm. For extras, pre-grill arepas over medium-high heat for 1 minute on each side. Refrigerate the extra arepas and use within 3 days, or freeze for future use.

5. To make the huevos pericos, crack the eggs into a bowl. Add the milk, salt, pepper, and garlic powder. Beat with a fork or whisk for 1 to 2 minutes, until blended.

6. Heat the butter in a nonstick skillet over medium heat. Once the butter is sizzling, add the tomatoes and scallions. Cook for a few minutes, until the scallions just start to brown. Add the eggs and let sit for a few seconds, then use a spatula to lift the cooked eggs from the skillet, allowing the runny eggs to coat the bottom of the skillet. Repeat this step until the eggs are cooked, about 5 minutes in total.

7. Break up or scramble the eggs with the spatula and serve on top of the arepas.

AREPAS DE QUESO
Cheese Arepas

For Danny, arepas de queso are the Colombian equivalent of French toast: "It's something you make on weekends with the family to bond together." They marked a weekly tradition for his family. Arepas de queso can also be found at all hours of the day from food carts that line city streets.

Makes about 12 arepas

2¼ pounds (1.1 kg) dried white hominy corn (maíz trillado blanco)

1 cup (200 g) granulated sugar

1 tablespoon salt

2 pounds (900 g) queso de nata**

Butter, for grilling

** Queso de nata is a soft cream cheese made from cow's milk that can be found in some Latin grocery stores. Low-moisture mozzarella can be substituted for a nearly identical end result.

1. Rinse the hominy corn until the water runs clear.

2. Transfer to a large pot and just cover with water (about a gallon/ 3.75 L). Cook over medium-high heat until the corn is soft, about 45 minutes. Transfer to a large strainer and rinse with cold water.

3. Run the corn one time through a corn or pasta grinder on the lowest setting. (Any kind of grinder will work, but precooked cornmeal can also be substituted if no grinder is available.) Mix in the sugar and salt by hand.

4. Flatten the dough by hand to about ¼-inch (6 mm) thickness and form about 25 disks, 5 inches (13 cm) in diameter.

5. Place about 2 ounces (50 g) of the queso de nata between two disks and press together between your hands.

6. Heat some butter on a griddle or flat pan over medium-high heat. Grill the arepas for about 3 minutes on each side, until they begin to brown. For extras, pre-grill arepas over medium-high heat for one minute on each side and refrigerate to use within three days or freeze for future use.

7. Serve and enjoy, but be careful about the hot, gooey cheese inside!

AGUAPANELA CON LIMÓN
Sugarcane Limeade

Aguapanela con limón is a common drink in Colombia. This beverage is sweetened with panela and pairs well with savory arepas. Panela is made by boiling sugarcane juice and letting it harden in molds. It's sold in solid blocks or cones and is available at any Latin grocery store. Baby bottles are often filled with aguapanela, without the lime.

Makes 4 servings

8 ounces (225 g) panela (unrefined cane sugar)

Juice of 4 limes

1. Roughly chop the panela into small pieces. Transfer to a saucepan and add 4 cups (960 ml) water. Boil until the panela has dissolved, about 10 minutes, depending on how small you chopped it. Remove from the heat and let cool. (However, aguapanela can also be served hot.)

2. Pour over ice and add lime juice to taste. Stir and enjoy!

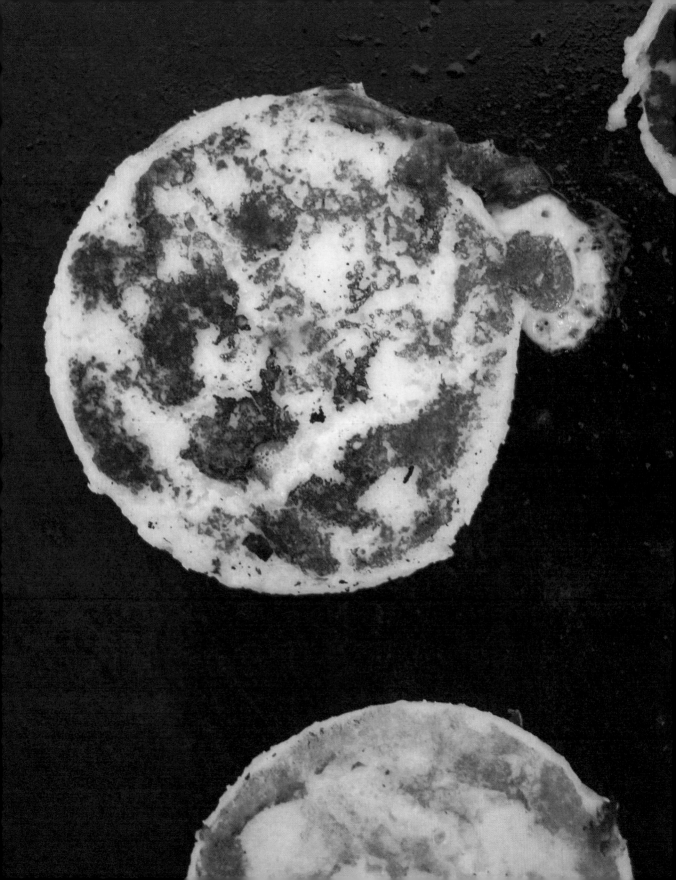

Stephen Kanhai

GEORGETOWN PATTIES

⑩ GUYANA

Georgetown Patties was a happy but brief 2017 experiment for Institute of Culinary Education–trained professional chef Stephen Kanhai, in which he first tried his hand at making and selling the street foods he nostalgically recalled from his childhood in Guyana to a diverse New York public at the Queens Night Market. When Stephen was offered an executive chef position at a well-known nonprofit that summer, however, he felt he could not refuse the opportunity, and that was the end of Georgetown Patties—for the time being. . . . Although Stephen hasn't made Guyanese food for the public since then, sticking with dependable catering and chef jobs in hopes of soon supporting a family with his wife, he is constantly developing his skills and deepening his understanding of his homeland's cuisine. Georgetown Patties was just the appetizer—Stephen hopes to eventually serve New York City a whole Guyanese-inspired culinary experience such as it has never tasted before. We can't wait.

"My name is Stephen Kanhai. I'm originally from Guyana. I came over here in 2001 at the age of eleven, straight to New York City—Queens—and I've been living in Queens ever since.

From a young age I loved food. I enjoyed being in the kitchen: You know, the typical watching your grandmother or your mother prepare a meal—sneaking in, stealing something from the pot or the oven—that typical experience. I enjoyed eating a lot, you know: I was a very chubby child, still am a chubby adult. I really loved food. Coming over here to America, I watched Food Network. That was my favorite network to watch—you know, Emeril, Wolfgang Puck. As much as sports, I enjoyed watching food programs.

I wasn't the best student. When you're, like, 'fresh off the boat,' as people would say, it was tough. You know: You spoke differently, so you would be the center of attention, and you get picked on a lot. So it was a lot of that. You had to become tough. Sometimes I would cut school and come home to watch Food Network or whatever's on PBS. There was this Italian lady who made Italian food. That was always my interest, watching all the Food Network shows. And it just continued.

I went to LaGuardia Community College after I graduated Hillcrest High School—in the top ten as the worst high school in New York City, because of gang violence and crimes. I was gonna become a teacher, but I really didn't enjoy that as much as I thought I would. So I eventually went to culinary school at ICE— the Institute of Culinary Education—and it was the most beautiful experience I'd ever had up until that time. I enjoyed everything about it: putting on the chef coat and using knives, learning about techniques. I was fascinated. I did a lot of externships, too, working in professional settings, and being exposed to that was amazing. The only problem I had with culinary school was that it was too short!

I really believe in, you know, 'bloom where you're planted,' so I did my externship at a restaurant called Quaint in Sunnyside, Queens, because I wanted to represent Queens, as well. It was really wonderful. I made their pastries; I prepped; I worked on the line; and I remember the first time I made something—I think it was an apple tart—and I made it. When it went out

"I REALLY BELIEVE IN, YOU KNOW, 'BLOOM WHERE YOU'RE PLANTED.'"

to the customer, I put a scoop of ice cream on top of it, and a little bit of caramel sauce, and seeing the customer eat it was the most amazing thing I ever experienced. It was like: *Wow.*

Right after that, I wanted to get into catering. So I moved on to a huge commissary kitchen—a lot of production going on there. I did a lot of events. I saw how the industry was: It was really tough. Most of the kitchen staff were from immigrant communities, most of them from Mexico. I thought I knew what hard work was till I saw them. Most of them just work in the kitchen and would go home to a small room, so their whole thing was working as hard as possible to send home money for their families and all that. And that taught me a valuable lesson. Seeing that just opened my eyes that this is much more than just cooking to them— it's not just a passion.

They would tell me their stories and I'd hardly understand, but you could tell there was a lot of real feelings behind them. I learned my work ethic from these Mexican cooks and chefs. It was something I needed; it gave me a jolt—to not just look for the glamorous parts of the food industry, but to respect the craft as well. Because many of them are craftsmen: They work so hard, they're so diligent, and they pay attention to the details. And that was very important. I didn't realize all these things. While I was in culinary school, it seemed more glamorous. You didn't see the hard work that went into it."

GUYANESE BEEF PATTIES

Butter is hard to come by in Guyana, so Guyanese pastries often use lard or margarine. Stephen reverse-engineered this beef patty recipe to re-create the taste he loved from his childhood, but he uses butter instead of lard or margarine. He feels this imparts a better flavor and yields a flakier crust. There are a lot of beef patties in Caribbean cuisine, but one thing impossible to replicate in Guyanese beef patties is the tangy, fruity, hard-to-describe taste of *wiri wiri* chile peppers (or Guyanese peppers), unique to Guyana. We hope you manage to procure some for this recipe.

. . . .
Makes 12 patties
. . . .

PASTRY DOUGH

2¼ cups (315 g) all-purpose flour, plus extra for rolling

1 teaspoon salt

1 teaspoon granulated sugar

1 cup (240 g) cold unsalted butter, cut into ½-inch (13 mm) cubes

¼ cup (60 ml) ice water, plus 1 or 2 tablespoons more, if needed

1 egg

FILLING

2 tablespoons vegetable oil

1 medium yellow onion, chopped

1 wiri wiri chile* (or ½ Scotch bonnet chile), chopped

6 garlic cloves, minced

2 tablespoons fresh thyme, chopped

1 pound (455 g) ground beef (80 percent lean)

2 tablespoons tomato paste

1 tablespoon paprika

1 tablespoon brown sugar

1 tablespoon salt

1 teaspoon ground black pepper

EGG WASH

1 egg, whisked with 1 teaspoon water

* Wiri wiri chiles can be hard to find outside Guyana. Check out your West Indian or South American store, or go online. Rehydrating dried wiri wiri chiles is also an option.

1. To make the pastry dough, pour the flour, salt, and granulated sugar into a food processor and pulse a few times to mix.

2. Add half of the butter and pulse several times. Add the remaining butter and pulse 6 to 8 times, until the largest chunks of butter are pea-sized.

3. Add the ice water (with no ice) and the egg to the mixture and pulse once or twice. Add more ice water 1 tablespoon at a time between pulses until the dough just barely holds together but is still crumbly. Pinch a small amount between your fingers to test: When it just holds together, it is ready.

4. Transfer the dough onto a dry, flat surface. Gather it into a pile and divide into 2 equal mounds. Carefully knead each mound into a disk that just barely holds together without cracks. Be careful not to over-knead, which leads to a tough crust. You should see specks of butter sprinkled throughout the dough, which is a good thing.

5. Sprinkle each disk with flour, wrap with plastic wrap, and place in the refrigerator for 1 hour or up to 2 days.

6. Remove 1 disk from the refrigerator and let it rest for 5 to 10 minutes to soften. Roll out to ¼-inch (6 mm) thickness. Using a 4-inch round cutter, cut out six 4-inch (10 cm) circles, and return to the refrigerator. Repeat with the second disk.

7. Preheat the oven to 350°F (180°C). Line a baking sheet with parchment paper.

8. To make the filling, heat the oil in a large skillet over medium-low heat and sauté the onion and chile until softened, about 4 minutes. Add the garlic and thyme and cook until the garlic has softened, for about 4 minutes.

9. Add the beef, tomato paste, paprika, brown sugar, salt, and pepper, and cook on medium heat until the beef is cooked through, about 4 minutes. Remove from the heat and let cool to room temperature.

10. To make the patties, take the dough circles out of the refrigerator and add about 3 tablespoons filling to the center of each circle. Fold the dough over the filling into a half-moon shape and seal by pressing the edges together with the tines of a fork.

11. Brush each patty with the egg wash. Bake on the lined baking sheet for 15 minutes, or until golden brown. Remove from the oven and serve warm or at room temperature.

GUYANESE PINE TARTS

These pine (pineapple) tarts bear some resemblance to apple pie, but unlike with the beef patties, there's no real Caribbean or South American equivalent of the Guyanese pine tart. Stephen fondly remembers picking up fresh, warm tarts in Georgetown to enjoy with music on the long ride home to his village. According to Stephen, most Guyanese pine tarts in the US are made with canned pineapple, so do yourself a favor and use fresh pineapple for this recipe.

Makes 12 tarts

- 1 pound (455 g) peeled and cored fresh pineapple, diced into ½-inch (13 mm) cubes (about 3 cups)
- ¼ cup (60 ml) fresh lemon juice
- ½ cup (100 g) packed light brown sugar
- 3 tablespoons granulated sugar
- 2 tablespoons dark brown sugar
- 1 teaspoon vanilla extract
- ½ teaspoon ground cinnamon
- ¼ teaspoon ground nutmeg
- 1 batch Pastry Dough (page 56), rolled into dough circles and refrigerated
- 1 egg, whisked with 1 teaspoon water

1. Combine the pineapple, lemon juice, sugars, vanilla, cinnamon, and nutmeg in a saucepan over medium-low heat and cook until the pineapple is soft and nearly translucent, about 15 minutes. Transfer to an uncovered container and refrigerate for 1 hour.

2. Preheat the oven to 350°F (180°C). Line a baking sheet with parchment paper.

3. Take the dough circles out of the refrigerator and add about 3 tablespoons filling to the center of each circle. Take a point at the edge of the dough circle and fold over the filling so that the edge stops just shy of the center of the filling. Repeat twice around the edge of the circle to create a triangular tart, leaving a small portion of the filling in the center uncovered. Each fold will slightly overlap the previous fold.

4. Brush each tart with the egg wash. Bake on the lined baking sheet for 15 minutes, or until golden brown. Remove from the oven and serve warm or cool.

Lenin Costas
DON CEVICHE

Deep in the Andes mountains near Machu Picchu, Lenin's grandfather was a gold miner at the height of the Peruvian gold rush in the 1940s. He died of cancer at age thirty-eight: "In those times, when you work in a mine, you go inside for maybe two, three months, and you're back maybe for one week. They don't work with no protection, because they don't know too much about all the kinds of sickness you can get later."

His young widow—Lenin's grandmother—had already been selling soups out of a pushcart on weekends to supplement her income from cleaning mansions in Lima, so she stepped up her cooking game, first adding ceviche to her pushcart menu, then opening her own restaurant in the Surquillo neighborhood of Lima in 1970—a restaurant that would thrive under her management for the next thirty-three years.

Little Lenin lived with his grandmother from age eleven to sixteen, and often helped

Lenin with childhood friends Karolina, John, and Javier (above); Abuela Adela working her pushcart (right)

her out. His grandmother's restaurant-running routines became second nature to him: "Six AM: Wake up, do the potatoes. Go to meat market, come back, start to do all the breads. Around eleven: the ceviches. So for me it was an inspiration, you know?"

At age sixteen, in 1995, Lenin was sent to join his mother in NYC, who was working as a nanny and a housekeeper. He quickly found a dishwasher job and has remained in the lively NYC restaurant industry ever since, working his way up to top server and manager at some of the finest French and Latin restaurants. Don Ceviche was born as a weekend passion project in 2017 at the LIC Flea & Food Market, and at the Queens Night Market, and has also been running out of a stall in the Essex Market on weekdays since May 2019.

Lenin still visits Peru every year and loves learning about the latest culinary innovations: "The ceviche in my grandma's time was so simple—it was orange juice, salt, and onions. They don't put lime. Around 1980, they changed orange juice to lime, maybe pepper. . . . Ceviches are evolving with the times. So my ceviche is now completely different than my grandma's was thirty years ago.

My dream is trying to do this Don Ceviche thing here in New York. Then, after that, maybe two or three years, open the restaurant in Lima and continue with the legacy, you know?"

PERU

PERUVIAN CEVICHE
WITH LECHE DE TIGRE

Peruvian cuisine is in something of a golden age in terms of global recognition and appeal. Lenin thinks ceviche is "going to be like sushi" in popularity and availability over the next decade—and he hopes to help spur the trend in NYC. When he was growing up in Peru, ceviche was simple: fish, lime, salt, and pepper. Nowadays it incorporates more flavors and ingredients and continually reinvents itself. The *leche de tigre* in this recipe adds a fiery zing to the ceviche. And, according to Lenin, it is also an aphrodisiac.

Makes 4 to 6 servings

LECHE DE TIGRE

4 ounces (115 g) white fish fillets

¼ cup (60 ml) lime juice

½ celery stalk

1 teaspoon minced garlic

CEVICHE

1 small red onion, thinly sliced into slivers

1¼ pounds (680 g) white fish fillets,* cut into 1-inch (2.5 cm) or smaller cubes

1 or 2 Peruvian *ají limo* chiles, seeded and finely diced

¾ cup (180 ml) freshly squeezed lime juice

2 teaspoons salt

Cilantro, minced, to taste

Lettuce leaves, such as romaine

1 package of *cancha* (toasted corn)**

1 to 2 ears fresh Peruvian white corn (*choclo*), boiled and kernels cut off cobs

1 medium to large sweet potato, peeled and boiled until tender and cut into 1-inch (2.5 cm) cubes

* Find fish from a reputable, trusted seafood retailer. Freshness is essential.

** Cancha can be purchased at Latin grocery stores.

1. To make the leche de tigre, combine all the ingredients with 2 tablespoons water in a blender or food processor. Blend on medium until liquefied.

2. To make the ceviche, place the red onion in a bowl of salted water for 10 minutes, then rinse.

3. Place the fish, onion, and chiles in a bowl. Pour the lime juice over the fish, sprinkle with the salt, and mix with a spoon to combine.

4. Add the cilantro and leche de tigre for a stronger taste and mix lightly.

5. Serve immediately over a bed of lettuce and garnished with a handful of the cancha, the boiled corn, and sweet potato.

Ruben "German" Montenegro

CHORI & CHIMI

ARGENTINA

German Montenegro found out about the Queens Night Market in 2018 when one of his best food-biz friends, Lenin Costas (see page 61), invited him to check out his ceviche tent there. When German saw how well his friend's business was doing, and took in all the exciting smells, sights, sounds, and tastes of dozens of other international food vendors selling that night, a thought occurred to him: Nice; this would be a cool place to sell Argentinian food. So he wrote John an email. Just like that, Chori & Chimi was born.

"I love the restaurant business—*love*—so I hope in the future to open my own restaurant here: Argentinian with other South American food, with my business partner, Roberto. He's from Peru. The vending business is a way to get into the kitchen, a step towards running a restaurant—you need experience on both sides.

I was born in 1976 in Mendoza, Argentina. A lot of people know Mendoza 'cause it's the wine city in Argentina, the Malbec city. My father—the third generation of immigrants from Spain and Italy—worked for the government for almost thirty-five years, controlling the wineries for the INV—Instituto Nacional de Vitivinicultura. My mother's father was born in Sicily, Italy, and came to Argentina around 1938.

I'm the last one of six—five brothers and one sister—so I remember when my mom cooked, going to the kitchen, taking a look at what she's making. I tried to learn. I grew up in a very poor family, so we ate meat only one time a week, but pasta maybe five times a week: homemade pasta—ravioli, gnocchi—and sauce. Basil and tomatoes from her garden. Everything from the garden. Pesto, too. *Tuco* is what we call marinara sauce—put some meat in it. Sunday, we made a *parilla*: asado steak.

When I was ten years old, I remember the light, the electricity—every three days—blackout. And we had to go to the deli to buy some candles and turn on the candles, because we had no light. It's OK now, but back then, it was a poor city. It was so difficult to study, because sometimes we didn't have any light at night.

In University I did graphic design, but to pay my university—it cost $200, which was a lot for us—I worked in restaurants, and I loved the business. In 2001, Argentina was going through a depression—it was crazy, the economy— so at that time I was twenty-four. All my friends: They have no job, they have no future. So a lot of people go to different countries. When I come to this country in 2001, graphic design was very difficult, because you had to learn the language . . . but in restaurants, it's the same thing around the world.

All my life here—eighteen years—I've been working in restaurants. When I came to this country I started working as a busboy, then server, then manager, and now I'm a bartender—for almost ten years.

I put up an Argentinian flag under our tent and always wear my special hat with the flag, so the Argentinians find us. We have a lot of Argentinian customers right now. One guy comes every Saturday. He eats two *choripanes*, and then takes home four more to his family.

I played soccer—football in Argentina— when I was younger. I love it. So I watch every Argentinian game wearing my hat and shirt. I was in Russia for the World Cup to support Argentina. And I just went to China to watch the basketball World Cup—I know, crazy!"

ARGENTINE CHORIPANES
WITH CHIMICHURRI

Choripanes—or choris, for short—are as Argentine as hot dogs are American. Choris are a staple at Argentine football matches and in Argentine street-food culture. The sausage-in-a-bun is even served as an appetizer while making asado (grilled steak). German's father's recipe hails from Mendoza, but the spices can vary according to region. For instance, some recipes call for cloves and cinnamon. If you don't have a meat grinder or metal grinder attachment at home, ask your butcher to grind the meat or even to make the chorizo for you!

Makes about 12 sausages

CHORIZO

10 feet (3 m) hog casings

2¼ pounds (1 kg) pork shoulder

2 pounds (900 g) venison or beef

12 ounces (350 g) bacon ends (or chopped bacon)

1 tablespoon plus 2¼ teaspoons kosher salt

5 garlic cloves, minced (about 2 tablespoons)

3 tablespoons Spanish paprika

1 tablespoon plus 2 teaspoons coarsely ground black pepper

¾ cup (180 ml) red wine

CHIMICHURRI

2 cups (100 g) fresh Italian parsley leaves, minced

4 garlic cloves, minced

¼ cup (32 g) fresh oregano leaves, minced, or 2 tablespoons dried oregano

1 cup (240 ml) extra-virgin olive oil

2 to 4 tablespoons red wine vinegar

½ teaspoon red pepper flakes

½ teaspoon kosher salt

Freshly ground black pepper, to taste

Baguettes or other crusty bread, toasted

1. **To make the chorizo,** soak the hog casings in warm water for 10 minutes.

2. Cut the meats into chunks you can fit into your meat grinder. Mix in the salt until evenly distributed. Let sit in the refrigerator at least 1 hour, but overnight is preferred.

3. When you are ready to grind, add the garlic, paprika, and pepper to the meat and mix well. Place in the freezer until it is between 30 and 40°F (−1 and 4°C). Place your grinder parts (auger, dies, blades, etc.) in the freezer as well, and place a large bowl in the fridge.

4. If you have multiple dies for your grinder, grind a quarter of the mixture through a very coarse die; 9 mm will do. Grind the rest through a 6.5 mm die. (If you don't have anything larger than a 6.5 mm, which is the standard "coarse" die, just use that for all the meat.) As the meat is ground, place it in the large bowl from the refrigerator.

5. After grinding, if your meat mixture is still at 35°F (1.7°C) or colder, you can go right to binding. If it has warmed up above that, place in the freezer again until the temperature is between 30 and 35°F (−1 and 1.7°C).

6. Add the red wine to the meat and mix well with very clean hands for 2 to 3 minutes; it is at the right temperature if your hands ache with cold when you do this. Mix until the meat binds to itself.

7. Stuff into the casing, twisting the casing after each sausage is sufficiently stuffed. Each sausage should be 5 to 6 inches (13 to 15 cm) long and about 1½ inches (3.8 cm) thick.

8. **To make the chimichurri,** combine all the ingredients in a mixing bowl and stir well to blend. (Leftovers can be stored at room temperature for up to 5 days. Otherwise, store in the refrigerator.)

9. To make the choripanes, grill the chorizo on a charcoal grill or grill pan for about 10 minutes, flipping as necessary, until cooked through.

10. Serve inside the toasted baguettes, topped with chimichurri.

Europe

Joey Batista

JOEY BATS CAFÉ

⑬

PORTUGAL

After working in a foundry for years, Joey's dad eventually owned a bar, then bought a butcher shop from his in-laws, who had run it since immigrating to the US in the '70s. Joey's uncles run a restaurant called Come e Cala-Te, which means "shut up and eat" in Portuguese. And everyone back home knew his mom, Isabel Fernandes,

was a master baker and chef. But Joey didn't get into the food business himself until he was in his late thirties. Since premiering his mother's Portuguese pastries at the Queens Night Market in 2017, Joey has opened cafés in Manhattan and Ludlow, Massachusetts, and now even offers nationwide shipping for his popular pastel de nata (or pastéis de nata for plural).

"I'm thirty-nine—born in Ludlow, Massachusetts, just outside of Springfield. I lived there for thirty-three years and worked a ton of jobs: bakery, construction with my uncle, bank teller, waiter, bartender, UPS, made pizzas on the side. . . . I'd failed out of community college, working third shift at the time. I was just so tired. So I went back to school at UMass to study computer science and math, and ended up with a nice career in IT at a large finance company. So many options here in New York: I got recruited, worked for a Portuguese startup. . . . But I wanted more, something a little more challenging, more exciting.

All my friends had some kind of side hustle. So I asked myself, *What could I offer New York that they don't have here already?* Boom. My mom is a master baker back home. She gave me a recipe and I brought some of her cakes to a cafe next to where I live. Within a month, was selling to ten different restaurants, then twelve to thirteen bodegas. So I told Mom, *I think this has legs. Could you come back and help me do markets?*

Back home in Ludlow, everybody I grew up with is Portuguese. There were

"I asked myself, What could I offer New York that they don't have here already?"

some Polish immigrants as well, but the majority of us—like everybody I went to school with—was Portuguese, first generation. There's these little pockets all over the Northeast. In western Mass., it's Ludlow and Chicopee—and so many other communities. But they haven't been here longer than maybe fifty years. All fairly recent.

I believe most people left because we still had the dictatorship at the time. That ended in '75. If that had ended five years earlier, I probably wouldn't exist. 'Cause a lot of Portuguese wouldn't have left the country. They were afraid for their kids getting recruited to go to the war in Angola, so a lot of them left during that time—'60s and '70s.

Every other nationality comes and stays and then we learn about their food because of New York—Italians, Irish, Asian, Latin. Everybody learns that way. The Portuguese did not stay in New York, and because they didn't stay, nobody really knows what fresh sardines on the grill are like. But they go to Portugal now and they're like, *This stuff is so good!* We love codfish. We could eat it 365 days a year made 365 different ways, and people are going to Portugal and they're learning that now, because it's been such a hot spot for tourism in the last two years. But when I started doing this three years ago, I had a very difficult time pitching it.

And all of a sudden now people are recognizing the flags. They're like, *Ah, the Portuguese flag! I was just there in Lisbon. I got engaged there!* I love it 'cause I get to be kind of like an ambassador. This is the stuff I grew up with, man—I know it's good. I can't wait for you guys to try it."

PASTÉIS DE NATA
Portuguese Custard Tarts

In describing pastéis de nata, Joey instructs the unfamiliar to imagine a warm crème brûlée wrapped in a flaky croissant. These egg custard tarts, which originated in Lisbon in the early 1800s, are usually eaten for breakfast or as a snack with espresso, and are traditionally sold at Portuguese cafes and bakeries. In Joey's household, whenever guests were expected, pastéis de nata were usually sitting on the kitchen table, and guests were encouraged to take and eat as they pleased.

Makes 12 tarts

DOUGH

- 1 cup (125 g) all-purpose flour, plus more for working the dough
- ¼ teaspoon salt
- ⅓ cup (80 ml) cold water, plus more for shaping the dough
- ½ cup (1 stick/ 115 g) unsalted butter, at room temperature, plus additional as desired

CUSTARD

- ¾ cup (150 g) granulated sugar
- ⅓ cup (40 g) all-purpose flour
- ¼ teaspoon salt
- 1¼ cups (360 ml) cold milk
- 6 large egg yolks
- 1 teaspoon vanilla extract, optional
- Ground cinnamon
- Confectioners' sugar

1. To make the dough, combine the flour, salt, and cold water in a bowl. Mix until the dough becomes firm and easily separates from the sides of the bowl. Transfer to a floured flat surface and sprinkle additional flour on top of the dough. Knead into a firm ball, which should be quick, as you're not kneading to change the firmness.

2. Roll the dough into a square about ⅛-inch (3 mm) thick, roughly 10 inches (25 cm) long per side. Spread a thin layer of butter (about 2 tablespoons) across two-thirds of the dough but leave about ½ inch (13 mm) around the border unbuttered to keep butter from leaking out. Flip the unbuttered third of the dough over the middle and fold the opposite side over it.

3. Flip the dough over while lightly flouring. Roll into a 10-inch (25 cm) square again as before, being careful with the edges. Spread another layer of butter over the dough and fold as in step 2. You can repeat this step with more butter as many times as you like—the crust will become flakier (and tastier as well as more caloric!) with each iteration—but leave about 2 tablespoons of the butter for later.

4. When you've buttered and folded for the last time, place on a baking sheet and refrigerate until the butter has chilled, about 15 minutes.

5. Sprinkle a little more flour over the dough, roll into a 10-inch (25 cm) square again, and spread another thin layer of butter on the dough, leaving a border on the edges unbuttered. Lightly moisten the unbuttered edges of the dough with cold water. Starting at one edge, roll the dough into a log with a diameter of 2 to 3 inches (5 to 7.5 cm).

6. Spread a little more flour on the dough, wrap or cover in plastic wrap, and let rest for 30 minutes.

7. To make the custard glaze, combine the granulated sugar with 1 tablespoon water in a small saucepan. Heat over medium heat without stirring until the glaze reaches 215°F (100°C) and remove from the heat.

8. To make the custard, preheat the oven to 550°F (285°C) and grease a muffin pan or line it with paper liners.

9. Mix the flour, salt, and milk together in a pot. Cook over medium heat (at about 350°F/180°C) while whisking constantly until thickened. Remove from the heat and cool for about 15 minutes.

10. Whisk the egg yolks into the milk while adding the glaze and vanilla, if using, until the yolks have broken and the mixture is a consistent yellow color. Strain the custard into a measuring cup.

11. To make the tarts, unwrap the dough and slice into 12 circles about ½-inch (13 mm) thick.

12. Place each circle into its own prepared muffin cup. Dip your thumb into some cold water and use it to press the dough down in the center and flatten against the bottom of the cup. Slowly work the dough up the sides of the muffin cup by applying pressure, all the way to the top of the cup.

13. Pour the custard into the cups until three-fourths full.

14. Bake for about 15 minutes, until the custard is browned and caramelized and bubbling up in the middle. Start paying close attention after baking for 10 minutes.

15. Let the tarts cool for a few minutes and then serve warm with a dash of cinnamon and confectioners' sugar.

Wesley Wobles

DOTTY'S NORWEGIAN KITCHEN

14
NORWAY

Picking up dinner at the Dotty's Norwegian Kitchen tent at the Queens Night Market feels like walking into a rainbow. While low-key-famous Chef Wesley ensures that each dish is topped with a supercolorful array of fresh herbs and raw and pickled spiraled veggies, his artist-and-caterer partner, Mimi, juxtaposes stripes, polka dots, and all manner of pastel colors in their accessories and décor. And after dark, the colored light bulbs get turned on! The ultracreative duo also runs a unique little café/art gallery in the East Village called Pinky's Space.

"**F**ood is all I really know. It's everything that I love—I mean, besides my wife. And my sons and our pets and my friends. But food is everything to me. And my grandmother was my influence. She'd wake up at six in the morning and start making crepes for breakfast and make big batches of jams every summer—it was just heaven. And so I fell in love with food that way.

I was born in Waterbury, Connecticut, in '79, and my father was a marijuana grower for a former SNL cast member. I didn't know until he got caught when I was fourteen. We had a giant pond. It would help supply the water to the crop right next to there, but hidden in the woods. My pop told me they were tomato plants. I was like, *How come we never have any tomatoes?* He'd say, *We just don't have any luck right now.*

My mother was the main one around growing up, and she taught me about gardening. Her mother lived in Florida, and her mother came from Norway. My summer vacation was hanging out in a condo in Florida cooking with my grandma; hanging out playing cards; Scrabble; going to the beach. But food was always the focus, the plan. We'd wake up in the morning and we'd have a plan of what we were going to make.

My mother took it badly—Dad's arrest—but I was super happy to be moving to Florida to spend time with Grandma. I got into surfing,

"I GET JOY OUT OF SEEING PEOPLE EAT MY FOOD."

got a job in a restaurant as a prep cook and dishwasher and immediately felt the energy of the restaurant business, like a rush. I thought, *This is cool—things go by so fast, it's so exciting.* But then I got into marijuana, decided it was cooler than school, and left at fifteen and started cooking full-time in restaurants. At seventeen I saw I was a mess, started studying for the GED, got it, enrolled in culinary school at eighteen in Portland, Oregon: Le Cordon Bleu.

My first chef position in New York City was in Brooklyn, and I was about to turn twenty-one there for the millennium. We overbooked it and I underordered enough steaks for all the reservations—so that will forever be embedded in my mind, 'cause I had to run around to all the other restaurants at like 12:15, because people are just sitting! It's New Year's Eve, they're on dates, and this is a special moment for them. They paid a ton of money and I'm like, *Do you have any steaks? Could you please give me a steak?* It was like anxiety central. I just wanted to crawl into a hole and die 'cause I was about twenty short. I learned from that mistake.

Later—after being the opening chef for a dozen or so New York restaurants, and several throughout Paris, too—I worked as a private chef for billionaires. I would prepare food sitting above Central Park West on the top floor in a penthouse, with everything at my fingertips, and I'd make dinner, and then get a call right before

I'm about to serve it—*Going out to dinner tonight. See you tomorrow!* And I'd have prepared three different types of meals and it would all be garbage. I was like, *I hate this life. This is not my life. I don't want this.*

I went through a dark period. Had no problem getting work, but my heart wasn't in it. I turned to drugs.

It wasn't until I met my wife, Mimi, that I started to see things differently—stopped focusing on the negative and just realized things I wanted to do in life and how I wanted to live my life and spread good vibes and energy to everybody. And that's what happened: I went on unemployment and signed up for a government program for self-employment, complete with training and mentors—and that's how we opened our café, Pinky's Space, in the East Village, and then the Dotty's Kitchen pop-up on Saturdays at the Queens Night Market.

Such a breath of fresh air, to be surrounded by like-minded people that all know how to cook!"

FÅRIKÅL
Lamb and Cabbage Stew

If ever there was comfort food for cold winter nights, it would be Norwegian *fårikål*. Wesley picked up this recipe, which has been passed down for generations, from his grandmother. According to Wesley, with every bite of this lamb and cabbage stew, "you feel, smell, and taste a piece of the earth." Serve this with freshly boiled baby potatoes doused with melted salted butter.

Makes 6 servings

- ½ cup (1 stick/115 g) butter (omit for a gluten-free version)
- ½ cup (65 g) all-purpose flour (omit for a gluten-free version)
- 4¼ pounds (2 kg) lamb shank, whole or cut
- 4¼ pounds (2 kg) white cabbage, cored and cut into large wedges
- 1 yellow onion, sliced
- 3 tablespoons black peppercorns
- 4 garlic cloves
- 3 rosemary sprigs
- 3 thyme sprigs
- 4 bay leaves
- 1 tablespoon salt
- 1 cup (240 ml) red wine
- 1 tablespoon tomato paste

1. Melt the butter in a large pot on low heat. Stir in the flour and cook, stirring frequently, until it develops a nutty smell and an espresso color, about 60 to 90 seconds.

2. Place layers of the lamb, cabbage, onion, and seasonings in the pot in any order, alternating until you have used all the ingredients.

3. Add the wine, tomato paste, and 4 cups (960 ml) water.

4. Cover and bring to a boil, then return the heat to low. Cook, stirring occasionally, until the meat is tender and easily detaches from the bone, about 3 hours. Enjoy hot!

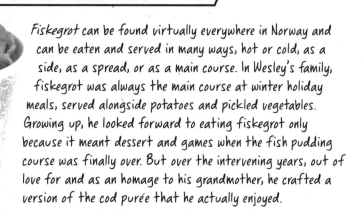

FISKEGROT
Fish Pudding

Fiskegrot can be found virtually everywhere in Norway and can be eaten and served in many ways, hot or cold, as a side, as a spread, or as a main course. In Wesley's family, fiskegrot was always the main course at winter holiday meals, served alongside potatoes and pickled vegetables. Growing up, he looked forward to eating fiskegrot only because it meant dessert and games when the fish pudding course was finally over. But over the intervening years, out of love for and as an homage to his grandmother, he crafted a version of the cod purée that he actually enjoyed.

Makes 6 to 8 servings

2½ pounds (1.1 kg) fresh cod

3 tablespoons potato starch

1 cup (240 ml) warm whole milk

½ cup (120 ml) buttermilk

½ cup (120 ml) heavy cream

½ cup (1 stick/ 115 g) butter, at room temperature

2 eggs

2 egg yolks

2 teaspoons salt

¼ teaspoon ground cardamom

¼ teaspoon garlic powder

¼ teaspoon onion powder

¼ teaspoon paprika

¼ teaspoon ground white pepper

SAUCE BLANCHE

2 parts yogurt

1 part mayonnaise

Lemon juice

Salt

Ground black pepper

Lemon wedges

Fresh dill

1. Cut the cod into small enough pieces for a food processor. Place the fish in a food processor and process until it becomes a smooth paste. Transfer to a large bowl.

2. Add all of the remaining ingredients to the puréed fish and combine. Transfer some mixture to the food processor until it is halfway full and purée until smooth. Repeat until all of the mixture has been puréed.

3. Divide the fish paste into one or more poach-safe bags or wraps. It's prudent to double-bag just in case of leakage.

4. Bring a large pot of water to a boil and turn the heat down to a simmer. Place the poaching bag(s) in the pot and cook for about 30 minutes or until the internal temperature of the pudding reaches 145°F (63°C).

5. Remove the bags and let rest for 30 minutes to reach room temperature. The texture and consistency should be similar to thick oatmeal.

6. To make the sauce blanche, combine the yogurt and mayonnaise in a bowl and season to taste with lemon juice, salt, pepper, and dill.

7. Serve the fiskegrot with the sauce blanche and more lemon and fresh dill, if desired. Eat with a fork.

LEFSE
Potato Flatbread

Like most thin flatbreads or crepes, *lefse* are very versatile. These potato flatbreads can be used in sweet or savory dishes, folded, rolled, stuffed, or eaten plain. Wesley has adapted the recipe for his tastes. For instance, he doesn't use the traditional grooved rolling pin for lefse, uses dehydrated potato flakes instead of mashing his own potatoes, and has added yeast as a leavener, as he likes the subtle fermented taste. His favorite way to enjoy lefse is with salted butter and jam.

Makes about 12 large lefse

1 cup (240 ml) warm water

3 tablespoons active dry yeast

3 tablespoons plus 2 teaspoons granulated sugar

3 cups (180 g) dehydrated potato flakes

2 cups (250 g) all-purpose flour, plus more for rolling

1 tablespoon baking powder

1 tablespoon salt

1 teaspoon baking soda

1 teaspoon ground cardamom

2 cups (480 ml) heavy cream

1 cup (240 ml) milk

2 cups (4 sticks/450 g) butter, cubed, at room temperature, plus more for cooking

1. Combine the warm water, yeast, and 2 teaspoons of the sugar in a bowl and let rest for 20 minutes.

2. Combine the remaining 3 tablespoons sugar, the potato flakes, flour, baking powder, salt, baking soda, and cardamom in a large bowl and whisk together.

3. Heat the cream and milk in a saucepan and bring to a boil. Remove from the heat and let rest until cool enough to handle.

4. Pour the cream along with the yeast mixture and the cubed butter into the dry ingredients and mix well.

5. If you have a cast-iron or heavy-bottomed skillet large enough to cook a lefse about 12 inches (30 cm) in diameter, form the dough into balls about the size of an orange and place on a pan or plate; you should have about 12 balls. If you don't have a large enough pan or skillet this size, make more, smaller lefse. Cover with plastic wrap and let rest for 30 minutes.

6. Roll out 1 ball on a well-floured pastry cloth until paper thin; large balls should be rolled to about 12 inches (30 cm) in diameter.

7. Heat the skillet on medium heat and add a little butter. Cook 1 lefse for about 1 minute, until brown spots appear on the bottom. Flip and cook the other side for 30 to 45 seconds. Repeat with the remaining dough.

8. Place the cooked lefse between damp kitchen towels until ready to eat.

9. Serve according to taste. Leftovers can be placed in an airtight container and frozen. Warm in the oven until soft when ready to serve.

Nicole and Carly Di Lena

DI LENA'S DOLCINI

ITALY

Born into a long line of Italian small-business owners, sisters Nicole and Carly Di Lena grew up in Fort Lee, New Jersey, surrounded by family. Their mother had immigrated from northern Italy—Santa Margherita, known for its pinot grigio. Their entrepreneur father had been born in Hoboken, New Jersey, but his parents were also from Italy—from Altamura, in the south, near Bari. The Di Lena sisters have been visiting family in both places their whole lives. They started their cookie company together with their grandmother's Italian cookie recipes and Nicole's severance pay after her garment-industry job had been outsourced.

Though neither of the sisters had worked in the food industry until a few years ago, the Di Lena sisters, serious amateur bakers since forever, have taken it on with gusto. They now have their own commercial kitchen space, featuring a ten-foot-high professional oven they bought in an auction that can bake two thousand cookies at once. They manage several employees, and their prepackaged cookie business is expanding well beyond the Queens Night Market—but they grew their clientele from the beginning by just showing up places with smiles, stories, and free cookies. In that spirit, the Di Lena sisters still love to show up at the Queens Night Market every Saturday to hand customers their cookies in person and share their own experiences with them.

Carly: In the morning, biscotti were a big thing for us in the house. We'd always have biscotti with our coffee. I mean, my grandmother was a three-times-a-day coffee drinker, so . . . always dip them in the coffee—but you have to get it right before it gets too soggy and breaks off!

Nicole: Also vin santo after-dinner wine with biscotti.

Carly: When we came home from school, actually, that was our treat: We'd have a biscotto dipped in plain wine—because that's what they did in Italy. It wasn't to get us drunk or anything. We'd just have one or two biscotti dipped in a watered-down rosé wine and we didn't think anything of it, and neither did our grandparents.

It was a European custom brought over here. And I think it helped us, too, because culturally we just really look at alcohol so differently from some of our friends.

Nicole: I studied abroad in Italy for a semester of college and met someone and wanted to stay there, and my grandmother was like, *I didn't make the sacrifice for you to go in reverse. You have to come back.*

Carly: My sister called her to tell her she was going to stay in Italy a little longer. It was this romance of a lifetime! And she's like, *No way. Not gonna happen.* She was the head of the family, and she told you how it was all the time—no sugar coating.

Nicole: So I came back shortly after that. It was sad, but in hindsight she was right: I would have lost my education.

Carly: You know, there are choices that you can make in life that can really catapult you to where you need to or want to be, and she knew that our opportunities would be here. I mean we go back there all the time, and it's wonderful, and it's fun to be in the *campagna* and to handwash my clothes for three hours—you know what I mean. Those are *Eat Pray Love* experiences. And you know we're in "The Motherland" when we go home, but at the same time, the opportunities you have being in America are incredible—and being first generation here, we appreciate that so much.

ALMOND BISCOTTI

Biscotti are cookies that are baked twice. Their hardness and sweetness make them perfect for dunking in espresso (or coffee). There might be something metaphorical in the association Nicole and Carly have of biscotti and their grandmother—she was full of tough love. After many years have passed, the sisters now believe her sternness and refusal to sugarcoat anything helped prepare them to eventually start their own cookie company. Biscotti are versatile. You can make them with any number of nuts and can even make them savory by adding cheese, pepper, and liquor.

Makes 20 biscotti

½ cup (1 stick/115 g) unsalted butter, at room temperature

¾ cup (150 g) granulated sugar

1 teaspoon Strega liqueur, optional

¼ teaspoon salt

2 eggs

2 cups (250 g) all-purpose flour

1½ teaspoons baking powder

1 cup (140 g) whole raw, unsalted almonds

1. Preheat the oven to 350°F (180°C). Line a baking sheet with parchment paper.

2. In a mixing bowl, cream the butter with a mixer for 1 minute while gradually adding the sugar. Continue beating until light and fluffy.

3. Mix in the Strega, if using, and salt. Add one egg at a time, beating until integrated. Gradually add the flour and baking powder while mixing until well combined. Stir in the almonds. The resulting dough should be firm enough to hold shape when formed into a log.

4. Place the dough on the lined pan. Shape into a 13 x 3-inch (33 x 7.5 cm) log.

5. Bake for 30 minutes. Remove from the oven and let cool for 30 minutes. Transfer the log to a cutting board and use a serrated knife to cut into slices ¾-inch (2 cm) thick.

6. Place the slices standing back up on the pan and bake for an additional 15 minutes for extra hardness, until dark golden-brown. Take out sooner if softer biscotti are preferred.

7. Cool and serve.

ORECCHIETTE
WITH BROCCOLI RABE

Sunday was pasta night in the Di Lena household, and a favorite in the rotation was "little ears" with broccoli rabe. The taste is bold and rustic, but also comforting. The broccoli rabe is bitter, the garlic pungent, the pepper flakes spicy, and the pasta, once coated in olive oil, are fun and slippery. Many Italians add sausage to this dish; pan-fry it separately and toss with the pasta.

Makes 4 servings

3 pounds (1.4 kg) broccoli rabe

⅓ cup (80 ml) olive oil

4 garlic cloves, crushed

1 teaspoon red pepper flakes

½ teaspoon salt

¼ teaspoon ground black pepper

1 pound (455 g) orecchiette pasta (preferably fresh-made)

Freshly grated Parmesan

1. Prepare the broccoli rabe by cutting off the lower, tough ends. Cut a 1-inch (2.5 cm) slit in the lower end of the remaining stem so it cooks evenly and is not as tough. Thoroughly wash in a large bowl and drain.

2. Heat the oil in a large pot over medium heat and sauté the garlic for 1 minute. Be careful not to burn the garlic or it will become bitter. Add the red pepper flakes, salt, pepper, and the broccoli rabe. Cover, reduce the heat to low, and cook until wilted, 10 to 12 minutes.

3. While the broccoli rabe is cooking, prepare the orecchiette according to the directions on the package. Drain the pasta and toss together with the broccoli rabe.
Plate and top with
the Parmesan.

CALZONE DI CIPOLLA

Onion Calzone

Nicole and Carly would often have these onion pies during Lent. Onion pie also reminds them of Christmas Eve, when Aunt Ria would be making anchovy doughnuts (*zeppole con le alici*) on the stove top and onion pies just below in the oven. They learned to make it from their grandmother as they prepared for the feast of Madonna del Buon Cammino, a tradition originating in Altamura, Italy. You can eat them when they're hot, but the sisters think they're best for breakfast, right out of the refrigerator. For optimal flavor, prepare the onion-tomato mixture the day before and let rest overnight in the refrigerator.

Makes 8 servings

2 tablespoons olive oil, plus more for baking

4 large Vidalia and/or sweet onions (2 each is ideal), thinly sliced into half-moons*

1 teaspoon dried oregano

1 teaspoon kosher salt

¾ teaspoon ground black pepper

1 tablespoon tomato paste

15 grape tomatoes, cut in half

1 pound (450 g) pizza dough, homemade or store-bought

1. Heat the oil in a large saucepan over medium-low heat. Add the onions, oregano, salt, and pepper. Sauté until the onions are caramelized, 7 to 10 minutes.

2. Stir in the tomato paste and add the grape tomatoes. Sauté for 3 minutes, until the tomatoes are softened.

3. Preheat the oven to 400°F (200°C). Oil a baking sheet that is larger than a 12-inch (30 cm) square.

4. Cut the dough in half. Using your fingers, stretch one half of the dough to form a 12-inch (30 cm) square. Spread the onion-tomato mixture evenly on top.

5. Stretch the remaining half of the dough and lay it over the onion-tomato mixture. Using your fingers, press the top and bottom dough squares together along the edges to enclose the pie. Brush additional oil on top of the dough and cut four 2-inch (5 cm) slits into the top to allow steam to escape.

6. Place the pie in the oven and bake for 35 minutes, or until the crust is golden brown. Remove from the oven and let cool.

7. Cut into squares and serve warm or at room temperature (or even cold as leftovers).

* If sweet onions are not available, add 1 teaspoon sugar to regular onions when cooking.

Kika Radz

BROOKLYN DUMPLING

(16) POLAND

Kika's parents moved the family from Poland to Connecticut, when Kika was just two years old, but they made sure she and her sisters grew up deeply connected to their Polish roots. They attended a Polish American elementary school during the week, extra Polish school on Saturdays to learn Polish grammar, writing, and history, and Polish church on Sundays. The girls weren't allowed to answer back in English when their parents spoke to them in Polish. And, of course, there was the food.

Kika's mother's pierogi were widely considered the best in their tight-knit Polish community, and she made sure her daughters learned all her culinary secrets. "My mom used to tell me, *You have to learn how to cook for your future family.* Very, very old school! Growing up I actually preferred to do the cleanup."

After her mom passed away, Kika's father opened up a Polish restaurant in their town. It felt like a fitting homage to his late wife, who had always wanted to keep strong Polish roots in the community. Though her father's menu had all sorts of traditional Polish food on it, "the *gołąbki*, the pancakes, everything," Kika was most excited about the pierogi—her mom's specialty.

Even as Kika moved to New York City and started to pursue a career in the film industry, she kept thinking about her mom's pierogi, wondering if they alone could be the foundation of a business idea. As her new on-set film world friends learned about Kika's Polish heritage and culinary skills, catering requests for pierogi started trickling in. As she shared her mom's pierogi with more and more enthusiastic friends and coworkers, she thought back on a trip she'd taken to see some friends in Kraków a few years back.

"There was this place called 24-Hour Pierogi. It's so popular at any given time of the day, especially after a fun night out, and no matter how long the line was you eagerly awaited your turn. I saw this about ten years ago and it never left my mind."

Why weren't pierogi fun and accessible like that here in the US? Everyone's favorite home-style on-the-go breakfast, lunch, dinner, and even late-night snack? Could she change that? Brooklyn Dumpling now plays with dumpling traditions from around the world and experiments with fusions, too, but the heart and soul of the endeavor is her late mother's classic recipe, with great attention to details like the perfect crispiness of the sautéed onions, the warmed sauerkraut.

So I've now taken her recipes and expanded with them. So it's nice, because it keeps a little piece of her memory alive. Every single time I'm working on them. I carry on her legacy, and it's constantly moving forward."

KOPYTKA
Polish Potato Gnocchi

Kopytka are a big hit with Polish children. They're simple, delicious, and fun to make and eat. Kika fondly recalls her mother calling them "little snakes." Recruit some young ones to help make these little snakes and top them with whatever their hearts desire!

Makes 4 servings (about 30 kopytka)

- 1 pound (455 g) russet potatoes, peeled
- 4 ounces (115 g) farmer cheese
- 1 egg
- ½ teaspoon salt
- 2 cups (250 g) all-purpose flour, plus more for rolling
- Butter-fried bread crumbs, homemade or store-bought, optional
- Crumbled bacon, optional
- Sour cream, optional

1. Boil the potatoes in a large pot of water until easily mashable, about 15 minutes.

2. Mash the potatoes thoroughly, then stir in the cheese, egg, and salt. Add the flour and combine into a smooth dough.

3. Break off portions of the dough onto a floured flat surface and roll into ropes ½ inch (13 mm) in diameter. Slice the rolled ropes diagonally at about ¾-inch (2 cm) intervals.

4. Bring a pot of salted water to a boil. Drop a handful of kopytka in at a time and remove with a slotted spoon when they float to the top, about 2 to 3 minutes per batch. They will be soft to the bite. For added texture and flavor, pan-fry in a little oil over medium heat until lightly browned on all sides, about 5 minutes.

5. Serve topped with the bread crumbs, crumbled bacon, and sour cream, if using.

POTATO AND CHEESE PIEROGI

Making pierogi together is a common Polish family tradition, as it was in Kika's family—especially around the holidays. Her home would become a "little pierogi factory." Kika has been making pierogi for as long as she can remember and has added some extra flavor to the traditional potato and cheese filling, such as garlic, parsley, and onion, in this recipe.

Makes 4 to 6 servings
(about 30 dumplings)

DOUGH

2 to 2½ cups (250 to 325 g) all-purpose flour, plus more for rolling

1 large egg

1 teaspoon salt

1 cup (240 ml) warm water, plus more as needed

1 teaspoon sour cream, optional

FILLING

2 medium russet potatoes (about 16 ounces/450 g), peeled, boiled, and mashed

8 ounces (225 g) farmer cheese

⅔ cup (110 g) diced yellow onion, sautéed

½ teaspoon garlic powder

1 teaspoon salt

½ teaspoon ground black pepper

3 fresh parsley sprigs, leaves only, chopped

Vegetable oil for frying, optional

Accompaniments, such as sauerkraut and/or crumbled bacon, optional

Sour cream

2 fresh parsley sprigs, leaves only, chopped

1. To make the dough, place 2 cups (250 g) of the flour in a large bowl and create a well in the center. Break the egg into the well and add the salt, warm water, and sour cream, if using. Stir to bring the dough together and knead well for 5 to 10 minutes, adding more flour or water when necessary. When done, it should be smooth and have an even consistency, and it should be soft but not stick to the hands. Cover and let rest for 20 minutes.

2. To make the filling, combine the mashed potatoes, cheese, sautéed onion, garlic powder, salt, pepper, and parsley in a bowl.

3. To make the pierogi, flour a flat work surface. Roll the dough out thinly to about ⅛-inch (3 mm) thick and cut out circles with a 2-inch (5 cm) glass. Gently stretch out each circle to about 3 inches (7.5 cm) in diameter to accommodate adding a tablespoon of the filling to the middle of each circle. Fold the dough in half and pinch the edges with a slight overlap on each pinch. Add a little twist as you pinch for extra design! This step will lead to thinly wrapped, bite-size pierogi; for thicker pierogi wrapping, cut out larger circles from the rolled dough.

4. Bring a large pot of salted water to a boil. Drop 6 to 8 dumplings into the water at a time. When they float to the surface (about 4 to 5 minutes), allow them to cook for an additional minute, then remove with a slotted spoon and set aside to cool.

5. For added texture and flavor, pan-fry in a skillet with a little oil over medium heat until golden brown on both sides, about 5 minutes.

6. Serve warm with your accompaniments, if desired. Finish with a dollop of sour cream and a sprinkle of parsley.

Alida Malushi

BALKAN BITES

KOSOVO

An Albanian born and raised in Kosovo, formerly of Yugoslavia; a student of literature who quotes Bourdieu; a journalist; an intellectual; a successful professional—Alida went to work one day in her mid-twenties amid the developing Kosovo War only to discover that her TV station had been entirely shut down.

That was the last straw. What else could she do with no means to do her work and tell her stories? She and her husband considered various places to move to, like Norway, where she had international journalist friends, but in the end warily settled on the US, since most of her family was going there.

Alida's only son was born soon after her move to New Jersey and helped give her a new sense of belonging and purpose in this strange place, so soon after her home had been destroyed. Skeptical of the American education system and its ability to give children of immigrants a robust sense of self, she worked hard to supplement her son's education with world history and language lessons, as well as philosophical concepts she was sad to see omitted from his public school curriculum. More than that, she wanted to make sure he never saw political disaster in his home as she had in hers. As soon as she got her citizenship, she exercised her right to vote—at every opportunity that presented itself.

She also found a new calling in food. "After journalism, food was my second passion. Whenever I cook, I feel it's like meditation. You know—you focus on what you're doing; you want to make people happy; you want to experience a new taste. So all my life is around food. When I came to this country I went to the French Culinary Institute in Manhattan and graduated in 1995, and since then I am in the food business—or industry—how they call it today. I worked in the Hilton Hotel, worked in a French restaurant, had for a short time my own pastry shop—I had all kinds of different experiences."

During this time, Alida always cooked at home. Family gatherings were a chance to share her favorite recipes from Kosovo with nostalgic family and fellow Albanian refugee friends, as well as with the younger US-born generation, and new friends and neighbors who were sometimes tasting these foods for the first time.

"Then I paused for some years: my mother had developed Alzheimer's, so somehow, for a couple of years, I was cut off from everything, because she lived with me and I had to take care of her. She passed away almost two years ago, and then my niece Ariana, my brother's only daughter, she had this idea."

Ariana asked Alida to learn traditional Albanian recipes that Alida's mother, Magbule, used to make. They would get together on Sundays to bake and share stories about Magbule. Then one Sunday while they were making burek, they decided that they should start selling their creations at pop-up markets. Now that's all Alida does, workwise.

"Our main idea doing this is to give people another experience. Because all people in the world are the same, except for three things that are unique and make them different: It's language, food, and music. Everything else is the same."

BALKAN ĆEVAPI
Grilled Meat Patties

Family BBQs in the US might evoke thoughts of hamburgers and hot dogs, but in the Balkans, family BBQs involve *ćevapi*. You might eat five or ten of these thumb-shaped meat thingies in a sitting, usually with *somun*, or *lepinja*—a fluffy, triple-rise flatbread made out of milk; *kajmak*, a Balkan clotted cream; *ajvar*, a red pepper spread; sliced sweet onions; and a shepherd's salad. Since Kosovo is majority Muslim, the ćevapi there are usually made of beef and lamb as opposed to pork. Ćevapi also freeze well uncooked.

Makes 4 to 6 servings

- 1¼ pounds (565 g) ground beef (90 percent lean if possible)
- 12 ounces (340 g) ground lamb
- 1 medium white onion, finely chopped
- 3 garlic cloves, minced
- 2 tablespoons bread crumbs
- 3 tablespoons cold water
- 2 teaspoons kosher salt
- 1 teaspoon ground black pepper
- ¾ teaspoon baking soda

1. Combine all the ingredients in a bowl, cover with plastic wrap, and leave to marinate for at least 1 hour in the refrigerator.

2. Remove the meat from the refrigerator and form into finger-length sausages; they should be as thick as your thumb.

3. Grill them over medium heat on a hot grill for about 10 to 12 minutes, turning them several times, until they are brown on all sides and cooked through. (A charcoal grill is recommended for the smoky flavor, but any grill or grill pan will work.)

4. Serve them hot, right from the grill.

BALKAN BAKLAVA

As Alida explains it, if handmade baklava comes to you as a gift, it means the highest honor and respect. Making baklava from scratch is a laborious process, especially with the layers and layers of paper-thin phyllo dough. These days, most people make baklava from store-bought phyllo because of the convenience. It is still delicious and will surely impress your guests. It's sweet, nutty, and flaky, and the tartness of the raisins helps balance out the sugary syrup.

Makes 24 pieces

- 1 cup (2 sticks/ 225 g) unsalted butter, melted, plus more for the pan
- 1 pound (455 g) walnuts
- 3 cups (600 g) plus ¼ cup (50 g) granulated sugar
- Zest of ⅛ lemon
- 1 pound (455 g) phyllo dough (24 phyllo sheets), thawed
- ⅓ cup (80 g) golden raisins
- 1 lemon, sliced
- 3 tablespoons honey

1. Preheat the oven to 350°F (180°C). Butter a deep 9 x 13-inch (23 x 33 cm) baking pan that has sides at least 2 inches (5 cm) deep. (If you use a smaller pan, just cut the phyllo sheets to fit.)

2. Pulse the walnuts, ¼ cup (50 g) of the sugar, and the lemon zest in a food processor until finely chopped. You should end up with about 4 cups .

3. Cut the 24 phyllo sheets in half crosswise. You should have 48 sheets that measure about 9 x 13 inches (23 x 33 cm).

4. Lay 4 phyllo sheets in the prepared pan, then spread about ⅔ cup (85 g) of the walnut mixture and about 1½ tablespoons of the raisins on the top.

5. Place 4 more phyllo sheets on top, then add the walnuts and raisins as in the previous step. Repeat this step 4 more times, ending with 4 phyllo sheets on top.

6. Melt the butter and pour over the baklava. Bake for 50 to 60 minutes, until golden brown. Remove the baklava from the oven.

7. Combine the remaining 3 cups (600 g) sugar, the lemon, and 2 cups (480 ml) water in a saucepan and bring to a boil. Cook over medium-low heat until it reaches a syrupy consistency, about 15 minutes. Add the honey, stir to combine, and remove from the heat.

8. Pour the hot syrup over the baklava. Let stand, uncovered, until it cools to room temperature, then refrigerate until serving.

9. Before serving, cut with a sharp knife into 24 squares (6 lengthwise by 4 widthwise) and serve at room temperature.

Radu Sirbu

TWISTER CAKE BAKERY

ROMANIA

Twister cake *might sound like it ought to be a silly food fad, but the Romanian equivalent, colac Secuiesc, points to their long history*: Colac means "cake" and Secuiesc, or Szekler, describes a region in Romania where Radu's cakes originated some three hundred years ago. Székely Land is a Hungarian-speaking part of Transylvania, hence the more common Hungarian name for the twister or chimney cake, kürtős kalács.

Bringing authentic chimney cakes to New York City fairs and festival-goers on weekends over the last decade has meant a lot to Radu, who has worked as a private chauffeur throughout the week since moving to the US in 2002. His cakes—made just the way his grandmother taught him—are so good, they once earned him an Instagram tag by a beautiful Romanian *stranger who tried them at a Romanian festival, came back for more to share with her family, and eventually became Radu's wife. Their two small children will have to learn to make the cakes themselves someday, considering their parents' how-we-met story. Radu's oldest daughter—from his first marriage—is already thinking of opening her own Twister Cake in Munich, where she lives.*

But for now, Radu loves his weekend cake-making ritual, selling cakes, seeing happy customers, and celebrating his grandmother's Transylvanian baking legacy far from home.

" I'm from the same part in Romania as the twister cakes, a town called Cugir. Very, very close—it's like not even an hour away—but I live in the same region in Transylvania, which is part of Romania: the central northwest of Romania, which borders Hungary. I was born in 1973—a Taurus. I grew up in that area, and I learned to make my cakes from my grandmother. She used to bake them the old-fashioned way, over the charcoal. She used to use some old, old, old tools, which remained in our family. Some I even have on display at the Twister Cake booth, like a 150-year-old wood cylinder. We had only one roll, so we used to make one cake at a time. Now I make eight cakes at a time in five minutes.

"I LEARNED TO MAKE MY CAKES FROM MY GRANDMOTHER. SHE USED TO BAKE THEM THE OLD-FASHIONED WAY, OVER THE CHARCOAL. SHE USED TO USE SOME OLD, OLD, OLD TOOLS, WHICH REMAINED IN OUR FAMILY."

In Romania, when I grew up, everyone was cooking at home—I think there was one restaurant in my hometown. Of course, I loved cooking and I always paid attention and I learned a lot from my grandmother. On weekends she was a chef at weddings, so she cooked a lot. She used to make these twister cakes on rare occasions because it takes a lot of time to do the charcoal, and then you have to do it by hand. . . . Back in the day, it was a slow process. Slow and good. Good stuff. These cakes used to be served as wedding cakes, three hundred years ago, and even while I was growing up.

You roll the dough around these custom-made wood cylinders made of maple, because maple has a very dense structure so doesn't burn fast. So we used to put a lot of oil on the wood cylinder, roll the strips of dough around the wood cylinder, sprinkle with sugar, and cook them over the charcoal, rotating very slowly by hand, until the sugar caramelizes. So when you take it off the wood cylinder it's like a hollow spiral. I remember when I was little putting my hand through it. It was like a bracelet going up my whole arm.

We didn't have any toppings back in the day. Sometimes walnuts or cinnamon, just a little bit. The last time I

remember she was making this for me was in '90 or '92, just before she passed away. Whenever we'd visit her, we'd ask her, *Can you please, can you please make us some?* So that's how I learned. *I'm too old,* she said, *you have to do it.* So me and my cousins, we gathered around the table and played with the dough, figured it out with my grandmother's help.

Prior to coming to US, I was a supervisor in a big gun factory: You know the famous AK-47? I used to work in the factory, then I was promoted to one of the security supervisors. My family, they all worked in the same factory basically—my parents and my grandparents. Even now, that factory is doing pretty much the same thing. They have a new addition: They make all the transmission boxes for Mercedes. So all the transmission boxes in the Mercedes cars right now are made in my hometown—all of them.

The job offered me the opportunity to have a second job, so I owned a computer store that did service, sales. . . . So I was working both jobs there, then, in 2002, I came to the United States. I had studied IT in Romania, but when I came here I became a chauffeur. And, you know, I really like it: It worked for me. I think a lot of Romanians coming to the United States, or Eastern Europeans, they get a chauffeur driver or taxi driver job 'cause it's very easy for us. Some people prefer to go to school and get a better job or work in a different field, but this worked for me—and I'm still doing it.

And I always loved to cook. Even when I'm home, I enjoy cooking. I cook every day if I have time. I have all kinds of herbs in my garden, and I like to add as much herbs and greens to my dishes as possible. I'm a Taurus; I like that kind of stuff—to sit in a corner, and eat my grass, not to be bothered."

KÜRTŐS KALÁCS
Romanian Chimney Cakes

Kürtős kalács are popular all over Romania and Hungary, and it's easy to understand their visual appeal. Radu remembers gathering around a metal bucket full of hot coal with his cousins as his grandmother roasted each chimney cake to the perfect caramel color and crusty exterior. Traditionally, kürtős kalács are served at weddings, triple the size of the ones in this recipe, and only topped with sugar. These days, entrepreneurs (including Radu) are getting more creative with toppings and fillings; you can roll the freshly baked cakes in walnuts, cinnamon, or chocolate, coat the insides with Nutella, or even fill with ice cream. To make these cakes, you'll need heat-resistant wooden or metal rollers, preferably with handles, to serve as spits. Special chimney-cake spits are also available, if you're inclined to make the investment. With the right equipment, these can also be made over hot coals, rotating often.

Makes 5 or 6 chimney cakes

- 1 cup (240 ml) warm water
- 1 tablespoon active dry yeast
- 3 cups (375 g) all-purpose flour, plus more for rolling
- ½ cup (1 stick/115 g) butter, melted and cooled to nearly room temperature, or ½ cup (240 ml) vegetable oil
- ½ cup (100 g) granulated sugar, plus more for coating
- 1½ teaspoons pure vanilla extract
- ½ teaspoon salt
- Vegetable or canola oil, for greasing

1. Combine the warm water and yeast in a large mixing bowl or stand mixer and let rest for 5 to 10 minutes. (You can also add 1 tablespoon sugar to help activate the yeast.) You should notice foam at the top after resting.

2. Add 1½ cups (185 g) of the flour to the mixing bowl. Mix with a paddle or whisk if using a stand mixer. Add the butter, sugar, vanilla, and salt. Use a dough hook on a low to medium setting and slowly add the remaining flour ¼ cup (30 g) at a time until the dough stops coming off with your hands but is still slightly sticky and soft; be careful not to add too much flour. (This kneading can also be done by hand and should take about 8 minutes.)

3. Oil a large bowl and place the dough in it. Cover and let rest for 30 minutes, or until the dough doubles in size.

4. Preheat the oven to 500°F (260°C).

5. Transfer the dough to a floured flat surface and roll out into a rectangle roughly 20 x 10 inches (50 x 25 cm) long and about ½-inch (13 mm) thick evenly throughout. Cut a strip about ½-inch (13 mm) wide from the long side. Roll back and forth with your hands to stretch the strip into a stick about 3 feet (90 cm) long, with uniform thickness.

6. Fill a bowl with oil and use a baster to thoroughly oil a roller that is about 9 to 10 inches (23 to 25 cm) long and 3 to 4 inches (7.5 to 10 cm) in diameter. Begin to wrap the dough around one roller (leaving the ends uncovered if there are no handles), flattening the end and overlapping for the first inch (2.5 cm) or so. Continue wrapping the roller, keeping the dough taut and leaving a small space in between each row. At the bottom, tuck the end in so it doesn't unwrap while cooking (also leaving the roller end uncovered if there are no handles). Roll the dough-wrapped roller and apply just enough pressure to fill in the spaces and even out the dough. (Too much pressure will make the dough too thin.) Repeat this step with more rollers until the dough is used up.

7. Pour sugar into a large pan or on a flat surface, brush oil on the dough on the rollers, and roll them in the sugar to coat completely. Let stand for about 10 minutes to rise again.

8. Suspend the rollers over a deep roasting pan or baking dish by resting the handles or uncovered roller ends on the sides of the pan, so that the sugar does not touch any surface. Bake for 5 to 6 minutes, until the sugar has melted and caramelized on the outside, and remove from the oven. Let stand for 30 seconds to 1 minute to cool. Turn each roller upside down, pull off the cake, and enjoy.

CHICORY COFFEE

When asked what pairs well with kürtős kalács, Radu immediately thought of his grandfather's chicory coffee. His grandfather would handpick the chicory, cut the roots, then roast and grind them himself. The woody bitterness is a perfect complement to the chimney cakes.

. . . .
Makes 4 or 5 servings
. . . .

3 tablespoons organic roasted
   ground chicory

Milk

Sugar

1. Bring 3 cups (750 ml) water to a boil in a saucepan. Add the chicory, lower the heat, and simmer for 3 minutes.

2. Remove from the heat and steep for 10 minutes.

3. Pour into cups through a fine-mesh sieve. Add milk and sugar to taste; Radu's preference is to use equal parts milk and chicory coffee, and 1 tablespoon sugar per serving.

Valentin Rasneanski

WEMBIE

MOLDOVA

"I was born in the Republic of Moldova, Soviet Union, in its capital, Chişinău. The Soviet Union got separated in '91, and I was born in '88, so technically I'm one of those people who were born in a country that doesn't exist anymore."

A true Eastern European ethnic melting pot himself, Valentin's heritage is Bulgarian-from-Ukraine on his mother's side and Ukrainian-Polish and Hungarian-Jewish-from-Moldova on his father's side. In 1988, when Valentin was born, Russian was the official language of his country, which matched the language he spoke at home, but when he was four and the Soviet Union crumbled, the Moldovan language, which he calls "Romanian," suddenly became the official language of the newly independent Moldova, and his family had to learn quickly to keep up.

The impact of the political change in '91 was not just linguistic. From one day to the next, as Russian speakers, Valentin's family's place in the Moldovan economy and society plummeted. His father got them through the tough times by selling whatever he could on the street in front of their house, waking up daily at 4:00 AM to claim his spot on the sidewalk with a tablecloth.

"So, imagine you live in a country, and you have a job, and you have your future, kind of. . . . And then, technically in one day, you don't have anything. You don't have a job, you don't have money—'cause all your money that was in the Soviet Union was transferred into your national currency. But it didn't mean that, let's say, the ruble in the Soviet Union would be equal to the currency of my country. It didn't mean

MOLDOVA

"SO, IMAGINE YOU LIVE IN A COUNTRY, AND YOU HAVE A JOB, AND YOU HAVE YOUR FUTURE, KIND OF. . . . AND THEN, TECHNICALLY IN ONE DAY, YOU DON'T HAVE ANYTHING."

that you can buy bread for the same amount of money. And me and my brother, we were like two and four years old. When you lose everything, and you don't have food for your kids, right? . . . And when my father had to go to Ukraine, buy the car parts, and bring them in the bags, and sell them on the street in my country just to make money for us to survive? That's a big deal."

The Rasneanskis considered moving to Ukraine, but the opportunity slipped away before they could grab it. Every summer, though, Valentin would get to spend two blissful months with cousins in his grandmother's idyllic town of Vil'shanka on the Syniukha River in southern Ukraine, cooking up feasts from scratch and spending long days out in nature, working up the courage to jump off little cliffs into the river below: These are some of Valentin's happiest memories.

After majoring in engineering in college in Moldova, Valentin won the green card lottery and took a restaurant job in New Hampshire, where

Valentin and his wife, Liia

he met his wife, Liia—a fellow Russian speaker, just arrived from Bashkortostan, Russia, herself. He realized it might be true love when he noticed how strangely comfortable he felt being his "weird" self around her. "If you're running after someone who just likes the attention, that's not a real relationship. The real relationship is when somebody just accepts you as yourself."

Though he quickly worked his way up from dishwasher to cook to kitchen-manager jobs in some of the best restaurants in New Hampshire, Valentin also knew working in restaurants wasn't what he wanted to do long-term and was getting antsy. After a few years working in construction in Massachusetts, then in the Florida Keys, where Liia completed her aesthetician training, the couple decided to experience New York City for themselves and were already searching for a business they could start together when they happened upon the Queens Night Market in 2017. They applied to sell their favorite desserts from both of their childhoods, 1,500 miles apart, but linked by the history of the Soviet Union. Inspired by his father's street-vending experience, as hard as it was, Valentin checks in with him often to trade stories and strategies, with the aim of eventually being, like his father was for twenty years, totally self-employed.

"The older I get, the more I don't want to work for somebody. I think freedom is what I'm looking for."

MOLDOVAN PLĂCINTĂS
Savory Cheese Pies

When Valentin was growing up in Chişinău, Moldova, his family of Russian speakers would celebrate many holidays and birthdays with their neighbors, a friendly Moldovan family, even though Valentin's family was just learning the Moldovan language after the fall of the Soviet Union. It was at one of these celebrations that Valentin discovered plăcintăs, a puff pastry with fillings. He would ask his mother to make them, and she would joke that only Moldovan women had the skills to make the dough as thin as it needed to be. Eventually Valentin learned a recipe for plăcintăs from his high school math teacher, Mogol Alexandru, who went on to start a bakery. This recipe is for a cheese-filled plăcintă, but a variety of fillings are possible, including mashed potatoes, pumpkin, and fruit. Valentin appreciates a good apple filling.

Makes 6 plăcintăs

DOUGH

2¾ cups (345 g) all-purpose flour, plus more for rolling

¾ cup (180 ml) warm water

1 tablespoon sunflower oil (or any neutral oil), plus more for cooking

FILLING

10 ounces (300 g) Brinza cheese*

1 handful fresh dill, finely chopped

Salt

1 large egg

* Brinza is a sheep's milk cheese commonly used in Eastern Europe. Substitute with a mixture of 2 parts feta to 1 part farmer cheese or mozzarella.

1. To make the dough, combine the flour, water, and oil in a large mixing bowl and knead until the dough is smooth and elastic.

2. Cover with a kitchen towel and rest in a warm place, or transfer to a covered plastic container and place in a bowl of warm water, to let rest for 15 minutes.

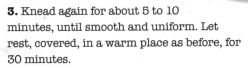

3. Knead again for about 5 to 10 minutes, until smooth and uniform. Let rest, covered, in a warm place as before, for 30 minutes.

4. To make the filling, combine the Brinza and dill with salt to taste. Set aside.

5. To make the plăcintăs, transfer the dough to a floured flat surface and knead into a large rope about 2 inches (5 cm) thick and 10 to 12 inches (25 to 30 cm) long. Divide into 5 or 6 equal pieces and form each piece into a ball.

6. Lightly oil a large flat surface. Flatten each ball on the oiled surface into a disk about 6 inches (15 cm) in diameter and about ¼-inch (6 mm) thick. Slightly oil each patty as you form a stack of them. Set aside for

Baaaaa!

10 minutes to allow the patties to absorb some of the oil for elasticity.

7. Stretch each patty as thin as possible so that it is paper-thin and translucent: Start by resting the center of the dough on one fist, and use your other fist to stretch the dough outward from underneath. When it becomes too thin to continue this way, place on a lightly oiled flat surface and carefully grab one side at a time, pull outward, and replace on the surface, repeating all around until it is nearly 2 feet (60 cm) across.

8. Fold each sheet into a square by grabbing the top side of the dough and folding down to the center of the dough. Fold the bottom edge and both sides toward the center, creating a two-ply square roughly half the size of the stretched dough.

9. Spread 2 to 3 tablespoons of the filling evenly on top of each square, leaving a small border bare.

10. Fold the dough into a smaller square, this time bringing down one corner slightly past center and doing the same with the opposite corner. Repeat for the two remaining corners, creating a roughly 5-inch (13 cm) square.

11. Heat a small amount of oil in a medium skillet over medium-low heat and fry one square with the folds down until that side is golden brown, about 2 to 3 minutes. Flip and fry until the other side is golden brown, about 2 to 3 minutes. Place on a paper towel to drain excess oil and repeat for the remaining plăcintăs.

Sam *and* Natasha Ilyayev

BLINTZ BOX

⊛ (20) UKRAINE

Natasha is from the Ukraine; Sam has been a New Yorker as long as he can remember. He and his parents left Tashkent, Uzbekistan as refugees from the crumbling Soviet Union when he was just three years old. The couple's collaborative food business draws from both culinary heritages, but it would be a bit of a mouthful to try to call it "Blintz Box: a taste of Ukraine—mixed up with diasporic Bukharian Jewish Russian-Uzbek culinary traditions and tweaked by a New Yorker's palate," so they just went with "Blintz Box" to be practical, for now. But the truth is, Sam and Natasha's marriage, like Valentin and Liia's of Wembie (see pages 100 and 110), brings together cultures and cuisines technically originating from two different continents, brought into communication by the former Soviet Union and the Russian language. For anyone who wants the longer version of their particular intercontinental origin story, Sam obliges.

"When I was three years old, I came here from Tashkent, Uzbekistan. Reagan had given refugee status to some Jews in the USSR. Everyone was fairly certain that the Soviet Union was going to collapse, or something was going to happen, so we decided to take the opportunity. We came to the States on refugee status in '89.

My grandparents were refugees, too. They had left Leningrad in the '30s—St. Petersburg now—to go to Uzbekistan. A lot of Bukharian Jews were leaving Russia at the time. There was like a purge. So prior to my kids, Tashkent was where a couple of generations were born, still under the Soviet Union umbrella. So my parents' cooking was influenced by that.

Once I met my wife, Natasha, we saw we had a lot of similar cooking, because of the Soviet influences. But we also have enough differences between our two countries that we were able to add to each other's recipes. Where I'm from, a lot more grains are used, and Asian spices. Where she's from, a lot more root vegetables. So we kind of combined our traditions and ingredients together.

First week Natasha immigrated here from Ukraine in 2006, she was working as a cashier at a grocery store my dad frequents, and he goes inside and sees her—he's like Norm from *Cheers,* knows everybody there—so he's like, *You must be new here; maybe you're looking for something else?* and he offered her a job at our family's bilingual day-care business. So she started working with us. Basically after a year of me annoying her, she decided to go on a date with me.

My Russian was really bad before I met my wife, and now it's OK. It's good enough that I would consider it fluent. I'd almost forgotten the whole entire language until I met her. I don't know how we spent that first year communicating, because she didn't speak a word of English and I barely knew Russian. I mean my parents always spoke to me in Russian, and I understood, but I wasn't very good at articulating my thoughts. My words were all over the place. I was only ever offered Spanish or Italian in high school. Never had an opportunity to study Russian. But I took it upon myself to learn to read and write it on my own over the past few years, and I'm up to maybe a fourth-grade reading level right now.

We enjoyed cooking for ourselves, you know, as a hobby. We enjoyed cooking for other people, especially my wife. But we were transitioning between businesses and jobs and thinking of something to do over the weekend. My father was actually a street-food vendor when we first came to this country. Nothing fancy like they have today—just hot dogs, the basics. I'd heard of food fairs and it felt like a good fit. We hardly ever saw Eastern European food at them. So we started selling *varenyky*—Ukrainian-style pierogies—on weekends in 2016, and now we sell blintz.

Our blintz is a Ukrainian-style crepe—a thin pancake similar to those found in other Eastern European nations. And we use a recipe that was started by my wife's family, and I added some things that my mother used and my grandmother used—kind of combined those recipes, and we have our own little version of it.

I often get questions about the food, but that's fine. Hopefully someday it will be as standard as pizza here. But until that day I have no problem answering those kinds of questions; I enjoy it. It's one of the main drives for my wife and I. Until pizza and burgers became what they were, they were maybe not as obscure, but an easy-to-eat item such as ours goes well as takeout food, goes well with any other dish as a side. So I think it fits the American lifestyle, especially the New York City lifestyle pretty well—on-the-go. We roll it and cut in half so you could eat it like a small burrito. Or with a fork and knife if you prefer.

When customers thank us for the delicious food, come back, and grab our business card—that's euphoria for me. It feels awesome."

UKRAINIAN BLINTZES
WITH CREAMY MUSHROOMS

For many Americans, the smell of pancakes hitting the skillet evokes vivid memories of family breakfasts. It's the same for Sam and Natasha. Their blintz recipes have been passed down for generations, with each iteration getting tweaked ever so slightly to accommodate contemporaneous tastes. The creamy mushroom filling in this recipe is savory, so this version uses less sugar in the batter than one might use for a dessert blintz. Serve with sour cream or your favorite hot sauce; it is common to eat these blintzes with *adjika*, a Ukrainian spicy salsa.

. . . .
Makes 10 blintzes
. . . .

FILLING

3 tablespoons unsalted butter

1½ pounds (680 g) whole portobello mushrooms, washed and thinly sliced

1 medium sweet onion, diced

1 tablespoon salt

¾ cup (175 g) mascarpone or sour cream

¼ cup (60 ml) heavy cream

BATTER

1¼ cups (300 ml) whole milk

1 tablespoon unsalted butter

2 medium eggs

1 tablespoon granulated sugar

½ teaspoon salt

1¼ cups (155 g) all-purpose flour

2 tablespoons canola oil

1. To make the filling, melt 1 tablespoon of the butter in a large skillet over medium-high heat and sauté the mushrooms, stirring frequently, until the liquid has completely evaporated, about 20 minutes.

2. Meanwhile, melt the remaining 2 tablespoons butter in a small pan over medium heat and sauté the onion. When it begins to caramelize, after about 15 minutes, remove from the heat.

3. Add the onion and salt to the mushrooms and cook for 2 minutes, stirring frequently. Turn the heat to low. Add the mascarpone and cream and cook, stirring regularly, until the cheese has melted and integrated with the cream and coated the mushrooms, about 5 minutes.

4. Transfer to a bowl to avoid overcooking the mascarpone.

5. To make the batter, heat the milk and butter in a small saucepan over low heat, until the milk is lukewarm. Remove from the heat.

6. Combine the eggs, sugar, and salt in a mixing bowl or stand mixer. Mix on low until completely smooth with no lumps.

7. Slowly pour the warm milk into the bowl, continuing to mix. Add the flour ½ cup (65 g) at a time, allowing the flour to blend thoroughly before adding more. Add the oil and mix on medium for a few minutes, until the batter is completely smooth with no dry lumps.

8. To make the blintzes, heat a 12-inch (30 cm) nonstick crepe pan over medium-high heat until hot. (Use unsalted butter to brush the pan if it is not nonstick.)

9. Use a 6-ounce (175 ml) ladle to add batter to the center of the pan while simultaneously tilting and rotating the pan to spread over the bottom. Keep rotating the pan until the batter is fully settled and does not spread any more.

10. Wait for the edges of the crepe to begin browning, about 30 seconds. Carefully flip by inserting a thin spatula under the center and lifting. Brown the other side, about 20 seconds, and transfer to a plate. Repeat with all the batter, or save the batter for later in an airtight container in the refrigerator for up to 1 week.

11. Add 2 tablespoons of the filling to the bottom half of each crepe. Fold the bottom edge over the filling, then fold both sides 1 inch (2.5 cm) toward the center, and roll it up. Cut in half and serve.

UKRAINIAN BORSCHT
Beet Soup

Historically, borscht made use of the most available vegetables and turned them into a hearty and healthy dish, served anytime in any season. Ukrainian borscht typically features less beet than its Russian counterpart, and it's common for Ukrainian borscht to contain meat, which Sam and Natasha have substituted with kidney beans to make the recipe vegetarian. The substitution also makes for a more appealing dish when served cold, since there is no animal fat congealing on the surface. This recipe is tomatoey, sweet, and tangy, with an undertone of beets. The vegetables should also be pleasantly al dente. Serve with a slice of bread or *pampushka*, which is similar to a garlic knot.

. . . .
Makes 6 servings
. . . .

1 cup (200 g) dried red kidney beans

4 tablespoons canola oil

2 medium beets, peeled and sliced like fries

3 large potatoes, peeled and cut into ½-inch (13 mm) cubes

1½ cups (360 ml) tomato juice

1 medium onion, diced

1 medium carrot, sliced like fries

1 tablespoon tomato paste

½ small white cabbage, sliced thin

¼ cup (40 g) diced red bell pepper

3 dried bay leaves

Salt

Ground black pepper

Sour cream

1. To clean and remove any impurities, pour the beans into a small pot, cover with water, bring to a boil, then drain.

2. Bring 7 cups (1.7 L) water to a boil in a large pot. Add the beans, reduce the heat to medium-high, and boil for 40 minutes.

3. Add the potatoes to the boiling beans and boil for an additional 15 minutes.

3. Meanwhile, heat 2 tablespoons of the oil in a skillet over medium heat. Add the beets and sauté until soft and easily broken with a spoon, about 15 minutes. Remove from heat.

4. Add the tomato juice to the boiling beans and potatoes and continue cooking.

5. Heat the remaining 2 tablespoons oil in a separate skillet over medium-high heat and sauté the onion and carrot until the onion begins to caramelize, about 10 minutes. Add the tomato paste and cook for 5 more minutes, stirring frequently.

6. Transfer the onion and carrot to the pot along with the beet, cabbage, bell pepper, and bay leaves. Season with salt and pepper to taste.

7. Bring to a boil and cook for about 3 minutes (to allow the bay leaves to cook), stirring occasionally. Serve with a dollop of sour cream on top.

Liia Minnebaeva

WEMBIE

BASHKORTOSTAN (RUSSIA) 21

Liia was born in 1993 in Oktyabrsky, a city of about a hundred thousand in the Republic of Bashkortostan in western Russia, built by the Soviets in 1937 to support the oil industry. Liia's mother is Bashkir and her father was Tatar, both from a long line of Muslim peoples who have called the region home for centuries and continue to speak their own languages and maintain their own traditions, despite being increasingly dispersed and discriminated against over the last century by their Russian neighbors.

The collapse of the USSR was tough for many Tatar and Bashkir families. Jobs were hard to come by, let alone maintain. Salaries became unreliable. Though her mother has managed to keep her teaching job for almost thirty years now, her father was not so lucky. When Liia was only eight years old, her father, Farit, who had exhausted himself working in factories and odd jobs, died of a heart attack in his early thirties, leaving Liia with a lifelong bitter association of her father's untimely passing with the USSR collapse.

When Liia was fourteen, she and her mother moved to Ufa, her mother's hometown and the capital of Bashkortostan. Eventually, she enrolled at Bashkir State University, where she studied mathematics and computer science for three years, until she realized she wanted more of an adventure out of life. She dropped out of college, and decided to test her luck in the US by going to stay with a friend in New Hampshire in the summer of 2014, without any clear plan beyond that summer. "You're always thinking that somewhere else could be a better life than here, right now. I thought: *I'm just going to move to the United States, and then I'll figure out what I want to do.* But so far it's not bad, so I think I made a good decision."

Liia quickly got a job working at a restaurant, where a week later she met her future husband and business partner, Valentin, a budding Moldovan chef (see page 100). They moved to NYC in 2017 and, when they came across the Queens Night Market in a listicle of NYC to-dos, decided to create a business where they could share their culinary traditions with the city that never sleeps. They called it Wembie, a mashup of "we," since they're a team, an "M" for "Moldova," a "B" for Bashkir, and "ie" because it's cute.

Liia's first contribution to the Wembie menu was her mother's Bashkir farm cheese donuts: "I remember when my mom used to make those donuts, she didn't make it a lot, because it was hard times to find the ingredients. It was expensive—sometimes we didn't have money, even for bread. . . . It's delicious, but sometimes you have to choose: Do you want to spend money on meat or a normal dish—or desserts? It's not going to make you full. And if you have kids, and you don't have a lot of money, you have to choose. So I remember that dish—it wasn't that often in my life, but when it was, it was always like a holiday."

"I REMEMBER WHEN MY MOM USED TO MAKE THOSE DONUTS, SHE DIDN'T MAKE IT A LOT, BECAUSE IT WAS HARD TIMES TO FIND THE INGREDIENTS. IT WAS EXPENSIVE— SOMETIMES WE DIDN'T HAVE MONEY, EVEN FOR BREAD."

BASHKIR FARM CHEESE DONUTS

Thinking back on her years in Bashkortostan, Liia doesn't have many fond memories, except for a special treat from her youth, usually reserved for holidays and birthdays: farm cheese donuts. Liia only recently realized the reason why these sweet and savory delicacies were so rare in her household: Despite the simple ingredients, the frying oil made them prohibitively expensive for her family in the aftermath of the USSR collapse. Each time she sells a set of donuts inspired by her mother, Gulnara, there is a bittersweet nostalgia but also satisfaction as she shares a rare shimmer of happiness from her Bashkir childhood with the world.

Makes about 30 donuts

7 ounces (200 g) dry farm cheese*

2 tablespoons granulated sugar

1 egg

⅓ cup (55 g) all-purpose flour, plus more for dusting

¼ cup (45 g) semolina flour

¼ teaspoon baking soda

Sunflower, vegetable, or other neutral oil, for frying

Confectioners' sugar

Sweetened condensed milk

* Farm cheese, aka "farmer cheese" or "farmer's cheese," can typically be found in Eastern European shops or grocery stores with well-stocked cheese aisles. It should be hard and crumbly to the touch. Dry cottage cheese is similar and can be substituted if farm cheese is unavailable.

1. Mix the cheese, granulated sugar, and egg in a bowl. Add both flours and the baking soda and knead until fully integrated and the dough does not stick to your hands. Sprinkle in more flour if necessary. Refrigerate for 15 minutes.

2. Remove from the refrigerator and form into balls about 1 to 1½ inches (2.5 to 4 cm) in diameter; this is easiest with a 2-ounce (60 ml) ice cream scoop. The donuts can also be formed by hand, but the bigger they are, the longer they take to cook.

3. Pour about 4 inches (10 cm) oil into a deep pot and heat over medium-high heat to about 325°F (165°C).

4. Carefully drop the donuts into the oil. Cook on one side for 2 to 3 minutes, then flip and cook for another 2 to 3 minutes, until they are an even golden brown.

5. Remove the donuts from the oil with a slotted spoon and place on paper towels or a wire rack to drain. Sprinkle with confectioners' sugar and drizzle with sweetened condensed milk to taste and serve warm.

Africa and the Middle East

Chef Ade

OBE KITCHEN

22

NIGERIA

Though she grew up in Lagos, Nigeria, in a family of internationally educated professionals, Ade had always been one of her family's most creative, hands-on members— and the one sibling who never went to boarding school: "During my younger age, I thought, *I'm not smart.* I just made up my mind that I'm going to use my hands to be successful, thinking, *It doesn't matter if I don't go to school.*"

Ade came from a big family that celebrated *everything*, so often upwards of two hundred people would come over for parties at their compound. For Christmas, for example, a whole cow would be slaughtered and cooked, then they would set up tents and chairs in the courtyard, and jollof rice would always be part of the feast. Starting at age eleven, Ade was already passionate about food and did what she could to help the hired cooks at every family party. "I would tell my mom, *No, we don't need to employ people to cook. I will do it!*"

Long after her siblings had all moved to the US, starting careers and families there, Ade stayed rooted in her family home in Lagos, where she was raising her own kids. Life was good: "I was used to living big. Before I wake up—I always had somebody living with me: my aunt, my friends—before I wake up, somebody tells me, *Your food is on the table.* At that time I had a shop. There is a driver waiting to take me to my shop."

Ade finally, semi-reluctantly, came to join the rest of her family in the US when her siblings managed to convince her that it would be good for her kids. Once she got here, she was shocked at how isolated people were from each other, how hard people had to work to get by. "So when I came here I said, *What is all this?* They tell me, *You can't live big at all. You can't do this, you can't do that. . . .* At first I was thinking, *Why did I come in the first place?*"

Determined as she was to be able to afford a good American college education for her kids, however, Ade rolled up her sleeves and started monetizing the one skill she knew would never fail to impress: her cooking. She had no trouble preparing feasts for three to five hundred people completely on her own, sometimes staying up all night for days in a row to do so. When clients asked for a recipe she didn't know, she'd do extensive research, compare and contrast different techniques, and would only use the freshest ingredients.

"For me, before I present food to someone, I eat it myself. I don't use any preservatives; I don't used canned anything—I make food from scratch. I don't mind if it takes a long time."

Her first catering clients and their graduation-party guests were so wowed by the flavors Ade put together that recommendations and more catering gigs soon started streaming in. Now Ade works as a nurse by day and caters by night, and enjoys sharing her culinary wisdom with her US-raised, fashion-professional niece, Mary Adeogun, who, with her creative director brother, David, started Obe Kitchen in 2017—a vending, pop-up, and educational project committed to preserving and celebrating Nigerian and West African cuisine.

Mary says, "My brother and I couldn't find the taste of our Auntie's food in New York City, and we thought, *I can't imagine how many other people are looking for those flavors and that familiarity of home*—and so that's what got us involved with the Night Market. And after that we realized that, yes, there's getting the food out there, but there are also ways to share stories and recipes about food so people can explore it on their own and do it in their homes and things like that. So we started cataloging recipes, and one of the first ones we did was jollof rice— Auntie's specialty.

I called up my Auntie, wrote down her recipe, and then started doing it in my apartment. I can't tell you how many times I tried and failed: I made funky jollof rice, tasteless jollof rice—even to this day I can't achieve the smoky jollof rice that Auntie makes. Even though I use a big heavy pot, it doesn't smoke the same way as an outdoor burner."

Ade added, "In Nigeria we have a special pot for cooking jollof rice. They call it *ikoko irin*. We don't have it here, so I have to improvise one similar to that. If I have to cook jollof rice, I have to do it on a gas stove outside. If some people tell you, *I cook jollof rice in the oven,* that is *not* jollof rice. . . . That is a *concoction!*"

> "IN NIGERIA WE HAVE A SPECIAL POT FOR COOKING JOLLOF RICE. WE DON'T HAVE IT HERE, SO I HAVE TO IMPROVISE . . . I HAVE TO DO IT ON A GAS STOVE OUTSIDE. IF SOME PEOPLE TELL YOU, *I COOK JOLLOF RICE IN THE OVEN,* THAT IS *NOT* JOLLOF RICE . . . THAT IS A *CONCOCTION!*"

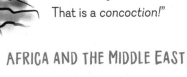

OBE ATA DIN DIN
Fried Stew

Walk into any Nigerian home and odds are you'll find a large pot of stew in the fridge or on the stove. *Ata lilo*, a sauce of puréed tomatoes and peppers, serves as the base for this and a whole family of related stews. Enjoy *obe ata* with a starch, such as white rice, *iyan* (cooked and pounded yam flour), or *eba* (cooked and pounded fermented cassava flour). It can also be served alongside other stews, such as *ila* (okra stew) or *efo riro* (vegetable stew).

Makes 8 servings

2 pounds (1 kg) assorted meats (such as goat, beef, beef offal, fish, chicken), cut into 2 to 3-inch (5 to 8 cm) cubes

1 medium sweet Spanish onion, roughly chopped

½-inch (13 mm) piece peeled fresh ginger, chopped

1 garlic clove, chopped

1 chicken or beef bouillon cube or 1 teaspoon Maggi seasoning, plus more as needed

Salt

ATA LILO

7 medium plum tomatoes

2 red bell peppers, seeded and roughly chopped

1 medium sweet Spanish onion, roughly chopped

2 Scotch bonnet chiles (*ata rodo*) or 4 habanero chiles

3 cups (720 ml) high-heat frying oil*

6 to 8-inch (15 to 20 cm) piece of *panla* (smoked stockfish), soaked overnight and torn into small pieces, optional**

1. Place the meats, onion, ginger, garlic, bouillon, and a pinch of salt in a large pot. Add enough water to just cover the meat. Bring to a boil and cook over medium heat until just barely cooked, 10 to 15 minutes, depending on the tenderness of the meat. Remove the meat and reserve the stock for later.

2. To make the ata lilo, purée the tomatoes, bell peppers, onion, and chiles in a blender or food processor on high until completely smooth. You may need to blend in batches and add 1 or 2 cups of water to help the mixture blend. Set aside.

3. To make the stew, heat the oil in a Dutch oven or large pot over medium-low heat and then fry the meat until the outer layer is browned and crispy, 10 to 15 minutes. A long low-heat fry is necessary to maintain the characteristic crunchy texture even upon reheating. Remove the meat and set aside.

4. Increase the heat to medium-high and add the ata lilo to the oil. You should hear the immediate sizzle of the ata lilo beginning to fry.

5. Add 1 or 2 ladles of the reserved stock to the pot and season with salt and bouillon as desired. Add the panla, if using. Cook, partially covered, until the stew has reduced by at least one-third and deepened to a dark red. Reduce further, if you prefer thicker stew. Return the meat to the stew and let simmer over low heat until heated through, 5 to 10 minutes.

6. Let the stew settle for 5 to 10 minutes. Skim any extra oil off the top of the stew and serve.

* It is traditional to use palm oil in this recipe and in much of Nigerian cooking. It has a high smoke point and imparts an undeniable and unique flavor to West African dishes. However, given the controversy surrounding it, we leave the choice of oil up to the reader. In addition, palm oil may need to be partially bleached, which is itself a tricky and dangerous process in a home kitchen.

** Panla is available in West African or pan-African grocery stores.

AKARA
Brown Bean Fritters

Akara are fritters made from *oloyin*, Nigerian brown beans or honey beans. Akara is typically eaten for breakfast, paired with *ogi*, a fermented corn porridge. It is also sold freshly fried by street vendors. For Mary, biting into akara, a crunchy exterior giving way to a hot, soft, savory interior, gives the same satisfaction as eating a perfect french fry. A Gambian friend of hers recently introduced her to eating akara inside a French baguette, topped with caramelized onions. If oloyin is not available, black-eyed peas can be substituted.

Makes 6 servings

- 2½ cups (480 g) dried oloyin (brown beans or honey beans)
- 1 small yellow onion, roughly chopped
- 1 Scotch bonnet chile (ata rodo)
- ½ teaspoon salt, plus more to taste
- ½ teaspoon adobo seasoning, Maggi, and/or chicken bouillon
- Vegetable oil, for frying

* If you forget to soak them overnight, add the beans and 1¼ cups (300 ml) water to a high-powered blender, then pulse for a few seconds. This starts to break down the beans so the outer layer releases just as easily as if they'd been soaked overnight.

1. Soak the beans in a large bowl of water, to loosen the outer layer, for at least 3 hours but ideally overnight. *

2. Peel the beans in the water by rubbing them against your hands and against one another. The loosened outer layers will float to the top. Discard these and continue agitating the beans until they are fully peeled. They should look uniformly beige or off-white.

3. Drain and transfer to a high-powered blender. Add the onion and chile. You may need to do this in small batches to avoid overworking the blender. Blend while adding a few splashes of water at a time as needed, up to 2 cups (480 ml), until just uniform but still a bit grainy; when you dip a spoon in the batter, it should still hold on the spoon, not flatten out completely and drip off.

4. Season the batter to taste with salt and adobo. Start with a ½ teaspoon of each and go from there.

5. Pour about 2 inches (5 cm) oil into a deep, heavy pan and heat over medium heat to about 350°F (180°C).

6. Carefully drop the batter in a tablespoonful at a time. Each spoonful should hold shape, drop quickly to the bottom, and then bob back to the top. If your batter sinks, the oil isn't hot enough. If your batter starts browning immediately, the oil is too hot. If your batter spreads out wildly, the oil is too hot or your batter is too thin. The pan should be full but not overly crowded.

7. Fry in batches until the undersides are golden brown, 4 to 6 minutes, then flip and cook until golden brown all around, 4 to 6 more minutes. The cook time will vary based on the thickness of your akara. If it still tastes of raw bean, lower the oil temperature and fry for longer.

8. Remove from the oil and place on a cooling rack to drain. Serve hot.

Peter Youssef

AMERICAN PHARAOHZ

(23)
EGYPT

After Peter's mother passed away from ovarian cancer, he was devastated. He was also worried about his father, Nassim, who had left his job and was in a bad place, dealing with his own health problems. Remembering that his parents had long nurtured a dream to someday open a restaurant together after his mother retired from the Department of Education, Peter said to his father, "We're both miserable: Let's go. You know how to cook; I know how to manage. Get up—I'm going to make this year into the biggest turnaround of our lives." He took out a $4,000 loan and American Pharaohz was born.

As Coptic Christians from Beni Suef, a small city about two hours south of Cairo, Egypt, Peter and his family wanted to showcase the range of Egyptian food beyond the halal street food that New Yorkers are becoming accustomed to. Peter's goal, beyond diversifying the culinary landscape, is to help foster a food culture with social impact. "What I want is a nonprofit restaurant. To hire refugees, give profits to City Harvest—whoever needs it." His own first American work experiences as a sixteen-year-old new immigrant in 2006 helped shape these ideals and his idea of what needs changing in the restaurant industry.

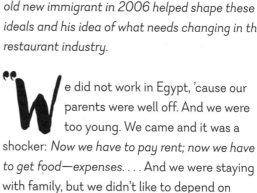

"**W**e did not work in Egypt, 'cause our parents were well off. And we were too young. We came and it was a shocker: *Now we have to pay rent; now we have to get food—expenses. . . .* And we were staying with family, but we didn't like to depend on nobody. And my dad did not know the language yet. And my mom, as well.

My brother was a little younger, so he could not work, and my sister was applying for college, so I always felt like I'm the—you know—*I'm the older son, I need to step in.* And I actually asked my family to send me to a Middle Eastern restaurant. I'm like, *Whenever you have a chance, find me a job, I'll go.* My dad's like, *You're too young, and you just came here, and it's been three days!* I literally did not unpack and I went to work—at the age of sixteen.

So I used to do twelve-hour shifts. Since that day, I never had a break.

I was a busboy, I was doing dishwashing, I was doing delivery in the snow. . . . And I didn't like the way I was treated. I did not yet have my green card or my citizenship, so I guess my boss felt like, you know, *I could take extra advantage of the situation—pay him two dollars less.*

At that time, the minimum wage was $5.15, if I'm correct. And I used to get $3.75 when I first started. And it was . . . it was crazy. I used to make like $250 a week. But it was my money. I felt proud of myself, providing for my family for a short period of time till my dad picked up a job."

TAAMEYYA
Falafel

Falafel is alleged to have originated in Egypt, created by the Coptic Christians, and Egyptian falafel is made with fava beans rather than chickpeas (garbanzo beans). Nassim's recipe keeps with that tradition. According to some, this makes the falafel moister on the inside and lighter. Peter's family would eat a lot of falafel during Lent, but mostly it reminds Peter of a local falafel shop about the size of a bedroom in Beni Suef. His grandmother would take him there almost every Saturday after church. Falafel can be served in a sandwich with fresh pita bread or alongside a green salad, hummus, or tahini.

Makes 2 to 3 servings (about 10 falafel)

- 1½ pounds (680 g) fava beans, soaked overnight and peeled
- 3 small white onions, roughly chopped
- 3 garlic cloves, roughly chopped
- ¾ cup (20 g) chopped cilantro
- ¾ cup (20 g) chopped parsley
- 2¼ teaspoons Vegeta seasoning
- 1½ teaspoons coriander seeds
- 1½ teaspoons dried parsley
- 1½ teaspoons ground black pepper
- 1½ teaspoons pomegranate juice
- 1½ teaspoons salt
- Sesame seeds
- Vegetable oil, for frying

1. Place all the ingredients except for the sesame seeds and oil in a large food processor or blender. Pulse until the mixture is bright green and smooth but still holds shape when handled. If the mixture seems too dry, or the ingredients are clumping together instead of blending, mix in 1 tablespoon water at a time, but be careful not to make it too watery or it will break apart when frying. Sprinkle the sesame seeds onto the falafel mix as desired.

2. Pour about 3 to 4 inches (7.5 to 10 cm) oil into a deep pot and heat over medium-high heat to about 350°F (180°C).

3. Scoop out some of the falafel mix and use your hands form into balls about the size of golf balls. Carefully add to the oil a few at a time. Fry each batch 3 to 6 minutes, flipping once if necessary, until evenly dark golden brown and crispy. Remove from the oil and place on paper towels to drain. Enjoy!

KEBDA ISKANDARANI
Chopped Liver Sandwich

The Alexandrian chopped liver sandwich is typical street food in Egypt—fast and affordable. Peter would always get these from a street cart near his church as soon as soccer practice ended. It's usually made with a mini baguette, but hot dog buns are sometimes used in the US. Although *kebda iskandarani* bears some resemblance to cheesesteak or sausage and peppers, the liver is undeniably front and center here in Nassim's recipe.

Makes 5 servings

- Juice of 1 lemon, plus more to taste
- 2 tablespoons ground cumin
- 1 teaspoon distilled white vinegar
- 1⅛ teaspoons red pepper flakes
- 1½ pounds (680 g) beef liver, cut into 1-inch (2.5 cm) cubes
- ¼ cup (60 ml) olive or vegetable oil
- 1 medium red bell pepper, seeded and sliced
- 1 medium yellow bell pepper, seeded and sliced
- 1 medium green bell pepper, seeded and sliced
- 1 Fresno chile, seeded and diced, or other, preferred chile
- 3 large garlic cloves, minced, or ⅛ teaspoon garlic powder
- 1 teaspoon salt
- 1 tablespoon ground black pepper
- 5 mini baguettes or hot dog buns

Tahini

Torshi (pickled peppers, olives, and cauliflower)

1. In a bowl, combine the lemon juice, cumin, vinegar, and red pepper flakes. Add the liver and mix well. Set aside to rest for 10 minutes.

2. Pour the oil into a large skillet and heat over high heat. Add the liver and its marinade, bell peppers, chile, garlic, salt, and black pepper, and sauté until the liver is fully cooked, about 10 minutes. Remove from the heat and let rest for a few minutes.

3. Serve hot in mini baguettes or hot dog buns, with a squeeze of lemon, if desired. Garnish with tahini and serve with a side of torshi.

Gladys Shahtou

SAMBUXA NYC

(24)

SUDAN

Born in Khartoum, Sudan, in 1990, in the middle of the Second Sudanese Civil War, Gladys Shahtou nonetheless enjoyed a quiet, comfortable early childhood surrounded by a happy, internationally educated, socially engaged family, until one day in 1994, an officer came to their house looking for her father—a lawyer and political dissident, who quickly fled to Switzerland where he had missionary friends from his international advocacy work. "My grandpa was still working at the UN at the time in Ethiopia, so my mother, my brothers, and I left to Ethiopia, and then we all came to New York. . . . I mean obviously, you know, our family couldn't be apart for too long, so we decided to move to be with my dad."

As a four-year-old in Ethiopia, Gladys loved bringing her Ethiopian nanny's injera (see page 132) to school for a delicious lunch, eaten carefully so as not to stain her all-white school uniform. As a five-, six-, seven-year-old in Astoria, Queens, Gladys attended PS 127, and gradually assimilated herself into the African American girls' clique, learning to emulate their Queens accents. "I'm also a quarter Haitian—I thought we were all black. I didn't understand the *Oh, you're African. You're, like, not from here.* . . . I didn't get that, so I hung out with all the other black girls. I thought I was one of them."

As an eight-year-old suddenly in Rafz, Switzerland, a small village near Zurich, Gladys had to start first grade all over again, for the third time now—this time in German. "It was hard. You just got used to a place. And Switzerland was totally different: It was like village life. Farms, new language—they didn't know what Africans, or even African Americans, were."

Her mother's Sudanese samosas helped win the Swiss over, however. At school or office events or home birthday parties, whenever she made them "they would always disappear—fast—and that's how we knew it wasn't just us: They were really good." Gladys had been helping her mother prep ingredients for as long as she could remember, but she wasn't allowed to do the delicate dough folding until she was ten. It was a big deal for Gladys when she finally learned how to fold a samosa: Now she, too, had the power to bring people together with food.

Years later, while studying international relations at the University of Geneva and interning at the UN Human Rights Council, Gladys started making and selling samosas on the side. Thanks to a few connections made through her boss, there were soon several UN departments that knew and loved the taste of Sudanese samosas.

A few years later, nearing the end of a temporary position at the Swiss Mission to the UN in New York, Gladys was stumped when the resumes she sent out for her next job got no bites. "I applied to tons of jobs, and I got frustrated. In Switzerland, you can just send your CV around and people will answer yes or no, you know? But I didn't get no answer, and that has never happened to me before. Based on just my qualifications. But I realized, in America it's not like that. You have to know people, you have to network, you go for coffee breaks with your bosses—and in Switzerland we're not used to that."

After a brief stint working for the Democratic Party in DC, Gladys was back in NYC in 2017 when she started noticing all the food festivals. *What if I had a little samosa stand?* she thought. She got right to it—first at markets, then at larger events. People kept asking her,

Grandma "Mama" Gladys hosting a reception at home, serving *fatayer* (Sudanese empanadas)

What else is on your menu? So she developed a more extensive menu based in the repertoire of Sudanese cuisine she had learned from her mother, mixing in some Haitian and Ethiopian dishes she had learned from her grandmother, and named her business Sambuxa—a name that just means "samosa" in Sudan but that any fellow Sudanese in New York would recognize.

In the past few years, Gladys has finally found home, not just in New York, but in a calling that brings her close to her Sudanese culture, working with her favorite foods, working with children, educating through nurturing, preserving, and promoting the culture she holds dear.

She remembers at thirteen her father, worrying his daughter was becoming too Swiss, suggested she dress more modestly and start wearing a headscarf, as Sudanese women do. She refused, with her mother's blessing, but "every other nonreligious part of Sudanese culture my parents made sure I learned—and I cherish that so much."

Gladys hopes in the next few years to find a way back to Khartoum, perhaps to start some kind of incubator and carry on her family's advocacy legacy. "Khartoum still feels like home. And Zurich is home. And New York is home. They're all home."

SALATA DAKWA
Tomato Salad

Salata dakwa is a common Sudanese salad and something Gladys has made almost every single day since she was six years old: "Since I was the only girl in the family, it was my duty." The salad can be flexible enough to include cucumbers or go without scallions, but it always has peanut butter. It is perfectly balanced, with sweetness from the peanut butter, fragrance from the cumin and sesame oil, zest from the lemon juice, and brininess from the "white cheese" (feta).

Makes 5 servings

- 1 bunch scallions, finely chopped
- 4 plum tomatoes, diced
- 1 cup (150 g) crumbled feta
- 3 tablespoons refined sesame oil
- 3 tablespoons unsalted creamy peanut butter
- ¼ cup plus 2 tablespoons (90 ml) warm water
- ¼ cup (60 ml) lemon juice
- 1 teaspoon ground cumin
- 1 teaspoon salt
- 1 teaspoon ground black pepper
- Pita bread

1. Combine the scallions, tomatoes, and feta in a salad bowl. Add the sesame oil and mix.

2. In a separate bowl, dissolve the peanut butter in the warm water. Add the lemon juice, cumin, salt, and pepper and mix thoroughly.

3. Transfer the peanut butter dressing to the salad bowl and toss. Serve with a side of pita bread.

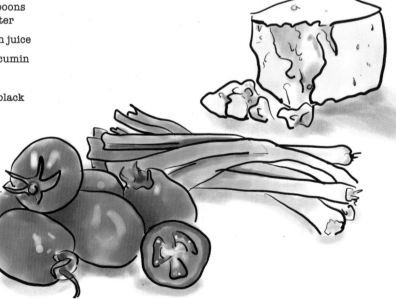

SALATA ASWAD
Eggplant Salad

The Arabic word for peanut literally means "Sudanese nut" or "Sudanese bean," and as that might suggest, peanuts are integral to Sudanese cuisine, used in stews, sauces, and salads. According to Gladys, salata aswad is a bit like baba ghanoush but richer from the peanut butter, balanced out with acid from the tomatoes, and more texturally varied from the eggplant peels, onions, and tomatoes. Eat with pita bread or as a spread for sandwiches.

Makes 5 servings

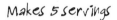

½ cup (120 ml) sunflower or vegetable oil, plus more for frying the eggplant

2 medium black or purple eggplants, peeled and sliced into ½-inch (13 mm) thick half-moons

1 medium white onion, sliced into half-moons

1 or 2 garlic cloves, minced

1 tablespoon ground cumin

½ teaspoon salt

½ teaspoon ground black pepper

2 plum tomatoes, sliced into half-moons

3½ tablespoons unsalted creamy peanut butter*

2 tablespoons lemon juice

* While Sudanese peanut butter has an earthier, less salty, and less sweet taste than American versions, Gladys still uses American brands when cooking in the US. She thinks the difference isn't so great as to warrant the difficult task of sourcing Sudanese peanut butter.

1. Pour about 1 to 2 inches (2.5 to 5 cm) oil into a deep pot and heat over medium-high heat to about 350°F (180°C). Fry the eggplant, in batches, until brown or slightly charred, about 2 minutes on each side. Remove from the pan and place on paper towels to drain.

2. Pour the ½ cup (120 ml) oil into a large pot over high heat. Add the onion and pan-fry until translucent, about 5 minutes. Add the garlic, cumin, salt, and pepper and stir to combine. Add the tomatoes, reduce the heat to medium, cover, and bring to a boil. Turn the heat to low and simmer, stirring occasionally, until the onions and tomatoes are stewed, about 10 minutes.

3. Melt in the peanut butter and add the eggplants to the pot. Add the lemon juice and mix well, mashing the solid pieces with a spoon, spatula, or masher as you stir. (You can also mash after the stew cools.)

4. Remove from the heat and let cool.

5. Serve chilled or at room temperature.

Eden Gebre Egziabher

MAKINA CAFE

Eden was born and raised in Addis Ababa, Ethiopia, until age fourteen. She spoke Amharic at school and in public, but with her Eritrean family and neighbors, she spoke Tigrinya. Her mother was an entrepreneur who founded private schools, her father an engineer for Shell Oil Company, and both parents traveled frequently for work.

Eden had lots of friends, both Ethiopian and Eritrean, and her home was often full of guests and relatives visiting from Eritrea. She loved when her cousins would stay with them, sometimes for months on end. They would make all sorts of traditional foods together, sometimes even lasagnas and pastas, a culinary heritage of the Italian colonists of Eritrea. "Aside from the Italian influence on Eritrean cuisine, Eritreans and Ethiopians have a very similar culture and cuisine—the main differences are in language, hairstyles, clothes."

When the Ethiopian-Eritrean war broke out in 1998, Eritreans residing in Ethiopia, including

Eden's family, were given two weeks to sell everything and leave the country.

Eden's parents had long been active in the Christian church and had hosted an older American missionary couple in their home in Addis back in the 1970s. So when Eden's mother got stuck in the US, Eden's dad called up their old American friends and asked for help. They immediately returned the favor, inviting Eden's family to come stay with them in Charlotte, North Carolina, where they sponsored them and helped them settle into a new American life.

"We ended up in America as refugees, and many people in the community came together to help our family get on our feet. Seeing people that didn't know us, who were willing to help us, created something in me. I told myself, *One day when I am in the position, I want to be able to give back the same way others did.* This journey took over a decade."

Going straight into high school in Charlotte was tough for Eden: There were only five non-Americans in her entire school, and she barely spoke English when she arrived. But when her new school took her on a class trip to New York, she saw people "of all colors, from all over the world" and loved it. She decided to someday make it her home, imagining herself working at the UN, fostering international peace, learning from other immigrants and refugees. In the meantime, she worked hard on assimilating into her new environment and mastered English within a year.

In 2016, with an MBA under her belt and a social mission in her heart, she decided to go into

Eden; her father, Gebremeskel; and her sister Emnet vacationing by the Red Sea in Massawa, Eritrea (above); Eden's father graduating from Addis Ababa University (right)

"I WANT TO BRING ETHIOPIANS AND ERITREANS IN THE US TOGETHER OVER FOOD TO CELEBRATE THEIR JOINT CULINARY HERITAGE AND APPRECIATE THEIR DIFFERENCES, TOO, LEAVING POLITICS ASIDE."

the food truck business, with a mission of fostering Ethiopian-Eritrean peace through food. "I want to bring Ethiopians and Eritreans in the US together over food to celebrate their joint culinary heritage and appreciate their differences, too, leaving politics aside." She also wants to educate Americans, many of whom may not even know that Eritrea exists, let alone that their cuisine is similar to Ethiopian cuisine, with the addition of some Italian influences.

Eden named her food business "Makina" because it sounds like the word for "car" or "truck" (as in "food truck") in Ethiopian Amharic, in Eritrean Tigrinya, and in Italian. After a few stints at the Queens Night Market, Makina is now a go-to food truck in midtown and downtown Manhattan, and Eden hopes it will grow into a brick-and-mortar restaurant before long, one that will specifically seek to give back and pay forward to Eden's community, as well as to her new hometown of New York City.

INJERA
WITH SPICY RED LENTILS

Eden says that "injera is our version of rice, so we eat it pretty much with everything." The moist, fluffy, spongy, versatile flatbread is eaten with hands and used to grab or sop up stir-fries, stews, and other tasty morsels. As a kid, Eden would be allowed to test her hand at making the last batch of injera batter, but it wasn't until she started Makina Cafe that she *really* understood all the factors that go into making injera, including temperature, humidity, and amount of water. Spicy red lentils (*misir wot*) are the quintessential Eritrean vegetarian dish, but you should consider making an array of dishes to go with injera.

. . . .
Makes 6 servings
. . . .

INJERA

3 cups (495 g) teff flour

¼ teaspoon active dry yeast

¼ cup (60 g) plain whole-milk yogurt

1 cup (125 g) self-rising flour

MISIR WOT

3 or 4 medium red onions, puréed

1¼ cups (300 ml) vegetable oil

2 tablespoons garlic purée or 6 garlic cloves, peeled and puréed

2 tablespoons ginger purée or one 5-inch (13 cm) piece peeled fresh ginger, puréed

1 tablespoon ground turmeric

¼ cup (65 g) tomato paste

⅔ cup (80 g) berbere

1½ tablespoons salt

1 tablespoon ground black pepper

2 cups (385 g) dried red lentils

3 tablespoons ground cardamom

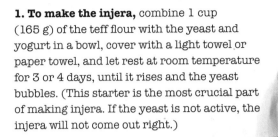

1. To make the injera, combine 1 cup (165 g) of the teff flour with the yeast and yogurt in a bowl, cover with a light towel or paper towel, and let rest at room temperature for 3 or 4 days, until it rises and the yeast bubbles. (This starter is the most crucial part of making injera. If the yeast is not active, the injera will not come out right.)

2. Combine the self-rising flour with 1 cup (200 g) of the starter and the remaining 2 cups (330 g) teff flour. Add some water, up to 4 cups (960 ml), and mix well until the desired consistency is reached: If you like thick injera, add less water; if you like thin injera, add more. Cover with a paper towel and let rest at room temperature for 12 hours, or until it begins to bubble.

3. Heat a skillet (with a lid) over medium heat, to about 320°F (160°C). The size of the injera will depend on the size of the skillet. Pour some batter into the skillet as you would for a pancake. Cover and cook for 2 or 3 minutes, until the edges start to lift up off the pan surface. Remove and let cool. The cooked injera should have many holes or air pockets and taste like sourdough; if it does not, stop cooking and let the batter sit for longer before trying again.

4. Continue cooking, stacking the injera on top of each other, and let cool. If using immediately, serve when cool enough to handle. If storing them, wrap in plastic wrap to prevent drying out and keep in the refrigerator or freezer. Put them in the microwave or oven to reheat.

5. To make the misir wot, heat the puréed onion in a medium pot over medium-low heat. Let the onion sweat out all the water until the onions are golden, 20 to 30 minutes.

6. Pour in the oil and garlic and cook for 5 to 10 minutes, allowing the garlic to cook. Add the ginger, turmeric, and tomato paste and mix well. Add a splash of water so the bottom doesn't burn. Cook until the flavors have married, about 10 minutes.

7. Add the berbere, salt, pepper, and a splash of water to prevent the berbere from sticking to the pan, and cook for about 5 minutes while stirring to mix. Be careful not to burn the berbere. Add 7½ cups (1.8 L) water to the pot, cover, and bring to a boil.

8. Meanwhile, rinse the lentils with cold water to remove any dirt.

9. Once the stew is boiling, add the cardamom to the pot and mix well. Add the lentils and cook until softened, about 7 minutes. Turn off the heat, cover the pot, and let rest for at least 20 minutes, allowing the residual heat and steam to finish cooking the lentils.

10. Plate the injera and spoon the lentils over it to serve.

Born and raised in Gaborone, Botswana, Charles Chipengule grew up thinking of himself as a foreigner because his father was from Malawi, his mother's parents were from South Africa, and he also had family in Zambia. Sometimes people in Botswana would shout at Charles or his relatives, "Mokwerekwere," a derogatory epithet for West African migrants. His South African grandmother would be especially offended by this, since she wasn't even West African.

But despite the social tensions that came with his foreign roots, Charles loved growing up multilingual, speaking Tswana in Botswana and with his mom, Chichewa with his dad, Zulu with his grandma, and English in school. His diverse heritage also made him familiar with not only local cuisine but also his grandmother's Indian-influenced South African food and his father's Malawi-style dried fish.

After getting tired of the meager electrotechnician job opportunities back home, he moved to New Jersey at age twenty-two, and his culinary world opened up even further as he entered the New York restaurant kitchen

Charles Chipengule
JAA DIJO DOM

26 SOUTH AFRICA

scene, working his way up from dishwasher to chef. When he started his catering company, Jaa Dijo Dom (which translates from Tswana to "a place to eat"), in 2017 with a mixture of Botswanan classics and a few of his grandmother's signature South African recipes, he gave himself the goal of exploring one new African cuisine per season—not only to educate the public about African cuisine, but also to get African immigrants in New York together to share recipes and learn to appreciate each other's cuisines.

Hiring cooks as necessary, according to the size of the catering order, Charles has had the pleasure of tapping into the African diasporic culinary talent pool, and over the last few years he has, with the help of new friends and collaborators from these countries, integrated recipes from Nigeria, Ghana, Senegal, and Morocco into his chef's repertoire. It's part of his mission: "Someday, I hope, Africans back home will see an African from elsewhere and instead of calling him 'mokwerekwere' will think, *Ah, he's from Senegal—great food!*"

BUNNY CHOW
Chicken Curry Bread Bowl

Bunny chow is a famous South African street-food sandwich. As food legend has it, this sandwich was invented in the 1940s when Indians migrated to Durban and needed a way to transport their hot curry for lunch. Hollowed-out bread filled with curry was the solution! It might be hard to find a loaf of white bread big enough to rival the traditional serving size in South Africa, but even with smaller portions bunny chow is fun to make and to eat . . . and to say!

Makes 4 servings

¼ cup (60 ml) canola oil

1 large yellow onion, diced

4 garlic cloves, minced

1 teaspoon grated peeled fresh ginger

1 tablespoon curry powder

1 teaspoon coriander seeds

1 teaspoon ground cumin

1 teaspoon ground ginger

1 teaspoon ground turmeric

2 cinnamon sticks

1 pound (455 g) skinless, boneless chicken breast, cut into 1-inch (2.5 cm) cubes

2 tablespoons tomato paste

2 medium russet potatoes, cut into ½-inch (13 mm) cubes

Kosher salt

Ground black pepper

1 loaf white bread (unsliced)

Sour cream

Chopped scallions

1. Heat the oil in a large pot over high heat. Add the onion, garlic, and grated ginger. Cook until the onion is golden, about 5 minutes.

2. Add the curry powder, coriander, cumin, ground ginger, turmeric, and cinnamon sticks. Cook until aromatic, 2 to 3 minutes. Add the chicken, tomato paste, and 1½ cups (360 ml) water and mix well. Add the potatoes and bring to a boil. Simmer on low heat until the sauce thickens, stirring occasionally, about 20 minutes.

3. Season with salt and pepper to taste. Remove from the heat.

4. Cut the loaf into four equal parts. Toast if desired. Create a well in each piece of bread by cutting a square or rectangle halfway down into one of the soft sides, leaving a 1-inch (2.5 cm) margin along each edge. Carve out the cube with your hand and set aside.

5. Fill the well with the chicken curry and garnish with sour cream and scallions. Top with the removed bread cubes and serve immediately. Eat with your hands by tearing off pieces of bread and dipping into and scooping out the curry.

With approximately 1.2 million citizens, the island of Mauritius lies east of Madagascar and is actually the most densely populated country in Africa. Due to its unique location and history, Mauritius is heavily influenced by Indian culture—but African, Chinese, and European culture have also indelibly left their mark on the small island nation.

Jaina's mother, Mira, was born in Port Louis, the capital of Mauritius, and her father, Vijay, in a small town called Pamplemousses. Vijay was recruited to teach in several small towns in Botswana, where Jaina was born and raised until age ten. Growing up, she regularly made the trip to Mauritius to stay with relatives. Her family made one final extended stay in Mauritius—to get papers in order before moving to the US in 2000, in pursuit of better opportunities for Jaina and her siblings.

Her father aimed for New Jersey, having seen pictures in magazines of big houses, cars, and fenced-in yards—but he had a cousin in Queens. After over a month of apartment hunting with Jaina's uncle—living first in a Queens Motor Inn, then at a YMCA, and using up most of their moving savings—Jaina's father found the perfect apartment in Kew Gardens, Queens, and the family has been there ever since.

Jaina Teeluck

PEREYBEURRE

27

MAURITIUS

Jaina experienced the sixth grade in three different countries and four different languages. After a British-style education in Botswana (taught in English with French as a second language), and a French-style education in Mauritius (taught in Creole with Hindi as a second language), Jaina was grateful her English was already fluent when she started school in Queens. However, she felt her Botswana-British hybrid accent marked her as a foreigner—as did her extraordinary discipline and introversion.

Two decades later—long after having mastered the American accent, and in the midst of establishing herself as a professional designer—Jaina got to spend a few weeks back in Mauritius for a cousin's wedding. Moved by the culture she felt was hers—but knowing she wouldn't have much opportunity to connect with it after returning to Queens—she started an Instagram account to display the photography she'd taken during her trip. She wanted to capture Mauritius as something other than "idyllic beaches for tourists." Connecting

INDIA

AFRICA

MADAGASCAR

MAURITIUS!

AUSTRALIA

"HAVING A PLACE WHERE MAURITIANS CAN GO AND FEEL AT HOME IS SOMETHING I WANT TO ACCOMPLISH—SHOWCASING OUR UNIQUE ISLAND CULTURE . . . I THINK THAT WOULD BE REALLY COOL, TO HAVE THAT KIND OF SPACE WE CAN SHARE."

with other diasporic Mauritians this way lit the fire for her culinary endeavors.

Jaina set out to create a project that could help represent the culinary traditions and innovations of her beloved Mauritius. She recruited her mother, father, aunt, brother, and

cousin to the cause and, playing around with the name of a stunning beach in northern Mauritius called Pereybere, came up with Pereybeurre (*beurre* is French for "butter").

The Mauritian population in NYC is small and scattered, but many of them began showing up at the Queens Night Market once it was announced that a Mauritian food outpost was approved. Jaina said, "It's funny because a lot of the Mauritians that we have just started to meet, they've been here for *years,* and are like, *I had no idea there were other Mauritians in New York!* Until they come to the Night Market and are like, *Oh, wow, there's a bunch of you guys here!*"

Perfectly ripe pineapples sold on the streets of Pamplemousses

CHICKEN BIRYANI
WITH TOMATO CHUTNEY AND CUCUMBER SALAD

Most people recognize biryani as a staple Indian dish, but it's also common in Mauritius. For Jaina, biryani evokes memories of huddling with cousins in her grandmother's kitchen, feasting at Mauritian weddings—when biryanis really took on elevated heights—and of course humble street-food versions found throughout the island. Jaina's mom's version has potatoes and peas, and the spices are subtler than you might find in other iterations. Nevertheless, this take on biryani definitely has a spicy kick, and goat or lamb can also be substituted for chicken if a gamier flavor is desired. This version is served with a side of tomato chutney and a cucumber salad, to complement the flavors as well as temper the spiciness.

· ·
Makes 5 servings
· ·

CHICKEN BIRYANI

6 or 7 garlic cloves

2-inch (5 cm) piece peeled fresh ginger

2 tablespoons olive oil, plus more as necessary

1 teaspoon salt, plus more to taste

1 teaspoon ground black pepper

1 cup (50 g) chopped cilantro

½ cup (10 g) chopped mint leaves

1 tablespoon biryani spice mix (such as Shan Biryani Masala Mix)

1 teaspoon ground cumin

1 teaspoon garam masala

½ teaspoon ground cardamom

½ teaspoon ground cinnamon

¼ teaspoon ground cloves

5 skinless chicken legs and/or thighs, cut into 1 to 1½-inch (2.5 to 3.5 cm) cubes and bone-in for best results

2 cups (390 g) basmati rice

1 cup (2 sticks/225 g) butter or ghee, plus 1 teaspoon melted

1 cup (225 g) vegetable oil

5 medium white potatoes, peeled and cut into quarters

2 teaspoons ground turmeric

2 medium red onions, thinly sliced into half-moons

5 hard-boiled eggs, optional

1 teaspoon saffron threads

1 green chile, chopped

TOMATO CHUTNEY

2 large tomatoes, chopped

½ cup (25 g) chopped cilantro

¼ cup (5 g) chopped mint

2 green chiles, chopped

2 garlic cloves, chopped

CUCUMBER SALAD

2 large cucumbers

1 large carrot

1 small red onion, thinly sliced

1 green chile, chopped, optional

1 tablespoon olive oil

1½ teaspoons lemon juice

Salt

Ground black pepper

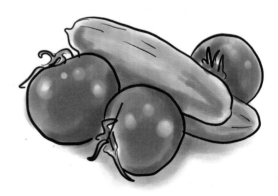

1. **To make the chicken biryani,** add garlic and ginger to a grinder or food processor and blend into a smooth, uniform paste, adding water or oil a teaspoon at a time, as necessary. Combine the olive oil, ginger-garlic paste, salt, pepper, most of the mint and cilantro (reserving a handful of each), the biryani spice mix, cumin, garam masala, cardamom, cinnamon, and cloves, and add the chicken to marinate for at least 1 hour, or overnight in the refrigerator.

2. In a large pot, boil the rice in 4 cups (960 ml) water until halfway cooked, 15 to 20 minutes. The texture should be semihard but not completely softened. Drain in a colander.

3. Heat a deep pot such as a Dutch oven over low heat, then add the chicken and just cook through but do not fully brown, about 15 minutes.

4. While the chicken is cooking, melt the 1 cup (225 g) butter in a deep skillet over medium-high heat. Add the potatoes, 1 teaspoon of the turmeric, and salt to taste and fry until lightly crispy. Remove the potatoes and set aside. Fry the red onion until golden brown, about 15 minutes, and remove from the heat.

5. When the chicken is lightly cooked, add half of the red onion and all of the potatoes to the pot and mix well. Add the rice on top, followed by the remaining red onion and the eggs, if using. Sprinkle the remaining teaspoon turmeric,

the saffron, the remaining mint and cilantro, and a few pinches of salt on top. Finally, drizzle the teaspoon melted butter over the rice, cover the pot, and cook over low heat until the rice and chicken are fully cooked, 30 minutes to 1 hour.*

6. **To make the tomato chutney,** blend all of the ingredients in a blender on high until the tomatoes are fully crushed, then pour into a bowl and season with salt. Set aside.

7. **To make the cucumber salad,** peel the cucumbers and carrot and, using a peeler, cut into long, thin slices, but only use the outer edges of the cucumbers if they're not seedless or seeded beforehand, and then squeeze out and discard any excess juice. Combine the carrot, cucumber, red onion, and chile in a bowl and mix well. Whisk together the oil, lemon juice, and salt and pepper to taste in a separate bowl. Toss the vegetables with this dressing.

8. To serve, plate the biryani with the tomato chutney and cucumber salad.

* The chicken tends to release water while it is cooking, so additional liquid should not be required during this step. If you are using goat or lamb, consider adding up to 2 additional cups (480 ml) water before adding the parboiled rice.

Jessica Spiegel and Amir Alerasoul

JOON
(28)
IRAN

Joon is the brainchild of Amir, an Iranian from Tehran who came to the US at age twenty-six for his MBA and now works in finance, and Jessica, an American architect originally from Florida. They met online and fell in love in NYC in 2010.

"We met on chemistry.com, which I don't think even exists anymore, and he's the only one who asked me to dinner," Jessica recalls. "So I thought that was cool. I didn't know anything about Persian food, but after we had been dating for a while, I met his mom—and she bought me a cookbook, *Food of Life,* the most famous Persian cookbook. And so I would cook from that, and just follow the recipes exactly, and it worked out pretty well!"

Since then, with the help of cookbooks and translated instructions from Amir's mom—and that universal driving force of wanting to please the in-laws—Jessica has become so proficient with Amir's favorite recipes, nailing the crispiness of the golden tahdig ("bottom of the pot" in Farsi) rice to go with stews, that they jointly launched Joon in 2016 to sell their crispy-rice-based dishes to the New York public at the Queens Night Market.

Joon, Amir explains, means "dear" in Farsi. "I think it's the same word in Armenian and Georgian. When you really like something or someone, you say *joon.* Like when my mother calls me and is feeling friendly, she calls me *Amir joon.* If you want to show that you're close, and that a person's dear to you, you say that name and followed by *joon.* If, for example, you go somewhere and they have made some food that you really like, you just simply say, *Joon!* It means, *Oh, I'm so happy that this food is here!*"

Joon! is what Amir always said when his mother would make his favorite beef celery stew. "It takes a long time to make, so it always felt special when she put in the time." Twenty years ago, when Amir still lived at home and would go grocery shopping for the ingredients, meals took even longer to prepare. "Back then, after going to two, three different places for different things, you had to get the vegetables, then you had to bring them home, separate the good ones from the bad ones, take an hour to wash them all, and *then* you could use them. Today they have supermarkets and the vegetables are sold clean, so it's much easier!"

"Tehran *is* so clean," Jessica remembers as she thinks about her first trip there a few years ago, "It puts New York to shame. It is immaculate! Everything is amazing: People are so nice—everyone wanted to talk to me. It's hard to make money there now, but if things were different, I could see myself living there. I really thought I knew what to expect of Iran—I had heard stories from Amir and his friends and family—but I was even more impressed than I thought I'd be!"

JOOJEH KABAB
Yogurt Chicken Kebab

Joojeh kabab can be found in most Persian restaurants and is made in many Persian households. The yogurt gives and helps the chicken retain moisture in a way that is rare with skewered meats. The charcoal imparts a smoky flavor, the saffron and turmeric add depth, and a sprinkle of sumac contributes subtle, citrusy notes that lighten up the dish. Add veggies basted with oil to the skewers before grilling, if desired, and serve on basmati rice or lavash or pita.

Makes 4 to 6 servings

2¼ pounds (1.1 kg) boneless chicken breasts, cut into 1 to 1½-inch (2.5 to 3.5 cm) cubes

½ cup (115 g) plain whole-milk yogurt, Greek preferred

½ yellow onion, diced

3 tablespoons olive oil

2 teaspoons salt

¼ teaspoon ground black pepper

⅛ teaspoon ground saffron

⅛ teaspoon ground turmeric

Lemon wedges

Sumac

1. Combine the chicken with the yogurt, onion, oil, salt, pepper, saffron, and turmeric and let marinate in the refrigerator for at least 4 hours but preferably overnight.

2. Thread the chicken cubes on skewers, with about 4 or 5 cubes on each.

3. Grill on a charcoal grill (preferred) or on a grill pan over medium heat until cooked through, 8 to 15 minutes.

4. Serve with lemon wedges and a sprinkle of sumac on top.

KHORESH KARAFS
Beef Celery Stew

You might not find *khoresh karafs* in Persian restaurants, as it's primarily served in homes, but this is hands down one of Amir's favorite dishes and something he requests his mom to make every time she's in town. Insofar as technique goes, it's fairly simple and mostly a matter of low-and-slow simmering. But the turmeric, saffron, dried limes, and abundant dose of celery make for an unforgettable, comforting, and satisfying dish.

Makes 6 servings

7 tablespoons olive oil

1 pound (455 g) chuck roast or stew beef, cut into 1-inch (2.5 cm) cubes

2 large yellow onions, diced

4 whole dried limes, a hole poked in each

2 teaspoons salt

¼ teaspoon ground black pepper

¼ teaspoon ground turmeric

1 bunch celery, chopped into 1-inch (2.5 cm) pieces, large strings removed with peeler

3 cups (180 g) finely chopped fresh parsley

¼ teaspoon ground saffron

Cooked basmati rice

1. Heat 3 tablespoons of the oil in a Dutch oven over medium heat and brown the meat and onions with the dried limes, the salt, pepper, and turmeric, about 5 minutes. Add 3 cups (720 ml) water, cover, and simmer on low heat for 30 minutes.

2. Meanwhile, heat the remaining 4 tablespoons oil in a separate pan over medium-high heat and sauté the celery until vibrant, bright green, about 10 minutes. Add the parsley and sauté until it turns dark green, about 5 to 8 minutes.

3. Transfer the celery mixture to the meat and onions and add the saffron. Cover and simmer on low for 1½ hours, until the meat is very tender and the celery has softened. Add more water to prevent burning, if too much liquid has evaporated.

4. Serve over the rice. Leftover stew can be refrigerated and reheated later.

After working at Tribeca's Duane Park Patisserie, under the first woman to work in the Plaza Hotel kitchen, doors opened for Zahra. She started out doing cookie and cake decorating, which evolved into years of baking cakes professionally. Her version of the Persian love cake garnered a glowing New York Times *review after her first time selling it at the Queens Night Market.*

Zahra Lee

SWEET ZAHRA

28
IRAN

"I was born in Tehran, Iran, in 1974, and lived there till I was eight. There was a revolution going on, so we had to leave the country. It was a multistep process. First, my brother went to England. Mom went with him—I didn't see her for several years. I stayed with my dad, who wanted us to leave legally, so we had to fill out a lot of documentation. I had to leave my dad and go to Germany to live with family for a few months, until my uncle tried to come and get me. That didn't work, but finally Mom succeeded, and I was able to go to New Jersey—and that's where I began living in the United States as an eight-year-old. It took a lot to get here, but I'm so glad that we were able to get the freedom that we wanted.

I really liked Jersey. I remember having this teacher, Mrs. Brinson, who would make decorated cookies with me. She used to live in the same complex as us. I remember this year we made cookies and they were the exact same color as Smurfs, and she was just the best teacher, because I didn't speak any English at all—*at all.* I think I knew three words: I knew *fish, strawberry,* and my name. And besides that, I didn't know anything. And she worked with me, even over the summer, until I was all up to speed by fourth grade. She was amazing.

My dad was doing really well in Iran, and when he came here, once you convert the money, it's like a joke: You have like no money to start with. So he had to start from scratch, and he really did it. I think he showed me a really strong work ethic. I think a lot of people who come to this country don't know if they can maintain the same lifestyle, and it's virtually impossible. But he was able to do it, and I'm really proud of him for that.

After college I worked in advertising, which was fun, but something was missing. I didn't really feel passionate, so I started to think more about my life and what I liked to do as a child, and I remembered the one thing that I always loved to do with my grandmother was to bake and cook. So I decided to enroll at the Institute of Culinary Education, where I did the work-study program, and that began my culinary career. I was in my thirties, at a time when it wasn't that cool to be a chef yet. But I had this calling."

PERSIAN HALVA
Saffron Fudge

The first known recipe for halva was written in the twelfth century, and in the 1500s Suleiman the Magnificent had a special kitchen built next to his palace named Helvahane, the house of halva. This unique, rich, sweet, and aromatic fudge contains saffron, pistachios, and rose water but has a bittersweet connotation, as it's typically eaten at Persian funerals. Zahra had her first encounter with halva at her grandfather's funeral about twenty years ago. Maybe the halva's sweetness is meant to make the sorrow more palatable or to remind one of fond times with loved ones. Zahra's recipe is a bit more liberal than others may be with pistachios, saffron, and salt. Enjoy with tea and bread.

Makes sixteen 2-inch (5 cm) squares

Baking spray with flour

1⅔ cups (335 g) granulated sugar

1 teaspoon kosher salt

¼ cup plus 2 tablespoons (90 ml) rose water

1½ cups (3 sticks/340 g) salted butter, cut into ½-inch (13 mm) pats

2¼ cups (280 g) all-purpose flour

½ teaspoon ground saffron

½ cup (65 g) raw unsalted pistachios, chopped and sifted*

* Roasted pistachios can also be used but won't be as bright green.

1. Coat an 8-inch (20 cm) square nonstick baking pan with the baking spray. Cut two 8 x 13-inch (20 x 33 cm) pieces of parchment paper and place in the pan overlapping each other. This will create handles for easy removal of the halva.

2. Combine the sugar and salt with ¾ cup (180 ml) water in a saucepan with a lid and bring to a boil over high heat without stirring. Cook covered until the sugar is completely dissolved and syrupy, about 7 minutes. Stir in the rose water, remove from the heat, and cool to room temperature.

3. Make a roux by melting the butter until bubbling in a large saucepan over low heat, stirring in the flour, and cooking until blond in color, stirring frequently, about 5 minutes. Once the roux is boiling, stir continuously and make sure there are no burned bits at the bottom. Pour into a mixing bowl or the bowl of a stand mixer.

4. Slowly whisk the rose-water syrup into the roux ⅓ cup (80 ml) at a time until smooth. Mix with the paddle on low in a stand mixer or with a hand mixer until emulsified into a smooth paste. Stop mixing and add the saffron. Beat for an additional 10 minutes on low.

5. Pour into the prepared pan and tap against the counter to get rid of air bubbles. Quickly cover with the pistachios.

6. Place in the freezer for a few hours, or refrigerate overnight, until firm enough to cut, remove the halva from the pan and cut into 2-inch (5 cm) squares.

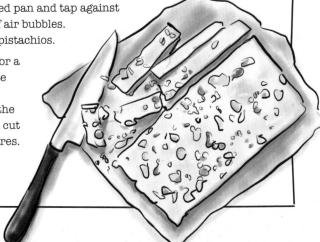

Sticky
Rice Wrap

Asia

Maeda Qureshi

THE PAKISTAND

㉑ PAKISTAN

Maeda trained at the Culinary Institute of America in Hyde Park, New York, graduating in 2011. While there, her curiosity for culinary nutrition through hands-on cooking experience brought her to believe in a "food first" approach that led her to enroll in Columbia University's nutrition program. Now she is a clinical dietitian at Elmhurst Hospital and the owner of the Pakistand, a pop-up restaurant that serves traditional and fusion-style Pakistani cuisine. All profits go toward charities supporting childhood education in Pakistan.

Women do have a hard time in this industry. I know I did. When I applied to places for my externship for the Culinary Institute of America, people couldn't tell from my résumé if I was male or female. There's this one place I showed up for my interview, and the guy said, *Oh, I didn't know you were a girl from your name.* And I was like, *Well, here I am. Are you gonna test me as a potential intern?* He said, *Yeah, I don't think you'd be good for this. It's really intense; it's hard for the guys. I don't think you'll be a good cook.* He didn't even check my skills out, just walked me out the door before I could get into the kitchen. Normally you do a stage—a one-day assessment of how you do in the kitchen: They give you stuff to do, like chop stuff, make a sauce. And he refused to let me prove myself, just because I was a girl. So that was really depressing.

When I was born, my parents couldn't figure out what to name me, so my dad went around different mosques in Brooklyn, where I was born, asking guys, like, *What should I name my daughter? And I want something unique, not something very common.* And someone said, *What about* Maeda *from* Sura Maeda? *Sura* means 'chapter.' It's a chapter in the Quran, our holy book. The guy said it's like 'feast' with an abundance of food, or a *dastarkhan,* which is a cloth that we typically put on the floor to eat. And it just symbolizes—you know—abundance, food, happiness. So my dad was in love with the name, came back to the hospital and told my mom, *This is what I want to name my daughter.*

When I was in kindergarten I was actually in ESL 'cause I couldn't speak English. My parents only spoke Urdu at home. I was always shocked—*I was born and raised here, how can I be in ESL?* But my parents knew I'd learn English when I went to school, and they wanted to make

sure I was in touch with my culture and the language—'cause that's not something you're going to learn in school.

All our neighbors were from Pakistan, so it was like a big cultural thing. Like Ramadan was amazing, 'cause we would share whatever we made and give it to our neighbors. There was always this floating plate that everyone had—

like my mom had her signature plate design, and let's say she made biryani: She would put biryani on that plate, cover it with paper towel, and say to me, *OK, go give it to them.* And that plate would come back to us later in the week with other foods that they'd made, just to return the plate, you know? You can't give an empty plate back to the people that gave you food!"

PAKISTANI TANDOORI CHICKEN KATI ROLLS

Kati rolls are traditionally sold as street food in Pakistan, but they're increasingly available in cafés and small restaurants. Typically they're made of tandoori chicken or grilled beef, topped with sliced onions and green chutney and wrapped in flaky paratha bread. Maeda's recipe doesn't call for the traditional clay tandoor oven, which creates a beautiful char with heat going up to 1,000°F (540°C). She's adapted the recipe to use in a conventional oven or on a charcoal grill.

Makes 5 servings

TANDOORI CHICKEN

8 ounces (225 g) skinless, boneless chicken thighs, cut into 1-inch (2.5 cm) cubes

¼ cup (115 g) nonfat Greek yogurt

Juice of 1 lemon

1 tablespoon olive oil

1 or 2 garlic cloves, grated

½-inch (13 mm) piece peeled fresh ginger, grated

½ teaspoon ground cumin

½ teaspoon ground turmeric

⅛ teaspoon Indian red chile powder (*lal mirch*), or cayenne pepper

⅛ teaspoon sweet paprika

¼ teaspoon cayenne pepper

GREEN CHUTNEY

1 bunch cilantro, leaves and stems

½ cup (120 ml) lemon juice

5 green Thai chiles, stems removed

¼ teaspoon salt

¼ teaspoon ground black pepper

5 frozen parathas

1 medium red onion, thinly sliced

1. To make the tandoori chicken, combine all of the ingredients in a large bowl, cover, and marinate in the refrigerator for at least 12 hours and up to 24 hours.

2. Preheat the oven to 350°F (180°C), or prepare a charcoal grill for a smokier flavor. Place the chicken on a baking sheet and bake for 20 to 25 minutes, or grill directly on the grill, until cooked through.

3. To make the green chutney, blend the cilantro, lemon juice, chiles, salt, and pepper in a blender or food processor on high until smooth, about 2 minutes, and set aside. If the mixture is too dry, add a splash of water while blending.

4. To make the kati rolls, thaw and heat the parathas in a dry skillet over medium heat until crispy, about 4 to 5 minutes each. Transfer each to a plate and place 4 or 5 pieces of the chicken, some of the red onion, and a drizzle of green chutney on the center. Fold in the sides, wrap up tightly like a burrito, and enjoy.

BEEF CHAPLI KEBAB

Chapli kebabs are Pakistani beef patties, served with naan or roti, often eaten as a snack or with tea. Meada brought her mother's chapli kebab to elementary school for lunch every day for six years and never got tired of it! These patties pack quite a punch, seasoned with ginger, garlic, cilantro, and Thai chiles. Maeda eases up on the use of oil in this recipe, choosing to pan-fry these patties rather than shallow-frying them.

Makes about 20 patties

CILANTRO YOGURT SAUCE

1 bunch cilantro, leaves and stems

Juice of 1 lemon

4 green Thai chiles, stems removed

½ teaspoon salt

2 cups plain yogurt

KEBABS

1 bunch cilantro, leaves only

1 medium onion, roughly chopped

4 green Thai chiles, stems removed

2-inch (5 cm) piece peeled fresh ginger

2 pounds (900 g) ground beef

2 tablespoons crushed coriander seeds

2 tablespoons crushed cumin seeds

1 tablespoon red pepper flakes

1½ teaspoons anardana (dried pomegranate seeds),* coarsely crushed in a spice or coffee grinder

½ teaspoon cayenne pepper

1½ teaspoons salt

1 tablespoon vegetable oil, plus more as needed

Naan

* Anardana can be found in Indian grocery stores.

1. To make the cilantro yogurt sauce, blend the cilantro, lemon juice, chiles, and salt together in a blender or food processor on high until smooth, about 3 minutes. Combine with the yogurt in a bowl with a spoon until fully integrated.

2. To make the kebabs, pulse the cilantro, onion, chiles, and ginger in a food processor until finely chopped, about 30 seconds.

3. Transfer to a large bowl and add the beef, coriander, cumin, red pepper flakes, pomegranate seeds, cayenne, and salt. Combine well with your hands. Shape some of the beef into a patty the size of your palm, about ½-inch (13 mm) thick and 4 inches (10 cm) in diameter.

4. Heat the oil in a sauté pan over medium heat. Place the patties, in batches, in the oil. Cook through, flipping once, about 6 to 8 minutes.

5. Serve with the cilantro yogurt sauce and naan on the side.

Daniel and Premalatha Nalladurai

DOSA MAMA

INDIA

Born and raised in Queens, New York, Daniel Nalladurai met Helena Kincaid (from Las Vegas and Southern California) while they were both studying film at Hunter College in Manhattan. Falling in love and finding they work well together, they got married and started a film production company together in 2016. Three years later, they asked Daniel's parents—immigrants from the Indian state of Tamil Nadu, who both work in hospitals during the week—to share their home cooking with the public on Saturdays at the Queens Night Market.

Daniel's mom, Premalatha, is from a tiny mountain village in Ooty in the south of India called Parson's Valley, formed as a result of the creation of the Parson's Valley dam. Premalatha's mother was the principal of the school in Parson's Valley, and her father had come to work for the electrical company at the dam.

Premalatha recalls a blissful childhood wandering the mountains and playing by a stream and a tall eucalyptus tree with her many pets—among them cats, dogs, and a cow. Although she was raised Christian and the rest of her family would eat meat or "non-veg" meals once a week, in contrast to many strictly vegetarian Hindu families, Premalatha was too attached to her many animal friends and remained a pescatarian.

Daniel said, "My dad used to vacation in Ooty and knew my mom through family friends. So they had an arranged marriage. That's when Dad moved to the US. Mom came later. They didn't live together until they came to New York. My mom grew up in a village of like a hundred, and then she got married and moved to New York, a city of millions of people. The

> "WE'RE THE WORKING PEOPLE OF NEW YORK—WE AIN'T RICH. WE HAVE ROOTS HERE."

contrast is wild. She was twenty-one at the time. I can only imagine how much of a change that was, and to live with a man you barely know, in a new city that he barely knows. . . ."

Premalatha recalls that at the time she didn't know what to think, just that she was up for a big adventure and was determined to make the most of it. One thing she was struck by in New York was how much meat everyone ate. Soon, she realized was raising American kids, too, and they liked meat more than she could have anticipated, so she fed them dosas with chicken curry and goat curry.

Premalatha said, "I remember when they were little, they used to beg me to make them Mickey Mouse–shaped dosas! So when Daniel asked me to make dosas at the Night Market, same thing, I said yes, of course. I didn't know it would become such a big thing! But it's fun, and the kids are getting better at making the round shape on the pan."

DOSAS
WITH CHICKEN CURRY

Dosas are typically eaten for breakfast and served with sambar, a lentil-based gravy, or various chutneys. But across some South Indian households, dosas are served with curries. This recipe is from Daniel's mother, who had learned it from her mother. The dosa is crispy, light, airy, and slightly tangy from the fermentation process. The chicken curry is layered with an array of flavors from the tomatoes, onions, cinnamon, cloves, garam masala, and much more.

Makes 4 to 6 servings*

DOSAS

2 cups (400 g) idli rice**

½ cup (100 g) split urad dal (white lentils)

¼ teaspoon fenugreek seeds

1 to 2 teaspoons salt

Vegetable oil, for cooking

CHICKEN CURRY

3 or 4 tablespoons vegetable oil

2 cinnamon sticks

3 green cardamom pods

4 cloves

2 medium yellow onions, diced

2 medium tomatoes, diced

2 tablespoons ginger-garlic paste***

1½ tablespoons ground coriander

1¼ teaspoons Kashmiri chile powder

1¼ teaspoons garam masala

1 pound (900 g) boneless skinless chicken breast or chicken thighs, cut into 1-inch (2.5 cm) cubes

1½ teaspoons ground turmeric

1 to 2 teaspoons salt

Cilantro

* This dosa recipe makes 15 to 20 dosas. Unused dosa batter can be stored in an airtight container in the refrigerator for up to 5 days.

** Idli rice is a parboiled, short-grain rice that can be found in Indian/South Asian grocery stores.

*** To make your own ginger-garlic paste, see page 139.

1. **To start the dosas,** rinse and soak the idli rice, urad dal, and fenugreek seeds in separate bowls of water for 4 to 6 hours, then drain.

2. Transfer the urad dal and fenugreek seeds to a wet grinder or blender and blend until smooth, 15 to 20 minutes. Add 1 tablespoon water at a time as needed while blending in order to make a smooth paste. To test whether it's ready, drop a spoonful into a bowl of water; if it floats, it's done. Transfer to a large bowl.

3. Transfer the idli rice to a wet grinder or blender and blend until smooth, 15 to 20 minutes. Add 1 tablespoon water at a time as needed while blending in order to make a smooth paste. (The floating test does not work on the rice.)

4. Add the rice paste to the urad dal paste and mix well to combine. Let rest in a container that is large enough to have at least a third of the container to spare, as the paste will rise as it ferments. Cover and leave at room temperature for 6 to 8 hours or overnight to ferment.

5. **To make the chicken curry,** pour the oil into a deep pot or pan over medium heat. When the oil is hot, add the cinnamon sticks, cardamom, and cloves and cook until the oil is fragrant, 30 seconds to 1 minute.

6. Reduce the heat to medium-low. Add the onions and cook until golden brown, about 8 minutes. Add the tomatoes and cook until very soft and combined with the onions, about 10 minutes.

7. Add the ginger-garlic paste and stir to combine. Stir in the coriander, chile powder, and garam masala. Add the chicken, turmeric, salt, and ½ cup (120 ml) water and mix well. Cover and cook over medium heat until the chicken is cooked through, 10 to 12 minutes. Remove from the heat and set aside.

8. **To cook the dosas,** add the salt to the batter and mix well. If the batter is not thin enough to pour, add enough water to reach the desired consistency.

9. Heat a nonstick or cast-iron skillet over medium heat. Add about 1 teaspoon oil to the pan and spread with a folded paper towel to coat the skillet. Use a large ladle to pour batter into the middle of the pan and immediately use the bottom of the ladle to spread the batter quickly and gently in a circular motion, starting from the center and working outward.

10. Drizzle about 1 teaspoon oil along the sides and on top of the dosa. Cook until nicely golden brown, 2 to 3 minutes. Gently flip and cook the other side until golden brown, about 1 minute. Transfer to a plate and repeat steps 9 and 10 to cook the desired number of dosas.

11. Fold each dosa in half and serve with the chicken curry, garnishing with cilantro.

"CAN FOOD BE AMAZING WITH JUST A FEW INGREDIENTS INSTEAD OF TWENTY-FIVE SPICES?"

Yuvika Bist

CILANTRO & MINT

(30)

INDIA

Born and raised in a Long Island suburb right outside of NYC, Yuvika (pictured right) loved her parents' home cooking but always wondered if it could be simplified a bit and made more accessible to the average person who isn't Indian. "Can food be amazing with just a few ingredients instead of twenty-five spices? So I took what my parents gave me and just deconstructed it a bit."

Yuvika's parents are both originally from India. Her dad's roots are in the Himalayan region, born in a "small town on a mountain, where your stove was a fire burning, and a pot on top," but ended up moving to the capital as he got older. On the

other hand, Yuvika's mom (pictured left) was brought up in New Delhi in a religious and strictly vegetarian household where "onion and garlic were frowned upon because of the odor they brought into the household, so you had to cook in very particular ways." When her parents make the same dish, Yuvika can taste the difference.

Her parents met at a hospital in Delhi where Yuvika's mom was working as a nurse and her dad was visiting a sick aunt. Defying all cultural norms of arranged marriages and caste consciousness, they started talking, fell in love, got married, and immigrated to the US together to start a new life.

Being the inspiration behind the recipes, Yuvika's parents are very invested in her new food business, too. They're always offering their help and ways to improve dishes, even ideas on new ones. *"How did we do?* they ask after a night at the Queens Night Market."

Now a banker by day, Yuvika started Cilantro & Mint with her childhood friend and fellow foodie, Felicia, as a weekend project, selling versions of her parents' recipes at the Queens Night Market while developing a line of chutneys to sell in grocery stores someday. All that takes long hours of careful trial and error, and, with demanding day jobs, free time is scarce. But so long as her parents' encouraging and helpful advice keeps coming, Yuvika feels confident growing her business one day at a time.

MIXED PAKORAS

When Yuvika's family had to stay indoors due to inclement weather, instead of ordering pizza, they would make pakoras with whatever veggies they had in the fridge. Warm pakoras are comforting snacks, especially paired with a hot masala chai. There are as many variations as there are vegetables, and you can make them in huge batches when you're expecting guests. Serve with green chutney, tamarind sauce, or Indian ketchup.

Makes 6 servings

- 2 cups (250 g) besan (gram or chickpea flour)
- 1½ tablespoons dried fenugreek (*kasoori methi*),* crushed by hand
- 2 teaspoons amchur (mango powder)
- 2 teaspoons ground coriander
- 2 teaspoons salt
- 1 to 2 teaspoons Indian red chile powder (lal mirch) or cayenne pepper
- ½ teaspoon asafetida (heeng)
- 1 pinch of garam masala, optional
- Juice of ½ lemon
- 1½ tablespoons vegetable oil
- 2 large white potatoes, peeled and cut into ½-inch (13 mm) cubes
- 2 medium yellow onions, sliced
- 8 ounces (225 g) paneer cheese, cut into ¼-inch (6 mm) cubes**
- 2 medium Asian eggplants, cut into ½-inch (13 mm) cubes
- 6 ounces (170 g) fresh spinach, chopped into ¼-inch (6 mm) strips
- Vegetable oil, for frying

1. Combine the besan, fenugreek, amchur, coriander, salt, chile powder, asafetida, and garam masala, if using (for a warm, smoky flavor), in a large bowl. Mix well to ensure an even blend of spices and flour.

2. Gradually add about 1½ cups (360 ml) water and whisk or use an electric mixer to blend until creamy but not too thick. A cake-batter consistency is ideal; add more water or besan if needed. Add the lemon juice and vegetable oil and mix thoroughly.

3. In a large mixing bowl, toss together the potatoes, onions, paneer, eggplant, and spinach until well combined.

4. Slowly pour the batter over the vegetables, mixing with your hands to make sure they are evenly coated in batter (but not immersed).

5. Pour about ½ to ¾ inch (13 to 20 mm) oil into a heavy pan and heat over medium-high heat to about 325°F (165°C). Grab a handful of the battered vegetables and carefully drop into the oil. Continue dropping handfuls into the oil, but do not overcrowd the pan. Fry until the bottoms of the fritters are golden brown, 3 to 4 minutes. Flip and cook the other side until golden brown, 3 to 4 minutes.

6. Remove from the oil with a slotted spoon, and drain on a cooling rack or paper towel. Fry in batches, until all the vegetables are cooked, and serve.

* The dry spices can be found in Indian/South Asian grocery stores or online.

** Paneer cheese can be substituted with firm tofu or even omitted entirely.

MASALA NOODLES

For Yuvika, masala noodles are a welcome alternative to the roti or rice typically served with meals in Northern India. While many types of noodles are used for this dish, rice noodles are not common. Yuvika uses them because they're gluten-free and hold up well in high heat for long periods of time.

Makes 6 servings

5 garlic cloves, peeled

1-inch (2.5 cm) piece peeled fresh ginger

2 thin green Indian chiles or green Thai chiles

1 pound (455 g) rice noodles (any thickness)*

2 tablespoons vegetable oil

2 teaspoons salt

½ head green cabbage, cored and sliced into small strips

¼ cup (70 g) frozen or fresh corn

1 green bell pepper, seeded, cut into ⅛-inch (3 mm) strips

1 yellow bell pepper, seeded, cut into ⅛-inch (3 mm) strips

1 red bell pepper, seeded, cut into ⅛-inch (3 mm) strips

¼ cup (60 ml) high-heat cooking oil

1 tablespoon light sesame oil

2 teaspoons cumin seeds

2 teaspoons mustard seeds

½ teaspoon asafetida (heeng)

1 medium or large onion, sliced

2 teaspoons amchur (mango powder)

2 teaspoons ground coriander

2 teaspoons "Meat and Vegetable" seasoning blend (such as Shaan brand)**

1 to 2 teaspoons Indian red chile powder (lal mirch) or cayenne pepper, optional

1¼ cups (140 g) grated carrots

Chopped cilantro

1. Combine the garlic, ginger, and chiles in a food processor and pulse into a rough paste. Set aside.

2. Pour the amount of water indicated on the noodle package into a large pot and add the vegetable oil and salt. Bring to a boil and remove from the heat. Add the noodles to the water and steep until al dente, 6 to 8 minutes. Drain and set aside.

3. Microwave the cabbage, corn, and bell peppers separately, for 1 minute each, and set aside.

4. Heat the high-heat and sesame oils in a wok or extra-large sauté pan over high heat. When the oil begins sizzling, lower the heat to medium. Add the cumin, mustard, and asafetida and sauté until fragrant and just starting to brown, about 1 minute. Add the garlic-ginger paste from the food processor and cook until fragrant, about 1 minute. Add the onion, amchur, coriander, meat and vegetable seasoning, and chile powder, if using, and sauté for about 1 minute.

5. Add the corn and sauté for 30 seconds. Add the bell peppers and sauté for 30 seconds. Add the cabbage and sauté for 2 minutes. Add the grated carrots and mix well.

6. Turn the heat to low and slowly add the noodles in batches, stirring to coat evenly. Serve garnished with cilantro.

* Use any noodles or pasta you want; just make sure they're prepared al dente according to the package instructions, steeping instead of boiling, if required.

** Can be found in Indian/South Asian grocery stores.

Sangyal Phuntsok

NOMAD MOMOS

(31) TIBET

"My parents are both from Tibet. We lost our country in 1959 to the Chinese. So that's why we escaped to all the neighboring countries: India, Bhutan. My parents moved to Bhutan, so I was born there, in 1974, more or less. It's a very small country. You might know that it's a very peaceful country: Its gross domestic happiness is the highest in the world.

In Bhutan my parents lived in a very remote, very hilly area called Bod Karnang. They were farmers—didn't have lights, gas, nothing—almost like a nomad style. So we work, and whatever we get from the field, we eat it. No cars. That was the memory: I enjoyed every day a lot. I used to go to school a few days and the rest I'd work as a shepherd or go into the forest, with Auntie or by myself, with some food and some water from the tree. We'd cut the tree and get the water. It's a little sweet. We enjoyed that a lot.

Around 1980, there was some political issue, and many Tibetans, including my parents, had to leave Bhutan. But we had a government in exile headed by His Holiness the Dalai Lama, so governments agreed India would take us—in the north part of India called Dehradun, in the state now called Uttarakhand. They had arranged some tents for us. Just on the ground. And some water for us."

In the resettlement colony in India, Sangyal's parents scraped by at first: "My father went to neighboring towns to work construction. My mother would go to the forest, cut and dry wood, and collect pieces for fire to make food. We had no oil or gas."

Nonetheless, Sangyal got to attend a Tibetan school in his new home, thanks to the government in exile and donations from international charities. He excelled at academics, earning himself a full scholarship to Delhi University, where he studied commerce, while his parents' resettlement colony grew and became more stable—turning tents into concrete houses, and street vending enterprises like his father's into successful businesses.

"My parents are illiterate, so they were happy I got a scholarship. They were happy I went to college, but they didn't quite understand what it was I studied."

After a year abroad studying in Utah, where he brushed up his English, and several years teaching computer literacy to the next generation of Tibetan students at his old boarding school in Mussoorie, he and his wife—who had taught science at the same school—decided to settle in the US, where his wife was pursuing a bachelor's in nursing: "I applied for political asylum because we had no land, no passport. All I got from India is travel documents. We had nothing of our own."

Sangyal had learned to make momos—Tibetan dumplings—on special occasions in his boarding school, which was created for Tibetan refugee children in the resettlement colony he was in. Culinary arts were a big part of their education for practical reasons: The kids had to eat, and the budget was low, so they took turns being in charge of meals for the dorm—and also for cultural reasons: As refugees in exile, the school administrators wanted to make sure their Tibetan traditions wouldn't be lost to the next generation.

When he first moved to NYC in 2009, Sangyal started making his momos again, selling them within the Tibetan community to get by while he searched for more stable employment. He was staying in a tiny room at a friend's apartment in Corona in 2018 when he looked out the window and noticed a lot of people on the sidewalk, walking cheerfully in one direction. It was a Saturday summer evening. He followed the crowds a few blocks and came across the Queens Night Market, bustling with international street food and happily chattering families and foodies. What a discovery! He searched quickly for a momo vendor and, finding none, decided to apply to become one himself.

Though he now has a full-time day job in the medical industry during the week, Sangyal looks forward to his Saturday evenings at the Queens Night Market, where he can preserve and share the Tibetan culture he holds so dear—one delicious, steaming dumpling bite at a time.

TIBETAN BEEF MOMOS
WITH HOT SAUCE

When Sangyal's family would make momos, they had to chop the meat by hand, and the repetitive whacks of the knife meeting the cutting board would signal to the whole neighborhood that momos were on the way. Beef is a common filling, but mixed veggies, chicken, and even yak are also typical. As in many cultures, making dumplings is often a family project, and the kids would compete to make them the fastest or in the best shapes, and even play pranks on each other by switching up the fillings. Momos can be served steamed or fried.

Makes about 20 to 25 dumplings

HOT SAUCE (SEPEN)

3 plum tomatoes

1 medium red onion, roughly chopped

5 garlic cloves

1 teaspoon minced peeled fresh ginger

¼ cup (60 ml) olive oil

1 tablespoon Indian red chile powder (lal mirch), plus more to taste

¼ teaspoon salt, plus more to taste

MOMOS

1¼ cups (155 g) all-purpose flour or whole wheat flour

½ pound (225 g) ground or finely chopped beef (about 85 percent lean)

1 small red onion, finely chopped

¼ cup (5 g) fresh cilantro, finely chopped (including the stems, if tender)

1-inch (2.5 cm) piece peeled fresh ginger, thinly sliced

¼ cup (10 g) thinly sliced chives

¼ cup (25 g) finely diced scallions

3 garlic cloves, minced

1 tablespoon canola oil

¾ teaspoon salt

1. To make the hot sauce, boil the tomatoes in a saucepan of water for about 5 minutes and drain. When cool enough to handle, peel and discard the skin.

2. Transfer to a blender or food processor, add the red onion, garlic, and ginger, and blend into a coarse paste.

3. Pour the oil into a saucepan over medium heat. Add the blended ingredients and sauté for 2 to 3 minutes, until they just begin to brown, adding the chile powder and salt about halfway through. Pour in ¼ cup (60 ml) water and cook for about 5 minutes to desired consistency (Sangyal prefers a consistency like thin mashed potatoes). Set aside.

4. To make the momos, combine the flour with about ¼ cup (60 ml) water in a bowl and knead until the water is absorbed. Keep adding water, a teaspoon at a time, and kneading until the dough becomes smooth and slowly bounces back when you poke it. Transfer to a plastic storage bag and let rest at room temperature for 15 to 20 minutes, until elastic.

5. Combine the beef, red onion, cilantro, ginger, chives, scallions, garlic, oil, salt, and ¼ cup (60 ml) water in a large mixing bowl. Mix gently by hand or with a large spoon until even and smooth. Let rest for 15 to 20 minutes to allow the flavors to combine.

6. Break off pieces of dough to form balls about ¾ inch (2 cm) in diameter. Roll each ball into a flat circle about 3½ inches (9 cm) in diameter and ⅛-inch (3 mm) thick.

7. Place a tablespoon of the beef filling in the center of each circle. Close the dumpling by starting at one edge, pinching together a small section of dough. Move along the edge in small increments, making a fold and pinching that fold against the previous fold while also slightly turning the bottom of the dumpling in the opposite direction. This will eventually form a rounded dumpling, enclosed by overlapping pinches at the top.

8. Lightly oil a steamer tray and place the dumplings in (in batches, if necessary), making sure they do not touch. Bring water in the steamer to a boil, place the steamer tray in, cover and steam for about 15 minutes, until the dough wrappers are slightly translucent.

9. Remove the dumplings and serve immediately with the hot sauce.

  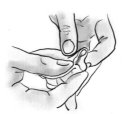 

When Mahfuzul is vending at the Queens Night Market, he's really teaching. When he sets up his tent, he hangs a picture of the great writer and artist Rabindranath Tagore, stacks his little information sheets on the table, and prepares to answer any questions his hungry customers may have about the food in such a way as to really give them access to Bengali culture.

A professor of Asian American studies, sociology of religion, and macroeconomics by day, he started Jhal NYC with his cousin both to educate the New York public about Bengali culture—and street food!—and to raise money to benefit his Queens-based Bengali community. The endeavor has already provided the funds for a Bangladeshi girl to go to college.

Mahfuzul was born and raised in Queens in a family-oriented Bengali Muslim household with lots of cousins around. In the summer of 2015, he was back in Queens on summer break from Harvard grad school, and his home was full of family, mourning the loss of an aunt. Mahfuzul wanted to get his bereaved cousin out of the house for a bit. So the two cousins wandered

Mahfuzul Islam

JHAL NYC

32

BANGLADESH

over to the Queens Night Market on a whim. Delighted with the whole scene, and seeing only one South Asian vendor, they started dreaming up their own food stall in giddy what-ifs.

A few days later, those daydreams had turned into feasible plans that would benefit everyone they could think of involving. They split practical tasks (such as applying for licenses), persuaded their talented mothers to oversee the culinary production, and quickly founded Jhal NYC to bring New Yorkers the Bengali street food you simply can't find in restaurants.

Before grad school, Mahfuzul had worked in sustainable development at the UN and hoped to enter the foreign service to make use of his intimate knowledge of two very different cultures and ways of life. Now, running Jhal NYC has provided him a launching pad for his own sort of independent, sustainable, development-oriented diplomatic mission—developing innovative teaching materials around food and intercultural storytelling—and, of course, the opportunity to share delicious Bengali food New Yorkers for too long have missed out on.

"WHENEVER YOU HAVE GUESTS, YOU HAVE TO FEED WHOEVER'S AT YOUR HOME. IT'S PART OF THE CULTURE. SO A QUICK SNACK THAT WE WOULD MAKE IS JHAL MURI."

JHAL MURI
Spiced Puffed Rice Snack

Jhal muri is cheap, quick, and easy to make, especially if you make the tempered oil in advance. Mahfuzul can't think about jhal muri without being reminded of the sounds of the bustling streets of Dhaka. It's traditionally served in a newspaper cone, and with the component spices all laid out in individual bowls, it can be easily customized to each person's tastes.

Makes **1 serving**

TEMPERED MUSTARD OIL

1 small yellow onion, roughly chopped

4 garlic cloves, roughly chopped

3-inch (7.5 cm) piece peeled fresh ginger

4 cups (960 ml) mustard oil

1¼ teaspoons ground coriander

¼ teaspoon ground cumin

Scant ¼ teaspoon Indian red chile powder (lal mirch)

Scant ¼ teaspoon turmeric

2 cardamom pods

1 cinnamon stick

1 bay leaf

JHAL MURI

3 cups (45 g) puffed rice

1 cup (about 60 g, depending on the brand) *chanachur* (Bengali seasoned snack mix)*

2 tablespoons chopped cilantro

1 tablespoon diced tomatoes

1 tablespoon diced onion

1 teaspoon thinly sliced green Thai chile, with seeds

Juice of 1 lemon wedge

1. To make the tempered mustard oil, combine the onion, garlic, and ginger in a food processor or blender. Blend into a smooth, uniform paste, adding water, a teaspoon at a time, as necessary. Combine paste with all the remaining ingredients in a large saucepan over medium heat and bring to a rolling boil, about 10 minutes. Remove from the heat, set aside, and store any excess in a glass container in the refrigerator for future use. There is no need to strain out the solids.

2. To make the jhal muri, pour the puffed rice and chanachur into a large sealable container such as a bowl or jar with a lid. Add all the remaining ingredients, as well as 1 tablespoon of the mustard oil, and shake vigorously so that the puffed rice and chanachur are evenly coated by the wet ingredients.

3. Serve in a newspaper cone for a traditional presentation, or otherwise in a large cup or a bowl. Eat with a spoon.

* Chanachur can be purchased at any South Asian grocery store.

Iqbal Ahmed

BENGALI STREET EATS

32 BANGLADESH

Born and raised in NYC's Lower East Side in 1987, Iqbal, the youngest of six siblings, grew up feeling like a typical '90s New Yorker kid: Streetwise beyond his years, he knew how to get around town on his own, enjoyed eating fast food with his friends after classes, and would talk back to his parents when they woke him up for school.

"I was one of those kids growing up, a know-it-all. I didn't know we were immigrants until I was like fifteen.

My parents were always telling us, *Hey, you guys are losing your culture.* Then my father took us to Bangladesh for the first time when I was fifteen, and that's when everything changed—

like a wake-up call. I went there and I saw kids scrapping for food and I was like, *Wow, we have it really good here in New York.* My dad literally said, *If I never left, you'd be here in this village, working as child labor.* And that humbled me.

My dad was a head chef for most of his life—that's how he actually got to America. He worked on cruises. He worked in Japan, in London—finally got to here. And I would never appreciate the stories until I got older and was like, *Wow, this guy did a lot.* The guy he was working for—at an Indian restaurant in the Upper East Side—that guy actually sponsored my entire family to come here, in the eighties. And when it comes to food, my dad actually taught my mom how to cook. Growing up, until I was fifteen, I would always go to KFC or like McDonald's, and I wouldn't appreciate the home-cooked meals. But as I got older, I would see the amount of work it took to make them, and my palate changed: I was enjoying it a lot more.

I fell in love with the food industry. My dad would tell us, *Hey if you don't do well in school, you're going to become a dishwasher.* And my first job out of high school was at a restaurant. I was a waiter at Dallas BBQ, and it got me through college. I learned how to bartend, I learned hospitality, I learned how to manage people. I got offers to manage places, and eventually ended up buying a place."

> *"YOU'RE ONE OF MY KIDS WHO WERE BORN HERE, MY DAD WOULD SAY. I WANT YOU TO BECOME THE PRESIDENT. I WAS LIKE, DAD, THAT'S HIGH HOPES."*

The place that Iqbal bought became Indi Thai—a little restaurant in the Lower East Side, specializing in both Indian and Thai cuisine—which he started with his sister Nasrin, who benefitted the most from their father's culinary teachings (and who wrote the following recipes), as well as his New York–childhood friend Emon Ullah, who helps manage the business side. Though Iqbal and Emon never imagined it as teenagers, now they are both married to Bengali women, whom they first met while visiting family in Bangladesh—and their wives have helped them reconnect with Bengali culture and food even more as adults.

"What led us to the Queens Night Market is Joey Bats (see page 71). He's actually a neighbor of ours, of Indi Thai restaurant. He's two doors down on Allen Street. And he was telling me about this market, with vendors from all over the world. . . ."

Bengali Street Eats, now a brick-and-mortar establishment around the corner from Indi Thai, was born as a pop-up for the Queens Night Market in 2019. Both Iqbal's and Emon's families got involved, putting their own culinary heritage front and center this time.

"We didn't lose our culture as much as our parents thought. My father's not here no longer, but I'm sure he'd be very proud of how all the kids turned out. We give back to the community, not only in Bangladesh but also here in New York. Coming from an immigrant household has been a true blessing."

SHINGARA
Vegetable Samosas

Bengali shingara tend to be plumper and have thicker wrappers than their samosa counterparts in other Desi countries. The division of labor for shingara in the Ahmed household: Jamal (dad) oversaw the fillings, Jahanara (mom) and Parvin (eldest sister) were in charge of the dough wrappers, and the other five siblings would stuff the wrappers with help from Jamal. The family tradition was a special treat because Jamal, head chef at an Indian restaurant, would rarely bring his talents home from work, but the kids marveled at his cooking chops when he did.

Makes 4 servings (8 samosas)

DOUGH

1 cup (125 g) unbleached all-purpose flour (gluten-free, if needed)

1 tablespoon soybean oil

Pinch of roasted ground cumin

Pinch of salt

FILLING

1 tablespoon vegetable oil

½ medium Spanish onion, diced

1 garlic clove, minced

1 medium russet potato, peeled and diced

1 small carrot, diced

⅓ cup (50 g) frozen corn*

⅓ cup (50 g) frozen peas*

½ teaspoon ground turmeric

Pinch of ground cumin

Pinch of salt, plus more to taste

1 tablespoon fresh cilantro, chopped

Soybean oil, for frying

Tamarind sauce (page 170)

Mint-cilantro chutney

* Whereas traditional shingara tend to contain only potatoes and peas, here corn and carrots are added to the filling for additional texture and flavor.

1. To make the dough, combine all the ingredients in a bowl. Transfer to a floured surface and knead, adding water, a tablespoon at a time, for about 5 minutes, until the ingredients are fully integrated and the dough is smooth. Usually about 3 tablespoons of water will suffice. Transfer dough back to the bowl, cover, and let rest while you make the filling. The dough is ready when it slowly bounces back as you poke it.

2. To make the filling, heat the oil in a skillet over medium heat, add the onion and garlic, and cook until the onion is translucent. Add the potato, carrot, corn, peas, turmeric, and cumin and stir until coated well. Add salt to taste. Pour in ½ cup (120 ml) water, cover, and simmer until the vegetables are tender and water has evaporated, about 15 minutes. Add the cilantro and stir lightly. Remove from the heat and let cool.

3. To make the shingara, cut the dough into 4 equal parts. Form each portion into a ball and roll out into a circle about 7 inches (18 cm) in diameter. Cut each circle in half.

4. Lay a semicircle of dough with the straight edge toward you. Bring the right corner up toward the very center of the dough, folding just beyond the halfway point. Moisten the vertical edge of the flap you just brought up, then bring the left corner toward the center, fold so it just slightly overlaps the moist edge of the other flap, and press to seal.

Lift the top of the folded flaps to open up into a cone that you can hold in one hand. Fill with 1 tablespoon of the filling.

Moisten the top edge of the cone and press together into a seam, creating a triangular shape.

5. Pour about 2 to 3 inches (5 to 7.5 cm) oil into a deep pan and heat over medium heat to about 350°F (180°C). Carefully drop in the shingara one at a time, but do not overcrowd the pot. Fry until golden brown and crispy, about 2 minutes on each side. Transfer to a colander lined with paper towels to drain.

6. Serve hot with the tamarind sauce and mint-cilantro chutney.

CHOTPOTI
Chickpea and Potato Stew

Chotpoti is a roadside favorite in Bangladesh. This potato and chickpea stew contrasts the crunch of raw onions, the zing of hot chiles, and the tang of tamarind sauce. When Parvin moved to Flatbush, Brooklyn, in the late '90s, she lived among a community of Bengali neighbors who celebrated Bengali culture. This is when she perfected this recipe, which has been passed down to Nasrin and Iqbal.

· ·
Makes 4 servings
· ·

TAMARIND SAUCE

5 tamarind pods, or substitute with ⅓ cup (80 g) tamarind pulp mixed with ½ cup water (120 ml)

2 red Thai chiles, roasted and dried, or 1 teaspoon red pepper flakes

1 teaspoon granulated sugar

Pinch of ground cumin

Pinch of black salt (kala namak)

STEW

1 cup (200 g) dried chana dal (split chickpeas), soaked overnight

1 teaspoon ground turmeric

¼ teaspoon salt

1 small russet potato, peeled, diced, and boiled until fork-tender

3 hard-boiled eggs, chopped or grated

½ medium Spanish onion, finely chopped

3 green Thai chiles, finely chopped

Fresh cilantro, leaves and stems, finely chopped

1 teaspoon chaat masala

1. To make the tamarind sauce, soak the tamarind pods in 1 cup (240 ml) water for 5 hours.

2. Crush the red chiles with the sugar and cumin in a separate bowl, then add the tamarind (along with its liquid) and the black salt. If the sauce is too runny, boil the sauce until it reaches the desired consistency.

3. To make the stew, drain the chana and transfer to a large pot. Add the turmeric and salt. Cover with about 4 inches (10 cm) water and bring to a rolling boil. Cover and cook over medium heat until tender, about 2 hours.

4. Add the potato and continue to simmer on low heat for 30 minutes, or until it reduces to the desired stew consistency.

5. Transfer the stew to a small serving bowl and top with the chopped egg, onion, green chiles, and cilantro. Top with the chaat masala and tamarind sauce.

FUSKA
Stuffed Semolina Crisps

Fuska is another roadside staple in Bangladesh, and it goes hand in hand with chotpoti, because the flavor profile and many of the ingredients overlap. Whereas the creamy, comforting texture of the stew is the foundation of chotpoti, it's the crispiness of the bite-size semolina shell, exploding with exciting fillings in your mouth, that characterizes fuska. Not only is it delicious, it is just plain fun to eat.

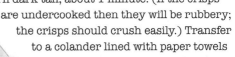

Makes 4 servings

1 cup (200 g) dried chana dal (split chickpeas), soaked overnight

1 or 2 pinches of salt

1 red onion, finely chopped

7 to 8 sprigs cilantro, chopped

5 green Thai chiles, finely chopped

⅓ cup (80 ml) lemon juice

3 tablespoons chaat masala

Pinch of black salt (kala namak)

24 ready-to-cook *puri papads* (semolina discs)

Soybean oil, for frying

4 hard-boiled eggs, grated

Tamarind sauce (page 170)

1. Drain the chana and transfer to a large pot. Add the salt and cover with about 2 inches (5 cm) water. Bring to a boil, cover, and cook over medium heat until the chana is tender and the water has evaporated, about 2½ hours. Remove from the heat and let cool.

2. Add half of the red onions, half of the cilantro, the chiles, lemon juice, chaat masala, and black salt to the chana and mix well. Set aside.

3. Pour about 3 inches (7.5 cm) oil into a deep pan and heat over medium heat to about 350°F (180°C). Fry the puri papads, stirring constantly until they puff up and turn dark tan, about 1 minute. (If the crisps are undercooked then they will be rubbery; the crisps should crush easily.) Transfer to a colander lined with paper towels to drain.

4. When the puri papads are cool enough to handle, poke a hole on top of each and fill halfway with the chana filling. Completely fill with a pinch of the remaining red onion and cilantro and the grated eggs.

5. Pour 1 teaspoon of the tamarind sauce into each crisp and enjoy immediately. Waiting too long will result in soggy fuska.

Hnin "Snow" Wai

DE' RANGOON

(33) MYANMAR (BURMA)

As a child, Snow (*hnin* literally means "snow" in Burmese) lived in Dawei, in the southern part of Burma close to Thailand, where her grandparents ran a traditional Burmese tea shop still in operation today. Her grandfather was Chinese and had run across the border in World War II. He'd set up the tea shop in Dawei as a way to make a living without any Burmese language skills. He eventually found a Burmese-speaking friend to help him, and met Snow's grandmother, a Burmese woman who had learned Hokkien in an afterschool program before the government closed down all the Chinese schools. She and eventually her daughter—Snow's mother—made Chinese, Burmese, and Indian food for the tea shop. Snow grew up eating their delicious food, three meals a day.

But the family business was struggling, so her father left to try to make money in Tokyo, and Snow went with her mother to Rangoon. She studied Chinese after school, with the hopes of someday getting a student visa and moving to China, but by the end of high school, a Chinese student visa seemed unlikely, even though her Chinese was good. She tried to find a way to join her father in Japan, but immigrating there was difficult.

Her uncle in the US suggested she try the green card lottery. She won and moved to New York at the age of twenty-one, tagging along with a friend and her family who were moving at the same time. Until that moment, she'd never traveled without her family.

Since Snow hadn't anticipated moving to the US, and had focused on Chinese instead of English, she had a hard time getting around the first year. She also had never worked before, or cooked, or done laundry—so the learning curve was steep on all fronts. A cousin she'd just met arranged for her to work at a Dunkin' Donuts,

but she couldn't understand the customers and got yelled at a lot. She was miserable and called her mom to tell her she was coming home.

Back in Rangoon, Snow decided she wanted to learn to cook and became her mother's apprentice, watching and copying her every move for six months, until she felt strong enough to give New York another go. This time, she enrolled in ESL classes and got a job at a Subway in midtown Manhattan. The manager was Chinese and didn't seem to mind her lack of English so long as he could direct her in Chinese. The customers, however, did mind.

"The first time a customer asked me something, and I didn't understand, he was so pissed off. He told me, *Can you put mayonnaise,* but I don't know what's mayonnaise; I don't know anything about any mustard, you know—I had a very hard time! I could not catch their pronunciation. Every night I came home and cried about the customers scolding me, and the boss scolding me in Chinese. That's why I went to ESL classes at LaGuardia. I worked till 4:00, so ESL classes 5:00 to 9:00, three or four days a week. I'd just eat Subway sandwiches on the way because they were free, but I did not like them."

Eventually, she got a better job as a waitress in a Japanese restaurant and connected with New York's Chinese-Burmese community.

Snow's husband, Win Htwe

She made friends and started attending community events like the Water Festival, or the Chinese New Year party where she met her husband in 2013. From a family of restaurateurs himself, Snow's husband took her seriously when she shared her dream of opening a tea shop in New York like her grandparents' and encouraged her to start small, with a pop-up shop or small-scale catering.

As Snow developed her menu for her debut at the Queens Night Market in 2017, she and her husband invited all their friends, Burmese and non-Burmese alike, to regular tasting parties at their home in Elmhurst. The tea leaf salad and Shan noodles always got the top scores and made their Burmese friends nostalgic, especially because there were no Burmese restaurants in New York since Mingala, the one run by Snow's husband's family, had shut down in 2016

De' Rangoon may yet revive it. . . .

LAPHET THOKE
Tea Leaf Salad

In Myanmar, tea leaf salad is available at almost every street stall and tea shop, and it's often offered as a complimentary dessert in restaurants. Fermenting leaves isn't something usually done at home, because ready-made fermented tea leaves can be store-bought. But here in the US, Snow had to teach herself to ferment dry tea leaves. We're glad she did, because the resulting salad is a great balance of salty, sour, spicy, bitter, and crunchy from the mixed beans and seeds.

Makes 2 servings

FERMENTED TEA LEAVES

10 cups (2.4 L) boiling water

2 tablespoons loose dry green tea leaves*

½ cup (120 ml) canola oil

3 Indian green chiles (or similar), seeded

Juice of ⅛ lime

½ garlic clove, minced

1 teaspoon salt

* The best and traditional way of fermenting tea leaves is using fresh tea leaves, but since fresh tea leaves are hard to find in the US, use loose dried green tea leaves, available in Chinese grocery stores.

** Boondi can be purchased in Indian/ South Asian grocery stores.

TOASTED BEANS AND SEEDS

1 teaspoon canola oil

3 tablespoons sesame seeds

¼ cup (16 g) *boondi* (fried chickpea flour puffs)**

¼ cup (40 g) salted, roasted peanuts

¼ cup (35 g) salted, roasted soybeans

¼ cup (30 g) roasted sunflower seeds

2½ tablespoons fried garlic chips (such as Maesri brand)

2 tablespoons roasted pumpkin seeds

1 teaspoon salt

SALAD

1 head romaine lettuce or Taiwanese flat cabbage, shredded

6 cherry tomatoes

14 small dried shrimp

½ jalapeño, seeded and finely chopped

2 lime wedges

2 teaspoons fish sauce, or 2 pinches of salt

1. To make the fermented tea leaves, place the tea leaves in a pot and pour in 5 cups (1.2 L) boiling water. Let steep for 20 minutes. Drain through a fine-mesh strainer; pick out and discard any tough bits like little stems. Place the tea leaves in cheesecloth and squeeze out the water. Repeat and then soak in cold water overnight.

2. Drain the leaves, squeeze out excess water, and place in a food processor with the oil, chiles, lime juice, garlic, and salt. Blend into a slightly textured paste, just nearly smooth. Keep in an airtight container in the refrigerator for 2 days to develop the fermented taste.

3. To make the toasted beans and seeds, heat the oil to a large skillet over medium heat. Add the sesame seeds and toast until light brown, about 5 minutes. Add the remaining ingredients and toast, mixing or tossing regularly, until shiny with a coat of oil, about 4 minutes. Remove from the heat, let cool to room temperature, and store in an airtight container.

4. To make the salad, divide the lettuce among two bowls. Around the edges of each bowl, arrange half of the cherry tomatoes, dried shrimp, and jalapeño, along with one lime wedge. Top each bowl with half of the toasted beans and seeds, then add 1 tablespoon of the fermented tea leaves, and 1 teaspoon of the fish sauce or a pinch of salt on top.

5. Serve, squeezing over the lime wedge and mixing well to eat. Leftover fermented tea leaves can be stored in the refrigerator for up to 1 month.

SHAN KHAO SWE
Shan Noodles

Shan noodles originate from the eastern state of Shan in Myanmar and are typically eaten for lunch or dinner. When Snow was growing up, there weren't many Shan noodle shops around, so her family would take long morning drives to enjoy them as a breakfast treat. This recipe is passed down from her aunt and is an umami marriage of soy sauce, tomato sauce, and chicken curry.

Makes 4 servings

CHICKEN CURRY

1 pound (455 g) boneless chicken thighs

Two ¼-inch (6.5 mm) slices peeled fresh ginger

2 whole garlic cloves

2 tablespoons salt

¼ teaspoon ground black pepper

3 tablespoons canola oil

1 large yellow onion, chopped

2 garlic cloves, minced

1 teaspoon smoked paprika

½ teaspoon Indian red chile powder (lal mirch)

¼ teaspoon ground turmeric

1 tablespoon fish sauce

½ teaspoon chicken bouillon powder

* Available at Asian grocery stores, black soy sauce is sweeter and less salty than regular, light soy sauce.

** Pickled mustard leaves are available jarred in Asian grocery stores.

TOMATO SAUCE

1½ tablespoons canola oil

1 large yellow onion, chopped

2 garlic cloves, minced

½ teaspoon ground star anise

½ teaspoon smoked paprika

1 tablespoon tomato paste

2 medium tomatoes, smoothly blended

1 tablespoon plus 4 teaspoons light soy sauce

1 teaspoon dashi

4 teaspoons dark black soy sauce (such as Dragonfly brand)*

16 ounces (450 g) rice noodles

Chopped cilantro leaves

Fried garlic

Crushed peanuts

Pickled mustard leaves**

Mung bean sprouts

1. To make the chicken curry, bring 3½ cups (840 ml) water to a boil in a large saucepan. Add the chicken, ginger, garlic cloves, 1½ tablespoons of the salt, and the pepper. Cook over medium heat for about 15 minutes, until the chicken is cooked through. Remove the chicken and let rest, until cool enough to handle. Shred with a fork.

2. Heat the oil in a large skillet over medium heat. Add the onion and cook, stirring frequently, until translucent. Add the garlic and cook until it begins to brown, stirring frequently, about 5 minutes. Turn the heat to low, add the paprika, chile powder, and turmeric, and stir until well incorporated. Turn the heat to medium-high and add the shredded chicken, fish sauce, the remaining 1½ teaspoons salt, and the bouillon powder. Stir and cook until the chicken is hot and well coated with the rest of the ingredients, about 5 minutes. Remove from the heat and set aside.

3. To make the tomato sauce, heat the oil in a large skillet over medium heat. Add the onion and cook, stirring frequently, until translucent. Add the minced garlic and cook, stirring frequently, until it begins to brown, about 5 minutes. Turn the heat to low, add the star anise and paprika, and stir until well incorporated. Turn the heat to medium, add the tomato paste, blended tomatoes, 3 teaspoons of the light soy sauce, and the dashi, and cook until the liquid has reduced and thickened to a pasta-sauce consistency, about 12 minutes.

4. To make the noodles, soak the noodles in a bowl of warm water for 20 minutes. Bring a pot of water to a boil and add the noodles. Stir with chopsticks to prevent sticking and cook until tender, about

3 minutes, depending on thickness of the noodles. Drain and rinse with cool water.

5. Divide the noodles among four bowls. Top each with 1 teaspoon of the light soy sauce, 1 teaspoon of the black soy sauce, a pinch of salt, 1 tablespoon of the tomato sauce, and 2 or 3 tablespoons of the chicken curry. Garnish with the cilantro, fried garlic, peanuts, mustard leaves, and bean sprouts.

Myo Thway

BURMESE BITES

MYANMAR (BURMA) 33

Growing up in the 1980s in Hinthada, in the northern delta part of Burma (now Myanmar), Myo was the beneficiary of his father's relentless curiosity about food. Every Sunday after church, Myo's father would launch into some culinary exploration or another, getting his kids to help out with the prep, and the resulting feast would never fail to entertain the large family. Over the course of Myo's childhood, his father would try and fail to launch seven or eight food businesses before hitting on one that stuck, thanks in part to these weekly culinary experiments.

One Saturday when Myo was in eighth grade, his father decided to learn how to make palata—a folded crepe-like flatbread with savory fillings—a popular Burmese street food akin to the Indian paratha. So he went out into the streets, found a palata vendor, and hired him to teach his techniques. Myo, as the eldest son—eager to prove himself useful to his father—joined in the lesson and eventually mastered the technique, too, though he never could have imagined then where his palata-making would someday take him. . . .

Decades later, in New York City, shortly before the city's only Burmese restaurant had finally closed, Myo started making and selling palata, first at street fairs, then at the Queens Night Market in 2015—its first year of operation. Burmese Bites gained an instant following of devoted fans, lines forming in front of his tent as soon as the market opened each week. A listing as number one of "The Top 10 Cheap Places to Eat in 2016" in The New York Times soon followed, and since then Burmese food businesses have been cropping up all over the city. A coincidence? We think not.

"My father and mother, they both were government employees. They both were teachers, high school teachers. When they got married, things were different. Their salary was enough to buy probably about like an ounce and a half of gold every month. But inflation hit. So every year the money value decreased and, you know. . . . They told me that they were used to people being able to spend one income and save another income. But not anymore. After a few years, they had to rely on both incomes for us to survive.

Another thing is I have altogether eight brothers and sisters, which is a big family. So at one point they said, *You know what, the government salary is good, but it's not good enough to [support] our family.* So my father decided to quit his job, which was the only job that he knows how to do. Then he went into business, but then . . . he tried this, that, seven or eight different things. He tried and failed, then finally was successful.

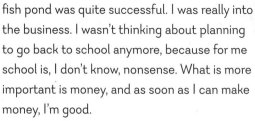

As a child, I know that my father had to borrow money from his relatives, all this stuff. And I don't really like it, but there's nothing really much that I can do about it. When I was in like, eighth grade, I decided, *OK, I'm gonna help a little more to my father so that, you know, I'll be helpful to the family.* So that's how I got more involved in the family business, because of the difficulty that my father went through.

When I became a tenth-grader, which is equivalent of twelfth grade over here—the final year of my high school—the political situation back in my country was kind of bad. There was demonstration and riots by students all over the place. And the government pressed down so the whole country was declared [under] martial law. All the schools were closed; all the colleges were closed. At that time, actually, I spent my time mostly working at my father's fish farm. After a while, they opened it back up—we go back to school and stuff—and, after a while more, things got bad again!

So this time they closed the schools for three years. And in those three years, I was at his fish pond most of the time, helping him out—and the

Myo and Rebecca (Myo's wife) making palatas for the Myanmar Baptist Church of New York's FunFair, around 1996

fish pond was quite successful. I was really into the business. I wasn't thinking about planning to go back to school anymore, because for me school is, I don't know, nonsense. What is more important is money, and as soon as I can make money, I'm good.

But after three years, unfortunately, the government situation was good again, so my father told me, *OK, you are to go back to school, go to college.* I said, *I don't want to go to school.* And he said, *Look, I'm a teacher, your mother is a teacher*—so why, by the time we got other people's children educated, you are the one who's not going to be educated? That's not how it's supposed to be. So he basically kicked me out to go to school—so, OK, I went to school.

I was studying engineering back in my country. The first year, I wasn't really into school, so I didn't study that hard—but, then again, I passed. I don't know how. The second year, it didn't look very good at all. And at the time, my sisters were in the US, so I wrote to my sister, *Why don't you call me, 'cause I don't really feel like going back to school over there either, and Dad is also not accepting me at home. He's not going to take the fact that I don't go to school and I do business.* I told her, *If I come to the States, if I go to school, that would be a little bit better.* Because my argument is that back home, even if I finish my school, my college, and if I got a degree in engineering, there is no way that I'm going to get a good job. There are a lot of educated people over there without jobs. So after you go to college, you're going to end up going back to your family business anyway.

So I said, *No, I don't want to waste my time. I'm gonna come to the US and at least study and after I got engineering degree I'm gonna get a nice job.* And she did call me, and yes, I came here, as a foreign student. I went to City College, and I was working and going to school full-time—I got $4.25 minimum wage at the time, selling hot dogs at the Port Authority Bus Terminal.

At that time, I don't know what is Snapple. I don't know which ice cream is what—vanilla, chocolate. Agh, it's killing me! I remember every time the kids come and ask me, *Do you have this ice cream?* I'd say, *You know what, look down in the ice cream box; if you find it, just take it,* 'cause I don't know how to look for any of them—'cause, I don't know, so many different kinds! I get a headache.

After that, somehow, the boss liked me, so I was promoted to his pizza store in Midtown on Fifty-Sixth Street between Fifth and Sixth Avenue, and I start taking phone calls for the order. I screwed up a lot, but I learned to know what is pizza, what is pepperoni, what is broccoli—and from that I learned little bit by little bit. And at the time my sister was working at a supermarket, so I joined her and I learned a lot more about all the foods and items that they sell. Then after a while I moved to the jewelry industry: I was selling rubies, sapphire, and emerald at one company, calling everybody and saying, *Hey, do you want rubies?* So my

communication skills got a little bit better at that time, I guess.

You know about the green card, right? You can get an H1 work visa for three years, and then you extend another three years—after that, that's all you can extend. You apply for green card or you leave the country. So the jewelry company was nice enough to apply for the H1 for me, and later the green card, and that's how I eventually got citizenship.

After I was working there—the Italian jewelry company—for fifteen, sixteen years, I said, *OK, you know, you do the same thing every day. . . . It's like, every day's the same for the past fifteen years.* I was like, *Is it what I really want?* And, another thing is that when I get old, what am I going to do? I don't have any, let's say, pension, or anything like that either—401(k), Social Security—I don't even know if there will be any Social Security left when I get old. Things like that.

So my wife and I discuss about this. That's where the street fair things come in. We were doing the street fair and didn't do very well, so we joined Queens Night Market and it was good. The second year, it was better. So I told my wife, *OK, you know what, should I go to the food industry like entirely?* She said, *Do whatever you want.* She told me, *I don't really want you to think,* Oh, I should have done this, I should have done that, *and when you are sixty years old regret what you didn't do.*

So I quit, and basically now I'm in the food business entirely. I have the Queens Night Market doing good, and now one pushcart in Long Island City. It's in its second year, and it's doing a lot better, as well. And I'm also thinking about expanding more this year."

Ohno kaukswe is typically eaten for breakfast, a snack, a light, late-night meal, or a party food. It's not typically eaten as lunch or dinner because those meals almost invariably mean rice. Myo admits that he didn't always appreciate soups, but after developing his own recipe, he now truly sees why this dish is regarded as one of the pillars of Burmese cuisine.

OHNO KAUKSWE
Coconut Chicken Noodle Soup

Makes 4 servings

MINCED CHICKEN

8 ounces (225 g) chicken breasts, diced

1½ teaspoons paprika

1 teaspoon salt

1 teaspoon dark black soy sauce (such as Dragonfly brand)

⅛ teaspoon granulated sugar

3 tablespoons vegetable oil

1 medium yellow onion

2 garlic cloves, minced

* Besan can be found in South Asian grocery stores or the Indian/Southeast Asian section of international grocery stores. It is widely used in Burmese cooking. In its raw form, it is often used to thicken soups and stews, whereas the roasted version is often used in salads to make them less watery.

BROTH

1 pound (455 g) bone-in chicken thighs

2 or 3 chicken backbones

1 medium yellow onion, diced

2 garlic cloves, flattened (use more, if desired)

1 tablespoon fish sauce, plus more to taste

2 tablespoons besan (gram flour)*

1 cup (240 ml) coconut milk

PAPRIKA OIL

1 cup (240 ml) vegetable oil

1 tablespoon paprika

8 ounces (225 g) wheat noodles

1 red onion, sliced into thin half-moons

4 hard-boiled eggs, halved

4 lime wedges

Cilantro

Red pepper flakes, optional

1. To marinate the minced chicken, combine ¾ teaspoon of the paprika with the salt, soy sauce, and sugar in a bowl or container. Add the chicken, combine, cover, and place in the refrigerator to marinate for at least 2 hours.

2. To make the broth, place the chicken thighs and backbones in a pot with the onion, garlic, fish sauce, and 9 cups (2.1 L) water. Bring to a boil, then reduce the heat to low and simmer for 30 minutes. Remove the chicken thighs and let cool before separating the meat from the thigh bones. Set aside the meat and add the thigh bones back to the broth. Simmer for 2 to 3 hours, until reduced by about a third.

3. Meanwhile, soak the besan in ¾ cup (180 ml) water for at least 1 hour.

4. To cook the minced chicken, heat the oil in a skillet over medium heat. Sauté the onion until brown, about 5 minutes. Add the garlic and remaining ¾ teaspoon paprika and cook until the garlic is just browning, about 3 minutes. Add the chicken and cook until the liquid has evaporated and the meat begins to sizzle, about 15 minutes. Remove from the heat and set aside.

5. To make the paprika oil, heat the oil in a saucepan over high heat until the oil just begins to smoke. Remove from the heat and let cool for about 1 minute. Add the paprika, stir, and set aside.

6. To make the noodle soup, slowly add the besan mixture to the pot while stirring. Simmer for 10 minutes; taste to ensure that the raw bean taste has been cooked out. Return the thigh meat to the pot and add the coconut milk. Add about 2 tablespoons of the paprika oil to make the soup pinkish red, adding more for desired color. Season with more fish sauce, if desired.

7. Cook the noodles in a separate pot of boiling water to desired firmness, about 7 to 8 minutes. Drain and divide among four bowls. Add 1 hard-boiled egg and lime wedge to each bowl along with some broth, diced chicken, red onion, cilantro, and pepper flakes, if using, and serve.

Joanne Franco

CATHAILINA

(34)
THAILAND

Both of Joanne's parents are from Thailand, and her older sister was born there, too, but Joanne was raised a New Yorker. Born in Brooklyn, she moved to Queens at age twelve, when her parents divorced.

After high school, Joanne went to Thailand on vacation and loved it so much she didn't come back for years. First, she stumbled into a career as a model. Joanne says, "In Thailand, there's really no middle class, like in America. In Thailand you're either 'somebody' or you're very, very poor. So the circle I was in in Thailand was more like the wealthier crowd, and I met this gay guy through a friend who'd lived in LA for a while and who was a makeup artist and owned a modeling agency, and his agency signed me."

Her modeling stint also led to her to meet her first husband, whose work took them to live in Dubai until she got pregnant. She then moved back to NYC, wanting her child to be a US citizen like her, and to be closer to her parents.

Her mother worked in nail salons for twenty years but was never tempted to open her own place. "My mom's not one to gamble with her money. You know, I guess when you didn't have any growing up, and then you make some, I think she was more frugal. *Let me save it.* It's a gamble to open up your own business. What if it doesn't work out?"

> "Nowadays everyone knows what Thai food is. There's a restaurant on every block. But when I was growing up thirty years ago in elementary school, people didn't know what Thai was. People would always ask, *What are you?* and you'd say, *Thai. Taiwanese? No! Thailand!*"

After years of being a stay-at-home mom, however, Joanne started getting antsy and decided she was ready to take a little gamble herself. Encouraged by her second husband, an Ecuadoran who had opened a popular bar in the East Village, she started Cathailina, a play on the name of her two-year-old daughter, Catalina. "The pun only works if you know us, but it's also nice when people ask," Joanne says.

On the menu are all the home-cooked Thai dishes she knows and loves but never saw on other Thai restaurant menus. She understands the hesitation many immigrant chefs have about serving unknown foods to an American clientele, but as a native New Yorker, she also thinks New York is finally ready to learn about Thai cuisine beyond pad thai and tom yum soup.

KAI LOOK KUEY
Son-in-Law Eggs

At your next cocktail party (especially any gatherings involving nuptials), consider serving these instead of deviled eggs. There's a story behind the name of the dish involving a mother threatening the jewels of her son-in-law. Whatever the actual origin of this Thai dish, these hard-boiled-eggs-turned-crispy-treat topped with a sweet and tangy sauce are sure to be a hit. Enjoy these by themselves or atop a bowl of jasmine rice.

Makes 12 pieces

- ¼ cup (60 ml) vegetable oil, plus more for frying
- 5 small shallots, thinly sliced
- 6 hard-boiled eggs
- ¼ cup (60 ml) fish sauce
- 3 tablespoons fresh tamarind juice or tamarind concentrate
- 1½ teaspoons grated palm sugar
- Diced red bell pepper
- Chopped cilantro leaves

1. Heat the oil in a large saucepan over medium-low heat. Add the shallots and cook, stirring constantly, until golden brown and crispy. Remove from the oil with a slotted spoon and drain on a plate lined with paper towels.

2. Pour about 3 to 4 inches (7.5 to 10 cm) oil into a deep pot and heat over medium-high heat to about 350°F (180°C). In batches, carefully add the eggs and fry, stirring occasionally, until browned all around, about 3 minutes. Remove from the heat and drain the eggs on a plate lined with paper towels.

3. In a separate small saucepan, combine the fish sauce, tamarind juice, and palm sugar. Bring to a gentle boil and reduce until the sauce has the consistency of honey or syrup, 3 to 5 minutes. Remove from the heat.

4. Cut the eggs into halves. Top with the sauce, shallots, bell pepper, and cilantro. Serve warm.

KHANOM PANG
Thai Toast with Cucumber Relish

Thai toast isn't easy to find in the US, but it's a simple and tasty snack, bursting with flavor. The cilantro roots and stems impart flavor without the wilting or discoloration of the cilantro leaves. The soft and warm meat paste contrasts with the pleasant crunch of fried white bread—a great way to use stale bread if you've got some sitting around. The toast pairs well with Thai fish cakes or chicken satay.

Makes 12 pieces

½ cup distilled white vinegar

¼ cup (50 g) granulated sugar

1 teaspoon kosher salt

2 medium cucumbers, peeled, split lengthwise, and thinly sliced into half-moons

2 small shallots, thinly sliced

1 red Thai chile, thinly sliced (seeded or unseeded, as preferred)

6 slices white bread, cut in half diagonally (preferably with crusts removed)

1 pound (455 g) ground chicken (preferably chicken thighs)*

5 garlic cloves, finely minced

1 egg

2 tablespoons soy sauce

1 tablespoon minced cilantro, root and stems

1 tablespoon fish sauce

1 teaspoon ground white pepper

Vegetable oil, for frying

* Ground shrimp or pork (or a combination) can also be used in this recipe.

1. To make the cucumber relish, bring the vinegar, sugar, and salt to a boil in a saucepan. Reduce the heat to medium and simmer for about 5 minutes, until slightly syrupy. Remove from the heat and allow to cool to room temperature. Mix in cucumbers, shallots, and chile. Cover and refrigerate.

2. To make the toast, toast the bread on the lowest setting in a toaster oven to remove moisture. It should be dried out but still white.

3. Combine the chicken, garlic, egg, soy sauce, cilantro, fish sauce, and white pepper in a large bowl and mix well to evenly distribute. Spread evenly onto the toast.

4. Pour oil about as deep as half the thickness of a slice of the bread into a deep skillet and heat over medium heat to about 350°F (180°C). In batches, place the toast meat side down first and fry until the edges start turning brown, about 1 minute. Flip and fry the other side for 1 minute. Remove from the oil and drain on a plate lined with paper towels.

5. Serve while hot and crispy, with the cucumber relish.

English, because he couldn't help but absorb it from his American surroundings, and Cantonese, because he went to a private primary school in Manhattan's Chinatown and picked up his friends' native language there.

Though his parents were born and raised in Vietnam, and Patrick's language collection has been steadily growing all his life, Patrick didn't really feel motivated to master the Vietnamese language until he met his wife, Ly Nguyen. Her Vietnamese language, culture, and culinary know-how is now at the very center of his existence: The couple runs two Vietnamese restaurants in New York and sells favorite soups and smoothies at the Queens Night Market on Saturdays in the warmer months.

Patrick Lin and Ly Nguyen

EM
35
VIETNAM

According to his parents, Patrick was a shy child who barely spoke at all until the age of five, when suddenly he spoke three languages fluently: first Teochew, the dialect spoken in the Chaoshan region of Guangdong, China (and at home in its diasporic communities such as the one where his parents grew up in Vietnam), then

"I was born in 1985 in San Francisco in the Tenderloin, moved to NYC at age two, and have been based in DUMBO, Brooklyn, since age five. My bike kept getting stolen when I was a kid, so I'm still really bad at riding bikes. . . . But now DUMBO is bikes everywhere, and I can't ride one!

I was in grad school getting a master's in accounting but graduated during the financial crisis and couldn't find a job, so I went to Vietnam for the

first time ever, working with my uncle in his fruit import business.

My parents are from Vietnam, but I'm ethnically Chinese—all four of my grandparents are from China and emigrated to Vietnam. My grandparents were actually pretty wealthy, and when the Communist Party won the Vietnam War, they put some of my uncles in prison. My grandfather was in prison for three years, so they hid any of the wealth that they had—as much as they could— and eventually the family was able to escape as refugees. They were basically boat people.

My parents used to sell meat to restaurants, mostly Vietnamese restaurants in New York City. So we would bring containers of beef bones— that you use to make the pho stock—to our warehouse in Williamsburg and then distribute it to the restaurants. We were getting them basically straight from farms in the Carolinas. So when I was a teenager I'd help out—make deliveries at restaurants, some butcher shops.

The USDA had just approved longans and lychees to come to the United States, and I was already bringing in dragon fruit. So I flew to Vietnam within a few weeks of that announcement and I was there wandering around and walked into a nail salon—and that's where I met Ly. I got her phone number; we went to watch a movie. I was still jet- lagged, so I fell asleep, and then we went to get smoothies

Patrick and Ly at their restaurant in Bensonhurst, showcasing a bowl of their hủ tiếu

afterwards—just like the smoothies that we sell at the Night Market and also at our brick-and-mortar store. It's a thing in Vietnam. And then I flew back to the States, we kept talking, and because I was still doing the longan and lychee business, I was flying back every month. In terms of hours, I spent a whole month of that year on airplanes.

So eventually I was there long enough and we were crazy in love, so I rented an apartment. Before, she lived in a place with no kitchen. I used to joke with her that I can't marry her if I haven't tasted her cooking. Just joking! But she kind of took that seriously and made hủ tiếu for me, which is our signature noodle soup at the restaurant, and that we sell at the Night Market.

It was an interesting choice, because hủ tiếu is actually a dish from the part of China my grandparents are from, where a lot of people immigrated to Vietnam in the early 1900s. And I was blown away—'cause my mom makes the same dish, and hers was better than my mom's. She kept making these amazing dishes now that she had a kitchen to work with.

I proposed to her a few months later. Then we were thinking, *What is she going to do when she comes to the States?* Share her wonderful cooking of course! We found a small space in Brooklyn and opened a restaurant, Em, and also started selling at the Queens Night Market in April 2019."

THỊT KHO
Braised Pork Belly

Thịt kho is the quintessential Vietnamese family dish, something almost every Vietnamese family will eat at home on a weekly basis. It's often served during Tet, first offered to ancestors, and then served at the table for the family. Ly is from Central Vietnam, where the style of cooking is different from the North or South. This recipe does not call for eggs, and black pepper is featured more prominently since it is produced in the region. The rich, savory sauce goes perfectly with rice, and it keeps for days, perhaps even getting better.

Makes 3 or 4 servings

½ cup (110 g) plus 2 tablespoons packed dark brown sugar

1 pound (455 g) sliced pork belly, cut into ¾-inch (2 cm) cubes

¼ cup (60 ml) fish sauce

1 tablespoon ground black pepper

Cooked rice

Chopped scallions

Diced Thai chiles or jalapeños

1. Heat 2 packed tablespoons of the brown sugar in a saucepan over medium heat, stirring constantly until caramelized, 60 to 90 seconds, being careful not to burn the sugar. Turn the heat to low and slowly add the pork while stirring. Continue stirring until the pork is cooked through, about 15 minutes.

2. Add the fish sauce, pepper, and the remaining ½ cup (110 g) brown sugar. Continue stirring over low heat until the sauce reduces to a dark brown color, about 10 minutes.

3. Serve over the rice with a generous helping of the sauce and garnished with the scallions and chile.

SINH TỐ BƠ
Avocado Smoothies

On Patrick and Ly's first date, they went to a movie, followed by a visit to a smoothie stand, where they sipped avocado smoothies, chatted, and people-watched for hours on the streets of Saigon. As far as smoothies go, sinh tố bơ is on the heavier side due to the avocado and condensed milk, and it is treated more like a dessert.

Makes 2 servings

2 cups (260 g) ice

1 Hass avocado, peeled and pitted

¼ cup (60 ml) half-and-half

¼ cup (60 ml) simple syrup,* or 2 tablespoons granulated sugar

¼ cup (80 ml) sweetened condensed milk

1. Combine all the ingredients in a large blender. Blend on high until pulverized into a smooth consistency.

2. Serve in two glasses with straws or spoons.

* To make simple syrup, boil and dissolve 1 part rock sugar in 1 part water.

Sokhita Sok

CAMBODIANOW

(36)
CAMBODIA

When her family moved to New York from Phnom Penh, Cambodia, in 2008, Sokhita had to start high school all over again—at age sixteen. No one had explained to her that if she scored poorly on the required ESL test, she simply would have been placed in a class along with other non-native English speakers, which would have helped her catch up to standard American high school English sooner. Instead, she cheated on her ESL test. "I thought it was a big deal. I thought . . . *Oh my God; I'm not supposed to fail this test,* so I copied my sister's test. She knew more English back then. So they thought that I knew English, when I didn't."

Though she barely understood English at the time, Sokhita was placed right into the mainstream ninth-grade class at her local high school in the Bronx. It was an incredibly alienating experience. There were only five Asian kids in her school, three of whom were her older cousins. She coped by becoming a bit of a

"teacher's pet," focusing intensely on her studies, determined to learn English fast so she could eventually break her silence in the classroom. She spent her lunch breaks either overdoing her community service requirement or in her teacher's office, with Cambodian food brought from home.

The move had come as a bit of a surprise to Sokhita. Her whole life, her parents had been grooming her older sister for an eventual move to the US, paying for her extra English classes, and the plan had always been for Sokhita to stay. She was an artist, had lots of friends in Phnom Penh, and wanted to be an art teacher.

When her divorced mother remarried a man with New York connections, however, the plan suddenly changed: everyone was moving to New York.

"There was nothing wrong with my life over there, you know. It's not like for them during the genocide or as asylum refugees: They *had* to leave. It was bad—really bad. There was no food; starvation; everything. But for me, I had my life together. It's not as modernized as over here, but I had my friends; I had my people; I knew my place. When I moved here everything was snatched away from me. I was mad at them. I didn't know any better until the last few years, when I see why I should be here—found a solid reason to be here."

In 2016, on break from her college studies in nutrition and dietetics, staying with her physics teacher father who also worked for the Cambodian Ministry of Education and international nonprofits, Sokhita volunteered as a teacher at a school in Cambodia and worked with Global Children, which provides college funds for Cambodian kids. Around 20 percent of the Cambodian population is still illiterate, and Sokhita wants to help change that. "It's not like I go there because I want to make up for what I missed. It's more like I want to bring something that I've learned from here and really bring it back to where it's needed. And as cliché as it sounds, that's what I want to do, give back to the community I came from," she said.

For now, Sokhita is elevating Cambodian cuisine in the US, creating interest in Cambodian culture by introducing a wide range of New Yorkers to Cambodian foods. She loves talking to customers about Cambodia. As the generation born well after the Khmer Rouge in Cambodia, she can present a much happier image of Cambodia than the one the West tends to hear about.

When she started her project selling food at the Queens Night Market, mere days after earning her nutrition degree, she thought that fish *amok* would be too strong for the American public, flavor-wise: "Until my family kind of insisted, *Amok is the national dish, go for it!* I wanted to sell something more subtle, lighter, for the crowd. But it turned out people

"CHICKEN IS NOT CHICKEN HERE; IT TASTES LIKE CARDBOARD. CHICKENS IN CAMBODIA ARE MUCH SMALLER, VERY FLAVORFUL. WHEN I VISIT MY AUNT'S PLACE, IN THE RURAL AREA, THE CHICKENS ARE WALKING AROUND, AND SHE'S LIKE, *JUST PICK ONE; IT'S GONNA BE YOUR CURRY FOR TONIGHT!*"

really liked the amok! I'm really surprised! . . . And now my family's trying to take credit for that, like, *I told you so.* But now that I know that people are more open, especially in New York City, I feel like there are more doors that can be opened."

AMOK
Fish Curry

Fish amok might be Cambodia's most recognizable dish globally. It's cooked with coconut cream inside a banana-leaf bowl. Whereas some Cambodian expats are opting to make this sweeter and without the fish sauce or shrimp paste, catering to Western palates, Sokhita prefers the salty, sour, and tangy flavors she remembers from Phnom Penh. Serve hot with rice.

Makes 3 servings

YELLOW KROEUNG (SPICE PASTE)

7 garlic cloves

1 small shallot, roughly chopped

2 lemongrass stalks, trimmed and roughly chopped

5 makrut lime leaves

1 thumb-size piece fingerroot (Chinese ginger or krachai)

1 thumb-size piece galangal

1 teaspoon salt

1 teaspoon ground turmeric

AMOK

¼ cup (25 g) chicken bouillon powder

2 tablespoons fish sauce

2 tablespoons granulated sugar

1 tablespoon dried shrimp paste (*belacan*)

1 teaspoon salt

2 pounds (900 g) tilapia or other white fish fillets, sliced into strips 3 to 4 inches (7.5 to 10 cm) long and ½ inch (13 mm) wide

2 eggs, lightly beaten

⅓ cup (75 ml) plus ½ cup (120 ml) coconut cream

1 tablespoon rice flour

1 teaspoon cornstarch

1 mild dried red chile (such as a guajillo chile), minced

Minced makrut lime leaves

1. **To make the yellow kroeung,** place all the ingredients in a food processor or blender and pulse until smooth and uniform, about 5 minutes. Set aside.

2. **To make the amok,** heat a skillet over medium heat. Add the kroeung and cook until the liquid has evaporated, about 10 to 15 minutes. Add the bouillon, fish sauce, sugar, shrimp paste, and salt and turn the heat to low. Cook for 10 minutes, stirring occasionally, until the sugar, salt, and bouillon have dissolved and the ingredients are well mixed. Remove from the heat.

3. Transfer to a large bowl and mix in the fish, egg, ⅓ cup (75 ml) of the coconut cream, and the rice flour.

4. Prepare three banana-leaf or ceramic steaming bowls that can hold at least 2 cups (480 ml). Divide the fish mixture among the bowls. Steam for 10 to 15 minutes, until the fish is white and firm.

5. Meanwhile, bring the remaining ½ cup (120 ml) coconut cream to a boil and stir in the cornstarch. Remove from the heat. When the fish is done (or very nearly done), add 1 teaspoon of the thickened coconut cream on top of each bowl to steam for 1 minute. Remove from the steamer.

6. Garnish with the chile and lime leaves and serve.

DOMLOUNG CHENNG
Caramelized Sweet Potatoes

In Cambodia, you can find *domloung chenng* on street corners, sold off of big metal platters. When Sokhita's mother went grocery shopping every day, she would always come back with snacks, and she would sometimes bring back these sweet potatoes in styrofoam containers with wooden skewers sticking out of each morsel. Sokhita uses Japanese sweet potatoes here in lieu of the sweet potatoes you would find in Cambodia.

Makes 5 servings

1 tablespoon white limestone paste*

2 pounds (900 g) Japanese sweet potatoes

8 ounces (225 g) solid palm sugar

1 teaspoon salt

1⅓ cups (110 g) grated fresh coconut (frozen is fine)

¼ cup (60 ml) coconut cream

1. Pour 5 quarts (5 L) water into a large bowl or pot and mix in the limestone paste.

2. Peel the sweet potatoes and cut into 3 x 2 x 2-inch (7.5 x 5 x 5 cm) strips. Soak in the limestone water for 30 minutes, then thoroughly rinse.

3. Combine the palm sugar, salt, and 1 cup (240 ml) water in a large pot and boil over high heat until the sugar caramelizes, 5 to 10 minutes.

4. Add the sweet potatoes, lower the heat to medium, and cook, stirring frequently, until the insides are the consistency of a baked potato, about 20 minutes.

5. Add the coconut cream, gently stir for 1 to 2 minutes, and then remove from the heat. The potatoes should be glistening in caramel.

6. Serve as dessert at any temperature.

* White limestone paste is used to stiffen the exterior of the potatoes for cooking, while leaving the inside soft and tender.

Carlos
Hon

Abraham
Chin

Calvin
Leong

THE MALAYSIAN PROJECT

MALAYSIA

Calvin, Abraham, and Carlos all went to the same culinary school in Kuala Lumpur, Malaysia, then moved to Providence, Rhode Island, to finish a BA through an exchange program with their culinary school—but it wasn't until years later, after pursuing different degrees and careers across the US, that the three first considered collaborating. When they all ended up roommates in a crowded apartment in Queens in 2015, they'd already been toying around with the idea of starting a food business together. They all thought, *We're all back together now, maybe it's time to start something. . . . You know what? Let's do it!*

Calvin completed his BS in culinary nutrition in Providence, Rhode Island, then earned an MS in nutrition in Dekalb, Illinois, leading to a career as a registered dietitian. Early on, he worked with the Northern Illinois Food Bank, which inspired him to seek work with community outreach programs in New York City—land of economic disparity, but also cultural diversity—where he now manages school food menu creation for children who have difficulty with access. He figures out how to get them balanced, nourishing meals they will actually enjoy, for under $2—including milk.

Growing up in Kuala Lumpur, Calvin always loved helping his grandma in the kitchen and that magical moment when the whole family would be together at the table, ready to eat dinner. "I'm not sure if it's a Chinese thing or just my family's thing—where you always address the elders to eat first—so we'd start with my grandmother: *Hey, Grandmother, it's time to eat now! You can go first.* And then I would say to my dad, *It's time for you to eat,* and then my mom, and then my sister. . . . It's a habit. Even when it comes to friends, if they're older than me, I'll say, *Go ahead first.* It's kind of like a sign of respect."

Abraham, originally from Batu Pahat, Johor, in the south of Malaysia, moved first to Providence with Calvin to earn a BS in sports entertainment events management, then settled into a New York job in the wholesale flower business, advising and connecting event planners and florists.

Abraham's mother was the cook in the family, and when he arrived in the US, he would call her for cooking tips. "Malaysia is a melting pot of cultures—Indians, Chinese, Malays, and some influence from Thailand. My mom would learn to cook different dishes hanging out with neighbors or friends—*What are you cooking tonight? Oh, give me the recipe!* And that's how my mom learned curry from Malay natives and Indians, and then she would try to combine two recipes to make her own recipes. And this is the joy that she had in cooking that I didn't understand as a kid, but at this stage of my life, I realize that is the beauty of food and culture."

Carlos, originally from Petaling Jaya, just

> **"WHEN I MOVED TO THE US, I HAD TO ALWAYS CALL AND ASK MY MOM, WHAT SHOULD I COOK, SINCE I MISS YOUR FOOD SO MUCH. I MISS HOME COOKING."**
> —ABRAHAM

outside of Kuala Lumpur, was also immersed in a culture of culinary exploration at home. "My dad loves diversity, so we would sometimes go to some Indian friends' house and taste Indian curry, or our neighbors are Malays, so we would also go to their house and experience their food, and our parents would invite them over to experience our food—so my parents were always open minded, exposing me and my brothers to different cuisines."

Carlos earned the same BS in culinary nutrition as Calvin in Providence, and got an Optional Practical Training temporary job in California. He couldn't find a permanent job he liked, however, and was about ready to give up on his American dream. "I was this close to buying a plane ticket back to Malaysia. I was checking out the websites, the price and everything. I'd decided the dates as well: My last step was buying the ticket. But I talked to some friends. They said, *You really like United States, why not give yourself another chance?*"

So Carlos went to NYC instead, moving in with his old schoolmates Calvin and Abraham and enrolling in a business program at the Long Island Business Institute, where he met his wife. "So that decision really changed my life! In New York, you can be whatever you want to be and you can do whatever you want to do. We all share this big amount of passion with food. From there it took off—the Malaysian Project was born."

BEEF RENDANG

Beef rendang is a staple in Malaysian cuisine and makes an appearance at many social and special occasions. The dish reminds Abraham, Calvin, and Carlos of their time as Boy Scouts, where the obligatory community service would require helping out at large weddings, which inevitably featured huge quantities of beef rendang. They began fine-tuning Abraham's mother's (Thia Bee Eng's) recipe when they spent some time in Rhode Island, and the closest Malaysian restaurant was a one-hour drive away. Beef rendang is traditionally served with *ketupat* (rice dumplings), *lontong* (rice cakes), or *lemang* (coconut sticky rice), but any rice or starch will do just fine.

Makes 8 servings

DRIED CHILE PASTE

½ cup (40 g) dried mild red chiles, such as Thai *prik ban chang* chiles

2½ tablespoons dried shrimp paste (belacan)

¼ cup (60 ml) vegetable or canola oil

CURRY PASTE

1 large red onion, roughly chopped

2 small shallots, roughly chopped

4 garlic cloves

½-inch (13 mm) piece galangal

½-inch (13 mm) piece peeled fresh ginger

1 lemongrass stalk, trimmed and chopped

2 tablespoons vegetable oil, plus more as needed

1 tablespoon Indian red chile powder (lal mirch)

1 teaspoon ground coriander

¼ teaspoon fennel seeds

¼ teaspoon ground turmeric

BEEF RENDANG

Leaves from 2 stems curry leaves

2 pounds (900 g) beef chuck or shank, cut into 1½ to 2-inch (4 to 5 cm) cubes

1¼ cups (300 ml) coconut milk

1. To make the dried chile paste, halve the chiles and soak in a bowl of water for 15 minutes. Remove as many seeds as possible and rinse to remove dirt. Transfer to a small pot and add enough water to just cover the chiles. Bring to a boil over high heat. Lower the heat to medium, cover, and simmer until the chiles are soft enough to blend easily, about 30 minutes.

2. Strain the chiles and transfer to a food processor or blender. Add the shrimp paste. Blend into a very fine paste. Add a few drops of water if the mixture is too dry.

3. Heat the oil in a saucepan over medium heat. Add the chile mixture and cook, stirring continuously to prevent burning, until emulsified, about 25 minutes. Remove from the heat, transfer to a small container, and set aside.

4. To make the curry paste, blend the red onion, shallots, garlic, galangal, ginger, and lemongrass in a blender or food processor, adding the oil as necessary to ensure a smooth blend. Add the remaining ingredients and blend into a smooth paste.

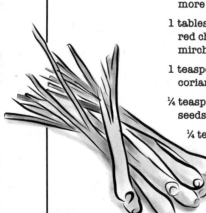

PANDAN KEY LIMEADE

This limeade is infused with pandan leaf, giving it an aromatic, leafy, vanilla-esque tones. Once you've made the syrup, it's quick and easy to make these refreshing crowd-pleasers in a hurry for guests.

. . . .
Makes 8 servings
. . . .

⅓ cup (65 g) granulated sugar

½ pandan leaf (about 12 g), cut into ½-inch (13 mm) pieces

Ice

8 whole key limes, halved

Drinking water

5. To make the beef rendang, transfer the curry paste and curry leaves to a Dutch oven or large heavy pot over medium heat and sauté until fragrant, about 5 minutes. Remove from the pot and set aside.

6. Turn the heat to high and sear the beef on all sides until nicely browned, 3 to 5 minutes. Add just a little oil to prevent sticking if necessary, but go easy in order to facilitate browning.

7. Add the coconut milk, curry paste, dried chile paste, and curry leaves. Mix until the beef is completely coated. Cover and cook over medium-low heat until the beef is tender, about 5 hours. Check the pot every hour or so to stir and test the meat for tenderness. If the sauce is too runny, you can remove the meat and reduce the liquid on higher heat before adding back the meat and returning the heat to medium-low.

8. Remove from the heat, add the pandan leaves, and serve hot.

1. Make a sugar syrup by mixing ¼ cup (60 ml) water and the sugar in a small saucepan over medium heat. Cook until the sugar dissolves. Remove from the heat, add the pandan, and stir gently. Set aside to cool for at least 30 minutes.

2. Place ice in 8 serving glasses. Squeeze two lime halves into each glass. Add 1 tablespoon of the syrup to each glass, fill with drinking water, stir, and serve.

Amy Pryke

NATIVE NOODLES

SINGAPORE

A recent graduate of Columbia Business School, Amy Pryke is on a mission to create a new kind of fast-casual Singaporean noodle shop in NYC. Her Queens Night Market tent is her testing ground; the famous hawker centers of Singapore, her inspiration.

"The hawker centers are basically semi-outdoor, huge communal dining spaces where you can find at least fifteen to twenty-five different kinds of cuisines. Usually each stand specializes in one or two things, so it could be a laksa noodle stand, like what I'm selling at Queens Night Market, or it could be like a grilled meat on a stick—what we call satays. Each one specializes and you can basically spend like two to four dollars for a dish and then share with like a whole table of people. Most working-class, or no . . . most Singaporeans in *general* would eat at least one meal a day at a hawker center. There are many—every neighborhood has one.

How you refer to Caucasians in Singapore commonly is *ang-moh*, which means 'redhead.'

It's also how a lot of Singaporeans would refer to me actually, if they didn't know that I spoke Mandarin, and I tried to order, they'd be like, *Whoa, why is that ang-moh speaking Mandarin?* English is my first language—all Singaporeans are fluent in English at least, because it's our language of instruction—and then you usually take a *mother tongue,* which tends to be the language your mother speaks. So in my case, my mom is Chinese, so I spoke and learned Chinese in school.

Ever since graduating from NYU, I had made decisions based on what outwardly looked nice, to check the box of *OK, yeah, I'm working in a big financial services company that will sponsor my visa—that's great.* I checked that box. Then the next step was *OK, now I've worked in this big financial services company; what's even more prestigious?* It's moving to a company that's hyped as one of the top places to work, so I went to BCG [Boston Consulting Group] after, and that was a personal accomplishment. But once I was there I realized this isn't actually what I want to do. And there's kind of a limit of things you can do to check the boxes.

I was in my consulting job and thinking, *How do I do something different now?* I wasn't ready to leave New York, and as an immigrant you can't just quit your job—you immediately lose your status and become an 'unlawful presence'—so I was thinking, *How do I buy some time and figure out what I'm going to do next?* And I knew it was going to be related to the food world, because someone had given me the advice to know your passion to figure out what you should try and pursue. Like if you have half an hour at lunch, what would you be reading, what would you be thinking about? And for me it was always related to the restaurant world and hospitality. I guessed business school would be a good way to plan out my next steps. . . . I wrote my essay on opening a restaurant, which is not very common for business school, and got in.

I got the laksa recipe from my nanny, Susila, who lived with us since my little sister was born—so maybe almost twenty years. She cooked for our family and is like family to us. She's actually from Sri Lanka, and we still have a very good relationship with her. We visited her family in Sri Lanka, and so it's not so uncommon for families in Singapore to have live-in helpers like nannies. She was an excellent cook.

Since I was little I would follow her to the market, and she had these amazing relationships with all the stall owners, and they would save the best parts of meat and the freshest vegetables for her. She learned a lot of cooking from my grandmother, too, and watched a ton of cooking shows—like she loved Jamie Oliver. She developed a repertoire of Singaporean recipes that we would eat at home, and one of them

Family dinner during a summer vacation at the beach: Pryke Family meals were nonnegotiable— they ate dinner together no matter what!

"SINGAPOREAN CUISINE HAS AT LEAST EIGHT TO TEN DISTINCT NOODLE STYLES, SO I STARTED WITH LAKSA, AND A RECIPE WHICH TO ME ENCAPSULATES A MULTI-ETHNIC SOCIETY."

was this laksa dish. When I went home a few summers ago, I learned it from her, and I kept it in notes on my phone. I also did some research on famous hawker center stalls' recipes and adapted my own version, refined by testing with friends.

My first time ever selling food commercially was April 2019 at the Queens Night Market, with the long-term goal of opening a fast-casual restaurant to create a scalable model, offering eight to ten noodle dishes that are to some extent customizable. Singaporean cuisine has at least eight to ten distinct noodle styles, so I started with laksa, and a recipe which to me encapsulates a multiethnic society. We have Chinese, Malays, Indians, and what you call 'others,' which I guess I would fall into, whether you're mixed race or Eurasian—and our food is a blend of all of those cultures.

My parents initially felt like, *Why are you choosing the hard way? What are you doing with your expensive degrees?* It's definitely a thing for Asian parents to overcome: first, entrepreneurship, then, even worse, in the food business. So it's a double whammy. I want to show my parents that I am serious about it and I have the grit to do it. A tough industry to be in, with not a lot of return, at least monetarily.

I struggle with feeling that I'm letting them down with my decision. But ever since the Night Market, and them seeing how I've done it myself, seeing that it's going well, my mom has been so supportive, she shares everything on her own Facebook page. She got even more likes than me, when she shared my first Queens Night Market post!"

LAKSA NOODLES

Singaporean laksa noodles are thick rice noodles swimming in a spicy, creamy coconut broth, usually garnished with shrimp or chicken, fried tofu puffs, and rau ram (Vietnamese cilantro). When Amy was growing up, her nanny would make the broth and noodles and lay out a big spread of garnishes, allowing each family member to customize their own bowl of laksa noodles. Slurping noodles around the dinner table with her family is her fondest and most indelible food memory.

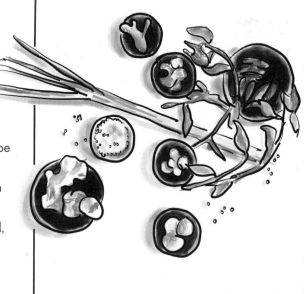

REMPAH (SPICE PASTE) *

1 cup (240 ml) vegetable oil

1 pound (455 g) shallots, peeled and chopped

7 dried medium-hot red chiles (such as Chinese "facing heaven chiles"), halved and seeded

6 ounces (170 g) dried shrimp

6 garlic cloves, peeled

7 candlenuts

2 tablespoons dried shrimp paste (belacan)

2 thumb-size pieces fresh turmeric, peeled, or 1 tablespoon ground turmeric

1-inch (2.5 cm) piece galangal, peeled and sliced

1-inch (2.5 cm) piece peeled fresh ginger, sliced

4 lemongrass stalks (tender white part only), or 1 tablespoon plus 1 teaspoon ground lemongrass

1 tablespoon plus 1 teaspoon granulated sugar

1 tablespoon salt

2 teaspoons curry powder

LAKSA NOODLES

8 shrimp (preferred size)

1 pound (455 g) thick rice noodles (lai fun)

1 tablespoon vegetable oil

⅔ cup (85 g) dried shrimp, diced

2¼ tablespoons rau ram (Vietnamese cilantro) chiffonade, optional **

2¼ teaspoons granulated sugar

⅔ cup (150 ml) coconut milk, plus more if desired

5 pieces fried tofu ("fried tofu puffs"), halved

Handful of bean sprouts

Fish sauce or salt

Crispy fried shallots, optional

1. To make the rempah, blend all the ingredients in a food processor into a smooth paste.

2. To make the laksa noodles, bring a medium pot of water to a boil and blanch the raw shrimp until pink and just cooked, about 30 to 45 seconds. Drain, peel, and set aside.

3. Bring a large pot of water to boil, add the noodles, and cook according to package directions. Drain and set aside.

4. Heat the oil in a large skillet over medium-high heat and stir-fry the dried shrimp until fragrant, about 30 seconds. Reduce the heat to medium-low and add 2 tablespoons of the rau ram, if using, and ¾ cup (170 g) of the rempah. Cook for about 20 minutes, stirring occasionally so the bottom does not burn.

5. Add the sugar and stir to combine. Add the coconut milk and turn the heat to medium, bringing to a light boil. Add the tofu puffs and bean sprouts and stir to combine for 1 minute. Add the blanched shrimp and cooked noodles and stir until well incorporated. Remove from the heat. Add the fish sauce to taste and mix well.

6. If you prefer a runnier soup, add more coconut milk. Serve in four bowls and garnish with the remaining rau ram and the crispy shallots, if using.

* You can use store-bought Laksa paste (common brands are Por Kwan or Tean's) instead of making the rempah spice paste from scratch, in which case you would start at step 2.

** If too difficult to find, the rau ram can be omitted.

*** The recipe for rempah makes more spice paste than is called for in the recipe. Excess will keep in the fridge for a month or in the freezer for 3 months. It works well with any seafood or vegetable stir-fry; simply heat equal parts oil and rempah over medium heat before stir-frying. Rempah is also a great marinade for fish.

ROTI JOHN
Omelet Sandwiches

Roti means bread in Hindi, and John was a common form of address for any Caucasian man in Singapore. Roti John embodies the melting-pot cuisine of Singapore. It is a toasty sandwich of minced meat and onions, wrapped in eggs, and slathered with a ketchup-based sauce. Amy considers it the perfect breakfast sandwich, although you can enjoy it anytime you feel like having an indulgent sandwich.

Makes 1 serving

SPICY KETCHUP

2 tablespoons ketchup

2 tablespoons sriracha

1 tablespoon granulated sugar

ROTI JOHN

⅓ large baguette or 1 hero roll (about 8 inches/20 cm long)

1 tablespoon plus 1 teaspoon canola or grapeseed oil

4 ounces (110 g) minced lamb, beef, or beef/lamb mix

⅛ teaspoon ground cumin

3 garlic cloves, minced

¼ small white or yellow onion, sliced

3 eggs

1 tablespoon sambal oelek chili paste

¼ teaspoon salt

Pinch of ground black pepper

1. To make the spicy ketchup, combine the ketchup, sriracha, and sugar with 2 tablespoons water in a bowl and set aside.

2. To make the roti John, split the bread lengthwise but do not cut all the way through, leaving a small hinge like a hot dog bun. Lightly oil a nonstick skillet with 1 teaspoon of the oil and toast the inside of the baguette by pressing down with a spatula until lightly browned, about 2 minutes. You can also toast the bread in your oven for 2 minutes on the broiler setting.

3. Combine the meat and cumin in a bowl and set aside.

4. Heat the remaining 1 tablespoon oil in the skillet over medium heat and fry the garlic until fragrant, about 30 seconds. Add the onions and cook over low heat until translucent, about 6 minutes. Turn the heat to medium. Add the meat and stir-fry until cooked through, about 6 minutes.

5. Crack the eggs into a bowl, beat lightly, then add the sambal oelek, salt, and pepper, and mix well.

6. Pour the eggs into the skillet, covering the meat. When the edges of the egg just start to firm up, after about 30 seconds, press the bread face-down lightly onto the mixture with a spatula for 2 to 3 minutes as the eggs continue to cook. The bread will absorb much of the egg mixture.

7. Flip the bread along with the omelet with a spatula and cook for about 1 minute. If the eggs are not cooked to desired doneness, flip the baguette back and cook until done.

8. Transfer to a plate and spread some ketchup in the center. Close the sandwich, slice into four pieces, and serve.

The Tham Siblings

LION CITY COFFEE

SINGAPORE

The brains and chefs behind Lion City Coffee, the brother-sister duo Chuin and Yeen Tham, remember the cold December day in late 1987 when their family moved from the Bedok South neighborhood of Singapore to Far Rockaway, Queens. Yeen was seven years old and Chuin was four.

"It was a huge culture shock. We were pretty comfortable in Singapore—our dad had a nice manager office job, our mom was stay-at-home, and our older sister was a driven high school student at the time. Our parents wore suits on the plane; they didn't know what the US was like. So we came in winter time—it was crazy. Singapore's, like, hot and humid!

When we first moved to New York, our dad's plan was to really immerse us in culture, pick up some education and some work experience for them, then return in five years—happier, richer, more fulfilled. But it didn't go like that. For one, just finding a place and a job was just a huge setback—there was a huge difference from what they had originally planned. And as kids growing up in New York, we got more acclimated to what's around here.

Our dad worked in Chinese restaurants. He was initially a dishwasher and worked his way up to a prep cook, and then a chef. In Singapore he was a manager at an office; he was well respected. To come to New York and to work as a dishwasher . . . and then to get fired because he wasn't fast enough . . . it was huge. Really, to his ego, it was pretty damaging. He

WELCOME TO NEW YORK
The Empire State

was pretty frustrated with a lot of things. Even getting a driver's license was a process he failed at many times. He could speak English, but it was very rough, a little bit 'Singlish,' if you will. So that had a negative impact, on, just getting around, getting to places.

Our mom worked as a seamstress in a factory in Ozone Park. Her factory was just a block away from home, so she could pick us up from elementary school, take us home, and check in on us if we got into trouble. Sometimes we would go into the factory when we were out of school. A lot of kids would do that because they had both parents working, and it was pretty hard to find after-school care. They were either horrible or just too expensive.

In the late 80s, it was not uncommon for children in Singapore to first learn English in school. We spoke Mandarin but practically no English at home. Entering a new school in New York, asking *where's the bathroom* required a bit of thought to translate for a seven year old. Our mom didn't even know she was referred to as *mom*. A year later, when Chuin entered kindergarten and bumped his head in the school yard because another student accidentally tripped him, he couldn't explain to the teachers what had happened.

But somehow we survived the early years. We even made great friends growing up, some of whom we are still very close to today.

We grew up so close together that we have this synergy. We feed off each other. When we're angry, we know how to deal with that—disagreements and all that. When one of us has a crazy new idea, we would know to bounce it off the other.

Lion City Coffee is new, currently serving at select pop-ups and special events. We test all our recipes on our friends—yes, we do blind taste tests! We would love to build a brick-and-mortar café . . . serving breakfast all day: *kopi*, our Singaporean-style coffee, with some signature Singaporean dishes, like a *kaya* toast, and some of the savory dishes we've been introducing at the Night Market. We would love to open that someday, either in Queens or Manhattan.

It's something our family had always wanted to do and is also an homage to our late father.

Outside of being a chef at Chinese restaurants, he would always experiment with different foods. Our mom loved to cook and bake, as well. She's into making sweet and savory cakes for special occasions. And our older sister, now along with her own children, bakes a really mean pandan chiffon cake.

Despite having made strides in our respective professional careers—Chuin, in finance, and Yeen, in law—we've always had a passion for our food culture. We kind of grew up being a cooking family, and we continue to live and remember our family stories through food. We're not culinary trained or anything, but we just love experimenting, and being more hands-on with food at home."

SINGAPOREAN NASI LEMAK
WITH FRIED CHICKEN

Nasi lemak is a popular dish in Singapore, and is considered the national dish of Malaysia: fragrant, fluffy, coconut rice accompanied by various sides—such as fried chicken, fried baby anchovies, roasted peanuts, eggs, sliced cucumbers, and a side of sambal chili paste—all plated as a single dish. It's iconic hawker food that Chuin and Yeen would often have for breakfast.

Makes 4 servings

FRIED CHICKEN (AYAM GORENG)

2 shallots

Two 2-inch (5 cm) pieces peeled fresh ginger, sliced ⅛-inch (3 mm) thick

1 red Thai chile, seeded

1 lemongrass stalk, trimmed

2 pounds (900 g) boneless chicken thighs (about 4 thighs)

1 egg, beaten

1¼ teaspoons curry powder

1¼ teaspoons ground white pepper

1¼ teaspoons salt

1¼ teaspoons ground turmeric

¾ teaspoon ground coriander

¾ teaspoon garlic powder

4 to 6 cups (1 to 1.4 L) vegetable or canola oil

¼ cup (65 g) cornstarch

COCONUT RICE

4 cups (720 g) jasmine rice

1 cup (240 ml) coconut milk

1 shallot, peeled and halved

Two 2-inch (5 cm) pieces peeled fresh ginger, sliced ⅛-inch (3 mm) thick

1 tablespoon granulated sugar

2 teaspoons salt

3 pandan leaves, tied in a knot

1 lemongrass stalk, trimmed

FRIED BABY ANCHOVIES (IKAN BILIS)

1 cup (240 ml) vegetable or canola oil

1 cup (40 g) dried small anchovies

1 teaspoon granulated sugar

Roasted peanuts

4 eggs, hard-boiled or fried

Sliced cucumber

Sambal oelek chili paste

1. To start the fried chicken, pulse the shallots, ginger, chile, and lemongrass in a food processor into a grainy pulp, about 3 to 4 minutes.

2. Transfer to a large bowl and mix in the chicken, egg, curry powder, white pepper, salt, turmeric, coriander, and garlic powder. Marinate for at least 2 hours, but overnight is preferable.

3. To make the coconut rice, rinse the rice thoroughly until the water runs clear. Place all the ingredients along with 4 cups (960 ml) water in a rice cooker or pot with a tight-fitting lid and cook. When done, discard the lemongrass, shallot, ginger, and pandan.

4. To fry the chicken, pour the oil in a wok or deep pot and heat over medium-high heat to 350 to 375°F (180 to 190°C). Lightly coat the chicken with the cornstarch. Fry until the underside is golden brown, 5 to 10 minutes. Flip and fry until uniformly golden brown, about 5 minutes. Remove from the oil and place on a cooling rack or paper towels to drain.

5. To make the fried baby anchovies, heat the oil in a separate wok or deep pot over medium heat to about 350°F (180°C). Carefully add the anchovies and fry until golden brown, about 15 minutes. Remove from the oil with a strainer, place in a bowl, and toss with the sugar.

6. To serve, arrange the coconut rice, chicken, anchovies, peanuts, an egg, and cucumbers on four plates and serve with a side of sambal oelek.

CHAI TOW KUEH
Fried Radish Cake

These savory stir-fried radish cakes are enjoyed any time of day in Singapore. *Chai tow kueh* comes in a white and a black version, the latter cooked with sweet soy sauce to add caramelized sweetness. Each bite is a texture and flavor adventure: slightly crispy on the outside, somewhat chewy on the inside, mixed with bites of scrambled egg, minced garlic, and pickled radish. Chuin and Yeen's late father was a master at making chai tow kueh, and they remember and honor his legacy each time they re-create his signature dish.

Makes 4 servings

RADISH CAKE

2 tablespoons vegetable or corn oil

3 garlic cloves, minced

1 daikon radish, about 12 inches (30 cm) long, grated and drained in a colander

1 tablespoon light soy sauce

1 teaspoon salt

1 teaspoon ground white pepper

6¼ cups (1.5 L) cold water

2¼ cups (360 g) rice flour

1 tablespoon cornstarch

* Available in Asian supermarkets

CHAI TOW KUEH

2 tablespoons vegetable or corn oil

2 tablespoons minced garlic

2 eggs, beaten

¼ cup (60 ml) light soy sauce

1 tablespoon minced preserved sweet-salted radish (*chye poh or choi poh*)*

1 teaspoon ground white pepper

½ cup (120 ml) sweet soy sauce, optional

1 tablespoon sambal oelek chili paste, optional

2 tablespoons chopped scallions

1. To make the radish cake, heat the oil in a wok or deep, heavy skillet over high heat. Stir-fry the garlic until fragrant, 1 to 2 minutes. Add the daikon radish, light soy sauce, salt, and white pepper, and and stir continuously for 2 to 3 minutes, until the radish becomes slightly translucent, then turn the heat to low. Pour in the cold water, then add the rice flour and cornstarch and stir continuously until it has the consistency of thick oatmeal, about 10 minutes.

2. Transfer to an oiled steaming pan or round cake pan that fits in a steamer but allows steam to circulate. Bring water to a boil in the steamer and carefully place the pan inside. Cover and steam for 45 to 50 minutes, until a toothpick inserted in the center comes out clean. Let cool to room temperature and then refrigerate for at least 4 hours, but overnight is preferable.

3. Remove the radish cake from the pan and cut into ½-inch (13 mm) cubes and set aside.

4. To make the chai tow kueh, heat the oil in a wok or large skillet over high heat and stir-fry the garlic until fragrant, about 1 to 2 minutes. Add the radish cake and let it sit for 1 to 2 minutes to develop a crispness. Stir-fry for 1 to 2 additional minutes, until the radish is evenly light brown. Stir in the eggs, light soy sauce, preserved radish, and white pepper. When the eggs are set, after 1 to 2 minutes, add the sweet soy sauce, if using, for the black version. Remove from the heat.

5. Divide among four plates, top with sambal oelek, if desired, garnish with scallions, and serve.

Hendra Lie

WARUNG JANCOOK

39

INDONESIA

In 2006, at the age of seventeen, Hendra Lie moved to the US from Jember, East Java, Indonesia, where he was born and raised—a third-generation Chinese-Indonesian. Food-obsessed from childhood, when he wasn't running around sampling street foods, young Hendra would often shadow his native Javanese housekeeper as she cooked, helping her make his family's favorite foods.

When the prospect of working at his cousin's Japanese restaurant in Queens presented itself, Hendra jumped at the opportunity, even though he'd never before left Southeast Asia. He adjusted quickly to New York life, working hard and constantly trying new foods. When his cousin's restaurant closed, he trained at New York City's Institute of Culinary Education, graduating in 2015, and soon worked his way up the NYC restaurant scene, cooking in such establishments as the Dream Hotel and the Musket Room. Eventually, Hendra married, became a father, and decided to take a break from the restaurant industry to be a stay-at-home dad while planning his own future Indonesian food business.

After several years of recipe testing at home for family and friends, Hendra's wife, Marshella, found out about the Queens Night Market and suggested he apply to be a vendor: The fire was lit and Warung Jancook was born the next day.

Warung is a common Indonesian word for a small business; *jancook* is a "fun" expletive used to mean "awesome"—at least in this context!

"*Jancook* in East Java describes anger, friendship, happiness—a word with a thousand meanings. A taboo—we curse with this word, but when you're with a close friend, you can say it in a fun way, like:

This satay is so good! Jancook! This satay is so good!"

TAHU GEJROT
Fried Tofu

Tahu gejrot is ubiquitous in Indonesia and always available as an appetizer on most any menu. In Cirebon, West Java, where the dish originated, it is often eaten with a tamarind dressing. This is the way that Hendra currently serves them, but he grew up eating them with a spicy sauce called sambal cobek, which is more common where he grew up in East Java.

· ·

Makes 3 or 4 servings

· ·

TAMARIND DRESSING

1½ cups (300 g) Javanese coconut palm sugar, or lightly packed dark brown sugar*

½ cup (120 ml) kecap manis (Indonesian sweet soy sauce)

Scant ½ cup (100 g) tamarind paste

6 shallots, peeled, plus more minced

4 garlic cloves, peeled, plus more minced

1 tablespoon rice vinegar

4 red Thai chiles or other red chile, plus more minced

FRIED TOFU

4 cups (960 ml) canola oil

One 16-ounce (454 g) package firm tofu, cut into 1-inch (2.5 cm) cubes

Salt

½ cup (65 g) finely diced cucumber

* Javanese sugar (gula jawa) is an unrefined coconut palm sugar typically produced in Java and can be found in Asian supermarkets.

1. To make the tamarind dressing, add all the ingredients except for the extra minced shallot, garlic, and chile to a pot with 2 quarts (2 L) water and bring to a boil over high heat. Reduce the heat to low to simmer for 45 minutes, stirring occasionally. Let cool, then strain through a fine-mesh sieve into a bowl.

2. Add the extra minced shallot, garlic, and chile to taste. Let rest overnight in the refrigerator before serving.

3. To make the fried tofu, heat the oil in a medium pot over medium-high heat to 300°F (150°C). Fry the tofu in batches of five to ten pieces, until light brown, 5 to 6 minutes per batch. Remove from the oil with a slotted spoon, and place on paper towels for a few minutes to drain.

4. Heat the oil to 350°F (180°C) and re-fry the tofu in batches of five to ten pieces until golden brown and crispy, 30 to 45 seconds per batch. Place on paper towels and sprinkle with salt to taste.

5. Serve drizzled with the tamarind dressing and garnish with the cucumber.

OTE-OTE
Vegetable Fritters

As a child, Hendra would often tag along with his housekeeper to traditional markets called *pasar*, which sell all manner of fresh produce and traditional snacks. It was at these markets that he developed a fondness for *ote-ote*: bowl-shaped vegetable fritters commonly topped with shrimp. They are traditionally made with cabbage, carrots, and bean sprouts, but Hendra has created a version that better suits his tastes after moving to the United States. He uses shrimp flour in the batter for extra depth of flavor, and the *saus sambal cabe* lends a sweet and spicy punch.

Makes 8 to 10 servings

SAUS SAMBAL CABE

2 tablespoons butter

⅔ cup (100 g) julienned Spanish or yellow onion

1¼ cups (300 ml) vegetable stock or water

2 cups (480 ml) *saus cabe*, such as Dua Belibis (a brand of Indonesian chile sauce)

BATTER

2 tablespoons dried shrimp

4 cups (500 g) plus 2 tablespoons all-purpose flour

3 tablespoons garlic powder

2 tablespoons rice flour, such as Erawan (a brand of Thai rice flour)

1 teaspoon ground coriander

1 teaspoon paprika

2 tablespoons salt

FRITTERS

1 pound (455 g) purple cabbage, cored and julienned

1 pound (455 g) white cabbage, cored and julienned

2 cups (180 g) julienned carrots

1½ cups (130 g) thinly sliced scallions

Scant 1½ cups (230 g) sliced Spanish or yellow onions

Canola oil, for frying

Kewpie mayonnaise, optional

Dried baby shrimp, optional

* Dried shrimp is available at Asian supermarkets. Ote-ote is often served with whole shrimp on top, but Hendra recommends infusing the batter itself with shrimp flavor.

1. To make the saus sambal cabe, melt the butter in a saucepan over high heat. Add the onion and sauté until it begins to brown, 1 to 2 minutes. Add about ¼ cup (60 ml) of the stock and stir. As the liquid evaporates, after about 1 minute, add more stock, repeating 4 or 5 times.

2. When all the liquid has evaporated, the onion should be brown and wilted. Remove from the heat and let cool.

3. Transfer the onion mixture to a blender or food processor and blend with the saus cabe and 1 cup (240 ml) water until liquefied. Set aside.

4. To make the batter, combine the dried shrimp and 2 tablespoons of the all-purpose flour in a food processor or spice grinder and blend into a uniform flour.

5. Transfer to a large mixing bowl and combine with the 4 cups (500 g) all-purpose flour and the garlic powder, rice flour, coriander, paprika, and salt. Add 3½ cups (840 ml) water and whisk until there are no lumps.

6. To make the fritters, combine the vegetables in a large mixing bowl. Add enough of the batter to submerge the vegetables and mix well.

7. Pour about 2 to 3 inches (5 to 7.5 cm) oil into a medium pot and heat over medium-high heat to about 25°F (165°C).

8. Dip a 1-ounce (30 ml) ladle into the hot oil, remove, and use to scoop the vegetables, molding a fritter in the shape of the ladle bowl. Carefully drop the bowl-shaped fritter into the oil and fry until golden brown, 3 to 5 minutes. You can fry in batches, but be careful not to crowd the oil. Remove and drain on a plate lined with paper towels.

9. Serve topped with the saus sambal cabe and,

if using, mayonnaise and dried baby shrimp, as desired.

Judymae Esguerra

KANIN NYC

⟨40⟩ PHILIPPINES

On August 21, 1983, Ninoy Aquino, opposition leader to the dictatorial regime of then President Ferdinand Marcos, flew back to Manila from the United States and was promptly assassinated on the tarmac, instantly invigorating the growing resistance movement. The University of the Philippines, where Judymae was entering her junior year as an interior design student, was a hot spot for political subversion.

Judymae's father, a newly minted US citizen based in Chicago, insisted that she and her siblings come join him there to keep clear of the political turmoil. Judymae said, "I was, I think, the most reluctant person to ever come here. I didn't want to come. I was in college having a great time. I had lots of friends, and I'd have to leave all of them."

But once in Chicago, at age twenty, Judymae was determined to make the most of her new circumstances and quickly found herself a bank job in order to go to community college and study architecture, which her parents had not allowed her to study back in the Philippines— too many years, too expensive.

After a few years, and a move to San Jose, California, to reunite with her mother and other siblings, she started to let go of her dreams of working in a creative field and focused instead on creating her own financial independence. With her attitude of "less than perfect is not good enough," she excelled in the fast-paced, male-dominated world of finance and was soon transferred to New York City, where she enjoyed an intense sixteen-year career as an assistant to traders at a major financial institution.

Maryhill Academy
HIGH SCHOOL DEPARTMENT

Award
Congratulations!

Name JUDY MAE C. CUETO
Year & Section IV B Date SEPT. 29, 1980
Award COOKING CONTEST (WINNER)
- HOMEMADE FOODS -

PRINCIPAL

Judymae won her high school cooking contest with her Lola Chayong's (maternal grandmother's) recipe for kare-kare (oxtail stew; above); Judymae, at seven years old, with her brothers, Kuya Lee and Lino (left)

"And then, one day, you realize: I actually have achieved everything on my checklist—of what I defined as success, but I'm not happy. That was the toughest time. You have everything to be thankful for, you reach all these goals—and yet I wake up every day and I'm not happy. So, ugh . . . that's why I had to quit. . . . It was hard for me to let go of the job, because I had that job before I had a family; I had a job before I met my husband, before the kids, you know? So that was hard to let go. Also because . . . I want to be independent, right? And all of a sudden, if I quit that, I'd have to be dependent on my husband. . . . But I felt like at that time I had to do this. Because if I didn't do it, then I would not be a good mom. Because . . . how are you supposed to take care of the kids when you don't even know yourself? . . . I had to do something. So I did quit my work, not to be a stay-at-home mom or because of the kids. I quit work for me. I gotta take care of me. So that's what I did."

Judymae gradually let herself indulge her creative side again, and cooking became a major outlet. After several years of preparation, in 2019, she decided to enlist her now-grown children to help her realize a dream: selling her food to the public at the Queens Night Market—and selling out every night, too.

"It's my medicine. And doing this with my family—they're supporting me with what I'm going through, right now, instead of me being the one who's always helping them out. It's the reverse. And it's a very good feeling as a mom, that they're taking care of me, too. Even if my daughter's in Boston, she's taking care of my Instagram!"

LUGAW
Rice Porridge

Lugaw, the umbrella term for rice porridges in Tagalog, is commonly eaten for breakfast but is also consumed any time of day. It's available in gotohan (eateries specializing in lugaw), street carts, and food courts. It's warming and comforting when you're feeling sick or when it's nippy outside. It's also a purported hangover cure. Two types of lugaw are presented here: arroz caldo and goto. You can really play with the amount of ginger and the preferred texture of the rice to match your personal preference.

Makes 6 servings

BROTH

One 3-pound (1.5 kg) chicken, cut into 8 pieces, for arroz caldo, or 2 pounds (900 g) tripe, for goto

1 medium yellow onion, quartered

2-inch (5 cm) piece peeled fresh ginger, julienned

1 tablespoon chicken bouillon powder for arroz caldo, or 1 tablespoon kosher salt for goto

1 teaspoon black peppercorns

LUGAW

1 cup (185 g) glutinous (sweet) rice, soaked in water for 1 hour

3 tablespoons canola oil

4 garlic cloves, peeled and crushed

2-inch (5 cm) piece peeled fresh ginger, julienned

½ cup (120 ml) patis (Filipino fish sauce)

1 teaspoon ground black pepper

6 hard-boiled eggs, quartered

Lemon wedges or slices

Thinly sliced scallions

Fried garlic

1. To make the broth, place all the ingredients in a large stockpot and cover with 8 cups (1.9 L) water. Bring to a boil, then reduce the heat to low and gently simmer the chicken for 1 hour or the tripe for 1½ hours.

2. Transfer the meat to a plate to cool. Strain the broth through a fine-mesh strainer and set aside.

3. Shred the chicken or dice the tripe into bite-size pieces and set aside. Discard the chicken bones.

4. To make the lugaw, drain the soaked rice, rinse with water a few more times, then drain well. Heat the oil in a large skillet over high heat and sauté the garlic and ginger until browned. Add the rice and sauté until the rice is translucent and dries out a bit, about 3 minutes. Transfer to a rice cooker, add 2 cups (480 ml) water, and cook.

5. Transfer the cooked rice to a soup pot, add 4 cups (960 ml) of the broth, and bring to a boil. Add the fish sauce and pepper to taste. Simmer, uncovered, on low heat, stirring frequently, so the rice does not stick to the bottom of the pot. Add boiling water if the lugaw is too thick. Remove from the heat when it has the consistency of overcooked rice, or has your desired consistency.

6. Divide among six bowls and top each with the reserved meat. Garnish with pieces of egg and lemon, sprinkle with scallions and fried garlic, and serve.

Leche flan is the Filipino take on the dessert inherited from Spanish colonizers. This flan is richer than its Spanish predecessor because it uses more egg and less milk. As kids, Judymae and her siblings would gripe to their mother about the tiny slivers of leche flan they were given and joke that the wind would carry away their stingy servings. Their mother simply responded that leche flan should be savored, not devoured. In the Philippines, this rich, eggy dessert is usually made in special tin or aluminum pans called *llaneras* or *liyaneras*.

LECHE FLAN

Makes 16 servings

CARAMEL

1 cup granulated sugar

CUSTARD

10 egg yolks

One 14-ounce (397 g) can sweetened condensed milk

One 12-ounce (354 ml) can evaporated milk

½ teaspoon vanilla extract

1. Preheat the oven to 350°F (180°C).

2. To make the caramel, set a metal 8-inch (20 cm) baking pan that is about 2 inches (5 cm) deep directly over a burner on the stove. Pour in ½ cup (120 ml) water and the sugar and boil over high heat until the sugar melts and starts to caramelize and you see brown bubbles, about 5 to 8 minutes. Lower the heat to medium. Use mitts to rotate and tilt the pan around continually over the burner until the caramel is spread evenly across the bottom of the baking pan and is a rich amber color, about 3 minutes. Remove from the heat and set aside.

3. To make the custard, whisk the egg yolks in a bowl just to break them up. Slowly whisk in both milks and the vanilla until well blended. Carefully strain through a fine-mesh sieve into the pan, on top of the caramel, then cover with foil.

4. Bring about 4 cups (1 L) water to a boil. Place the flan in a larger baking pan, such as a 9 x 13-inch (23 x 33 cm) baking pan or a roasting pan, and fill the outer pan with enough boiling water to come halfway up the small pan's sides.

5. Bake for 1 hour, or until the center of the flan is firm. Remove from the oven and water bath and let cool, then chill in the refrigerator for about 2 hours.

6. To unmold the flan, remove the foil cover and run a sharp knife around the sides. Cover the pan completely with a large plate or cutting board and quickly invert so the pan is resting on top. Slowly remove the pan, being careful not to spill the caramel. Serve chilled or at room temperature.

Jay and Jerrick Jimenez

GRILLA IN MANILA

⟨40⟩ PHILIPPINES

Happy Grilla in Manila customers at the Queens Night Market often come back to the tent after eating to ask Jerrick, Jay, their sister Dimple, or Mama Aida where their "real" restaurant is, so they can go visit it at some later date. This is it! Jerrick loves to tell them, You're here!

Their Queens Night Market tent on Saturdays is not just their restaurant, it's also an extension of their home, though the kids are all in their thirties and forties now, with busy lives and a variety of careers and households among them. They'd still mostly managed, over the years, to all get together weekly over a big meal full of laughter and stories with friends and neighbors, too—until Jay, the entrepreneur of the family, recruited the whole family to showcase their favorite Filipino recipes every Saturday at the Night Market. Since 2018, the Jimenez family weekly get-together just moved from Jerrick's or Dimple's house to the Night Market, where everyone's invited, and some of their friends still stop by every week to hang out at their tent, encouraging tentative new visitors to try their most daring specialty, balut—a cooked, fourteen-day-old fertilized duck embryo to be enjoyed straight out of the shell.

Jay: We are all originally from the south side of the Philippines: Las Piñas. We migrated here to the US—my parents first. I think in 1987. It was me and my other sister came here in 1991. And then you guys—

Jerrick: Two years after in 1993.

Jay: My brother and my sister Dimple moved here, to New York.

Jerrick: I was thirteen.

Jay: I was nineteen. I had my teenage years and a very little college in the Philippines. And then I moved here, so I could be with my parents. 'Cause my parents were always working abroad. My dad was in Papua New Guinea, Saudi Arabia. My mom was in Saipan [in the Mariana Islands]. They were overseas—

Jerrick: They were overseas workers.

Jay: So we used to grow up on our own. My older sister raised us, in my parents' absence. We have two more older sisters.

Jerrick: So there's six of us in the family.

Jay: My parents didn't have no TV back then, so—

Jerrick: As they like to say . . . so they had a lot of kids. They had time . . .

JAY **JERRICK**

Jay: There's two more older sisters—one right now in the Philippines; one's in Dubai. But the older one—in Dubai now—raised us when she was sixteen years old. Both my parents went to work abroad and she raised us. My mom and dad came home once in a while for six months at a time, would stay with us, then go back to work abroad. So we were mostly left with my sister.

Whatever job is available that they could perform, they got hired for. It's a contract job. You become a store manager, or a janitor—or in my dad's case, he was doing printing, material printing, and things like that. My mom was a medical transcriptionist. So she had a job in Saudi Arabia for a very long time and then Saipan, and then she moved over here.

Jerrick: So when they came here, that's when they both decided they were just going to stay. So that's when they decided, OK, they're ready to start taking the kids. So that's when the whole process started.

Jay: For me it was tough—back home I had a thing going on. I was a recording artist, I was an upcoming—

Jerrick: Rapper!

Jay: Rapper. I was in a rap group. Called Bass Rhyme. We're considered one of the pioneers of rapping in the Philippines. So the choice was between my career, which was that, or go to the US and be with my parents, which I hadn't done for a long time. Tough choice. So I stayed here [in the US] with them, started working . . . eventually raised a family. And this became my home.

Jerrick: It was hard for me too 'cause I was young, just turning fourteen. They sent me here. It was a culture shock. There you could be outside till three AM. The only thing that bothers you are the mosquitos. Over here, even in school, I didn't feel safe.

Jay: In the Philippines, you sit outside, and your friends will just come along. You sit outside; you always have something to do; you always have something to laugh about; you always have something to eat. You go outside, your neighbor has a mango tree. Everybody gathers under the mango tree. You hang out all day, pick up a ripe mango, just chop it up and eat there and have fun. Pretty much the lifestyle: It's calm, innocent—you're there with your friends, you just laugh about things, you talk about things a lot— and you come home before the lamplight turns on. My mom . . . if that light turns on and you're still not home for dinner, you'll see the slippers!

Jerrick: For me, it's my sister!

Jay: 'Cause our sister applied the same rule. If you're not at home yet when the lamplight turns on, you're in big trouble.

Jerrick: So you can do whatever you want during the day—

Jay: For boys.

Jay: Your neighbors will watch your kids for you outside—that kind of a neighborly environment. To this environment, you can't go out alone.

Jerrick: This is our pager—our cell phone: [claps] We clap, to call out our friends. For example, you live three houses down, you go outside, you don't see anyone. All you do is clap. Once you clap, you start seeing friends come out, then they clap, too, and then that's how the night goes.

Jay: It means *Let's go hang out.* Instead of calling, going house to house, you just clap.

Jerrick: We'd play hide and seek, basketball in the park. Here when it rains you gotta stay inside or you get sick. In the Philippines, it starts raining, you'd better call your friends 'cause we're playing volleyball, we're playing tag—out in the rain.

Jay: I just had a flashback last weekend when it rained over here when we were packing up—reminded me of my childhood: The last time I was outside getting showered in the rain, I was probably thirteen years old—and now here at the Queens Night Market. I'm so happy about it.

Jerrick: We just love to share—we take pride

"WE JUST LOVE TO SHARE—WE TAKE PRIDE IN THE FOOD THAT WE MAKE. I DON'T KNOW IF WE'RE BIASED WITH THE FAMILY, BUT: MY MOM MAKES THE BEST *DINUGUAN.*"

in the food that we make. I don't know if we're biased with the family, but my mom makes the best *dinuguan.* It's "Mama's Dinuguan." If Mom does not make the dinuguan for this week, we're not selling dinuguan. Mom has never given us the secret yet. We're waiting . . . until then—

Jay: All I know is she puts blood in it. That's it.

Jerrick: If you actually go to different restaurants and you order the dinuguan and you taste ours, you'll probably—

Jay: There's a difference in flavor.

Jerrick: Because we're the only ones that actually serve dinuguan as crispy-fried. Everyone else would serve it as a stew, pretty much.

Jay: The dinuguan actually came from my mom. Her name's Aida—and that's her baby, her dinuguan.

Jerrick: But everyone actually, even here at the Night Market, calls her Mama. 'Cause she's always here and everyone comes to her and gives her food. Mom has her favorites from some of the stalls here, so they call her Mama.

Jay: They send her food.

Jerrick: Yeah, they go, *Here, this is for Mama.*

DINUGUAN
Pork Blood Stew

The use of pork blood might frighten or turn away some readers, but dinuguan is a traditional Filipino dish often served at gatherings and special occasions, especially in December at Simbáng Gabi (Mass of the Rooster). After Simbáng Gabi, there are many stalls set up outside churches selling dinuguan with a side of *puto* (a Filipino rice muffin). This version uses pork shoulder instead of pork offal, and it's rich, savory, and pungent from the vinegar. Serve in bowls with white rice, garlic-fried rice, or puto.

Makes 4 servings

- 3 tablespoons vegetable oil
- 2 medium white onions, chopped
- 6 garlic cloves, minced
- 2 pounds (900 g) pork shoulder, cut into 1-inch (2.5 cm) cubes
- ¾ cup (180 ml) distilled white vinegar
- 3 bay leaves
- 1 pork bouillon cube
- 1¼ cups (300 ml) pork blood*
- 4 long hot green chiles
- 1 tablespoon granulated sugar
- Salt
- Ground black pepper

1. Heat the oil in a pot over medium heat. Sauté the onion for 30 seconds and add the garlic. Cook until the onion softens, about 10 minutes.

2. Add the pork and sauté until golden in color, 3 to 5 minutes. Add 2 cups (480 ml) water and bring to a boil. Add the vinegar and bay leaves and return to a boil. Add the bouillon, stir, and cover. Simmer for 1 hour over medium heat. Check occasionally and add water if the ingredients seem pasty.

3. Add the pork blood and chiles and stir. Cook over medium heat, stirring every few minutes, until the stew has the consistency of tomato sauce, about 15 minutes.

4. Stir in the sugar and season with salt and pepper to taste. Remove from the heat and serve.

* Head to butcher shops or Asian markets and ask for this. It may be sold in a coagulated state.

SISIG
Chopped Pork

Sisig is typically served as *pica-picas*, or tapas, at Filipino bars, and it's easy to see why. The dish is an explosion of textures and flavors. It's salty, spicy, vinegary, minerally, citrusy, chewy, and crispy. This recipe uses pork belly, but meat from a pig's head is commonly used in the Philippines. You can eat it by itself or serve it with rice topped with fried garlic, as the Jimenez brothers recommend.

Makes 4 servings

1 pound (455 g) pork belly, with skin, cut into ½-inch (13 mm) cubes

1 tablespoon salt

1 tablespoon plus ⅛ teaspoon ground black pepper

3 chicken livers, cut into ½-inch (13 mm) cubes

1 large red onion, finely chopped

Juice of 4 calamansi or ½ lemon, plus 1 sliced

2 long hot green chiles, seeded and minced

1½ teaspoons soy sauce

Vegetable oil, optional

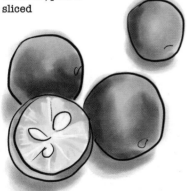

1. Season the pork belly with the salt and 1 tablespoon of the pepper and let rest for at least 30 minutes.

2. Stir-fry the pork and livers in a large skillet over medium heat until well done, about 5 minutes. The pork skin should be crispy. Remove from the heat and rest until cool enough to handle.

3. Finely chop the pork and liver into roughly ¼-inch (6 mm) pieces. Transfer to a bowl and combine with the onion, calamansi juice, and chiles. Season with the soy sauce and remaining ⅛ teaspoon black pepper.

4. Reheat in a pan with a bit of oil if desired. Garnish with a few calamansi slices and serve.

Alfredo and Marienits Pedrajas

LAPU-LAPU FOODS
(40)
PHILIPPINES

For three generations now, Alfredo's family has had restaurants in his hometown of Cagayan de Oro, a city on the southern Philippine island of Mindanao. As a kid, he would watch and sometimes help out at the restaurant his grandfather had started and that Alfredo's mother took over: Tivoli—a place famous for its chicken barbecue.

Alfredo studied agriculture in college and briefly went into poultry farming, but when he met his wife, Marienits, a talented baker who ran her own little business, the Honey Baked Café, he decided to help her transform it into a full-blown restaurant. For fifteen years, Marienits and Alfredo ran a successful restaurant serving a mix of Filipino and international savory dishes and pastries. Chicken adobo, the Philippines' national dish, was a mainstay.

In 2011, an opportunity came up for the whole family to move together to New York. They considered the better healthcare services offered in the US,

and decided to go ahead with the move, as comfortable as they were in the Philippines. Alfredo and Marienits sold their restaurant, knowing it might be years before they would be restaurateurs again, and willingly took whatever jobs they could get in the US.

In his job search, Alfredo noticed that Filipino-run grocery stores and delis always sold spicy fried peanuts—*adobo mani*—at the counter, but they were imported from the Philippines and often old and dried out. He knew he could get better quality peanuts in the US and make it fresh in New York, so he started a little side business making the spiced peanuts and delivering them to grocery stores.

Soon, Marienits and Alfredo were itching to serve whole meals again and founded Lapu-Lapu Foods to bring some of their best dishes from home to the New York public at the Queens Night Market. Now, having tested the waters through vending and catering, the Pedrajas family is hoping in the near future to open a "resto-bar" and music venue in Queens to showcase the emerging Filipino pop music scene in NYC.

CHICKEN ADOBO

Filipinos love their garlic and vinegar, and both are supporting stars in this dish. Chicken adobo is an iconic and familiar household dish in the Philippines, but it's also sold in many fast-food establishments. It's traditionally cooked in a wok. Serve this with white rice, a boiled egg, and a side of tomato and arugula salad.

Makes 5 to 6 servings

2 pounds (900 g) chicken thighs (bone-in, with skin)

½ cup (120 ml) cider vinegar or coconut vinegar

¼ cup (60 ml) Filipino soy sauce, such as Silver Swan Soy Sauce

1 tablespoon plus 1 teaspoon patis (Filipino fish sauce)

1 teaspoon onion powder

½ teaspoon ground black pepper

¼ cup (60 ml) canola oil

20 garlic cloves, minced

1 tablespoon black peppercorns

1 bay leaf

3 hard-boiled eggs, halved

1. Combine the chicken, vinegar, soy sauce, fish sauce, onion powder, and pepper in a bowl or container and marinate in the refrigerator for at least 1 hour, but overnight is preferable.

2. Heat the oil in a wok or medium pot over medium heat. Add the chicken (reserving the marinade) and pan-fry until golden brown, about 3 minutes on each side. Remove and set aside.

3. Add the garlic to the wok and sauté until fragrant and just browning, about 3 minutes. Return the chicken to the wok and add the reserved marinade. Add the peppercorns and bay leaf along with 1 cup (240 ml) water. Cover and bring to a boil. Simmer until most of the water has evaporated and the sauce turns dark brown and oily, about 45 minutes.

4. Uncover and continue to simmer until the sauce has reduced to the desired consistency, usually about 10 minutes. Remove from the heat, discard the bay leaf, and serve each dish with half an egg.

Wanda Chiu
HONG KONG STREET FOOD
(41)
HONG KONG

Wanda Chiu was raised in the '60s in Happy Valley, an area of Hong Kong filled with luxury apartment buildings and hotels. Celebrity-spotting was just as popular as watching horse races at the famous racecourse—from their rooftop, since minors weren't allowed in—and street food was all the rage.

When Wanda was seventeen, her father—fearing the potential spread of Chinese communism into Hong Kong—moved their family to New York City, choosing the "quiet, suburban" area of Flushing, Queens, as their home. Her mother found work in Manhattan's Chinatown as a seamstress, and brought groceries home from the Chinese stores near work.

There were virtually no Chinese or Hong Kong–style restaurants in Flushing when Wanda's family arrived. Wanda had only a handful of Chinese classmates, mostly from Taiwan, at her new school. She missed egg waffles, rice-noodle rolls, and the night markets back home—a place where everyone could gather to enjoy midnight snacks after the heat of the day had passed.

Over the next few decades, she started dabbling in and found a passion for cooking, taking pointers from cookbooks and the internet, hoping one day she'd be able to share the traditional Hong Kong flavors she loves with others. Since starting four years ago, her stand at the Queens Night Market—Hong Kong Street Food—has become a family affair: Her kids, three sisters, brothers-in-law, nephews and nieces, cousins, and friends have all worked at the booth, propelling her stall into popularity.

She didn't—and still doesn't—have any plans to commercialize her food. After decades of learning to re-create the memories she holds so dear, she just loves to share her hometown cooking with everyone else. She was a bookkeeper and a housewife, and now she works at an after-school center. And on summer Saturday nights, she sells under a tent with a bright-red label: HONG KONG STREET FOOD.

Wanda and her dad at their family farm in Hong Kong in the '60s

SEE YOW WONG CHOW MEEN
Soy Sauce Pan-Fried Noodles

For Wanda, pan-fried noodles evoke memories of breakfast on cold winter mornings before school. You might find these noodles at some Cantonese restaurants in NYC—but according to Wanda, most are disappointing in some way or another: Some don't have enough soy sauce, others are made too dark with cheap soy sauce, some are too salty, and others are too moist. A proper rendering of this dish requires premium soy sauce (as the Chinese name suggests), and the noodles should be dry and crisp.

Makes 4 servings

- 2 tablespoons premium light soy sauce
- 1 tablespoon premium dark soy sauce
- 1 teaspoon granulated sugar
- 1 pound (454 g) thin egg noodles for pan-frying*
- 1 tablespoon vegetable or canola oil
- ⅓ cup (45 g) shredded cabbage
- ¼ cup (25 g) shredded carrot
- ¼ cup (60 g) shredded snow peas
- ½ teaspoon toasted sesame oil
- 1 teaspoon toasted sesame seeds

1. Mix the soy sauces with the sugar and set aside.

2. Bring a large pot of water to a boil. Add the noodles and stir for 15 seconds. Remove from the heat, drain, and set aside.

3. Heat the vegetable oil in a wok or deep skillet over medium heat. Stir-fry the cabbage, carrot, and snow peas until soft, about 3 to 5 minutes. Add the noodles and stir-fry until they feel dry, about 2 minutes. (The noodles will become lighter and less sticky to toss and stir as they dry.) Add the soy sauce mixture. Stir quickly until the noodles are evenly coated.

4. Drizzle the sesame oil over the noodles, remove from the heat, and transfer immediately to a serving bowl. Garnish with the sesame seeds.

Variation: Street vendors in Hong Kong typically serve the dish without meat, but protein (such as roast pork, beef, chicken, or shrimp) can be added to your liking. These should be prepared in advance and added as the noodles are being stir-fried.

* The noodles can be found in the refrigerated aisle of Asian supermarkets.

CURRY FISH BALLS

Curry fish balls are about as Hong Kongese as burgers are American. For Wanda, curry fish balls remind her of the street vendor outside her school, where she would pick up a tasty snack after a long day of classes. Though they're simply seasoned fish paste shaped into balls—and fairly ubiquitous in Asian stews and hot pots—they take on new and exciting heights when deep-fried and then dunked into any number of bathing sauces just before eating. A go-to classic, and Wanda's favorite, is curry sauce.

1. Heat the vegetable oil in a Dutch oven or other large heavy pot over medium-high heat. Add the garlic, shallot, and ginger and stir-fry until they become fragrant, about 2 to 3 minutes. Add the chicken broth and curry powder and mix well.

2. Turn the heat up to high and add both soy sauces, the chili sauce, oyster sauce, soy paste, and sugar and bring to a boil. Add the fried fish balls and turn the heat to low to simmer.

3. Dissolve the cornstarch in ¼ cup (60 ml) water and slowly add to the pot while stirring. Simmer until the sauce thickens like gravy or to a consistency you prefer.

4. Drizzle the fish balls with the sesame oil. Each fish ball should be thickly coated with the shimmering curry sauce. Remove from the heat.

5. Thread the fish balls onto bamboo skewers, four or five per skewer. Serve immediately, while hot.

Makes 10 to 15 skewers

- 2 tablespoons vegetable or canola oil
- 2 teaspoons minced garlic
- 2 teaspoons minced shallot
- 1 teaspoon minced peeled fresh ginger
- 2 cups (480 ml) salted chicken broth or water
- 5 tablespoons Madras curry powder or other yellow curry powder
- 1 tablespoon light soy sauce
- 1 teaspoon dark soy sauce

- 2 teaspoons Asian chili sauce or sriracha
- 2 teaspoons oyster sauce
- 1 teaspoon soy paste
- 1 teaspoon granulated sugar
- 3 packages fried fish balls (about 18 fish balls per package)*
- 2 teaspoons cornstarch
- 1 teaspoon toasted sesame oil

* Fish balls can be found in the refrigerated aisle of Asian supermarkets.

Johnson barely knew his parents as a child. His mother, already a US resident, had worked abroad since he was a baby—and since his parents had separated early, he'd only see his father occasionally on weekends. Even then, his father would mostly just give him money to go play in the arcades or to buy some tasty snacks at a nearby night market. He was close to his grandmother, though—so close that when, after she suffered a stroke and had a hard time speaking, little Johnson was the only one who understood her and would translate for everyone else.

When Johnson was sent to go live with his mother in Singapore at age thirteen, he felt like he was leaving his family to stay with a stranger. A few years after that, she moved with him to Vancouver, and eventually to New York. Throughout all these moves, he was always a little homesick, never knowing where he was going to live next, but baseball was Johnson's constant comfort. He'd always find a way to watch when his team was playing, and it never

Johnson Hu

BSTRO

(42)

TAIWAN

Johnson was happy as a kid in Taipei, living with his grandmother and aunt. His grandparents spoke the Sichuan dialect, having moved to Taipei in 1949 to escape the Communists, and his Taipei-born aunt spoke both Taiwanese and Mandarin, but everyone spoke Mandarin to Johnson, so that was his only native language. They lived in a *juan cun*—a government-sponsored, temporary village for low-income military dependents, close to a military base.

"I ALWAYS ROOT FOR THE TAIWANESE BASEBALL TEAM; THEY ARE IN THE SOFT PART OF MY HEART."

failed to make him feel at home again. "I always root for the Taiwanese baseball team; they are in the soft part of my heart."

Johnson cherishes his team's baseball hat, too—it's dark blue with the five-petal plum blossom flower, the symbol of Taiwan. "Chinese Taipei" is the name of the team, "because of the politics there—but let's not get into politics!" he says.

"When I go to the Night Market, I wear this. I feel like this has the most homelike feeling for Taiwanese—helps tell people I'm from Taiwan, helps start conversations with my countrymen, 'cause you know baseball is the national sport in Taiwan. When I wear this, it makes me feel like I'm part of the team, like I'm in Taiwan again."

He hopes the food he sells at the Queens Night Market accomplishes the same for other full-grown Taiwan kids far from home.

DA JI PAI
Chicken Steak

Johnson remembers chicken steak bursting onto the Taiwanese street food scene about the time he was in fourth grade. His earliest memories of it involve getting dinner money from his grandmother and using part of it to buy a bento box and using the remainder to splurge on a chicken steak. These flavorful, crispy, and juicy chicken steaks fry up in a hurry. They're usually served on the go in a cookie bag.

Makes 4 servings

- 4 chicken breast fillets
- 3 garlic cloves, minced
- 1 scallion, chopped
- 2 tablespoons light soy sauce
- 1 tablespoon soy paste
- 1 teaspoon ground white pepper
- ½ teaspoon five spice powder
- ⅛ teaspoon granulated sugar
- 2 cups (250 g) coarse sweet potato starch,* such as Queen's Premium Sweet Potato Starch
- Canola or soybean oil

1. Flatten the chicken breasts with a meat tenderizer until about ½-inch (13 mm) thick.

2. Combine the garlic, scallion, soy sauce, soy paste, white pepper, five spice, and sugar in a large bowl or container and add the chicken. Add about a tablespoon of water to evenly spread the marinade. Cover and marinate for at least 1 day in the refrigerator.

3. Remove from the refrigerator and discard any large pieces of scallion or garlic clinging to the chicken. Coat the chicken with the sweet potato starch.

4. Pour about 2 inches (5 cm) oil into a large pot or deep fryer and heat over medium-high heat to about 325°F (165°C).

5. Fry 1 chicken fillet at a time until evenly golden brown, about 2 minutes on each side. Serve in paper cookie bags if you have some!

* Coarse (or "thick") sweet potato starch can be found in Asian groceries. Japanese panko bread crumbs can be used as an alternative if sweet potato starch cannot be found.

Han Kim and Woo Chung
SEOUL PANCAKE

(43) **SOUTH KOREA**

Born and raised in Seoul, Han Kim remembers as a kid generally preferring "American food—pizza, hamburgers" to traditional Korean cooking . . . until his family moved to Brooklyn when he was thirteen and he found himself being served those same foods, day after day, in his new school's cafeteria for lunch. His attitude changed: "When my little sister and I came home from school, my mom would make us kimchi pancakes, and it felt like we were home again."

Later, on visits back to South Korea as a young adult, Han got to experience the street-food version of his mother's kimchi pancakes—*kimchijeon,* often paired with *makgeolli* (a Korean rice wine) on a rainy evening served in a *pocha,* or street stall. This is the experience he hoped to eventually share with the New York public when he first started Seoul Pancake as a side-hustle project in 2015, working at markets throughout the city.

Two years into the endeavor, though, Han developed a bad cough that wouldn't go away—a possible consequence of inhaling too many cooking fumes and plain old burnout. He'd been working seven-day weeks, adding his weekend vending to his already

Han Kim (left) and Woo Chung (right)

demanding day job at a hospital. So he put Seoul Pancake on hiatus to focus on getting his health back on track.

Han's old friend Woo, however, had seen Han's Facebook posts about Seoul Pancake vending at the Queens Night Market and "couldn't love them enough!" He wanted in.

"DJ Woo," a gregarious, hip-hop-loving math fiend and lifelong foodie, had first come to the US from Seoul, South Korea, for college, then returned to Korea for mandatory military service. Then, having tried and repeatedly failed to satisfy his parents' career hopes for him, he returned to the US to complete his second BA in mathematical physics.

Having just settled into a stable, math-whiz-friendly career he enjoyed, working as a "quant" at a hedge fund in New York, he was free to realize his goal of reviving Seoul Pancake in his downtime, helping it reach an even larger audience with the addition of his aunt's homemade soy sauce recipe, some sauce innovations of his own, and, of course, his boundless enthusiasm and hard work.

> "When my little sister and I came home from school, my mom would make us kimchi pancakes, and it felt like we were home again."

Han took some convincing— six months, to be exact—but eventually agreed, and Seoul Pancake reentered the New York food scene in 2018 as a partnership. One summer evening, a year later at the Queens Night Market, it began to rain—usually a bad sign for food vendors. But instead of leaving, the customers in Seoul Pancake's line popped open their umbrellas and kept ordering, then huddled under an empty tent nearby to enjoy their hot kimchi pancakes. Han realized with joy that this was exactly the nostalgic image that had inspired him to start Seoul Pancake in the first place.

"In Korea, when it rains, people start craving kimchijeon and makgeolli and go eat it under pocha tents in the street. I was living my dream, feeding these people, making them so happy in the rain."

KIMCHI PANCAKES
WITH "MAGIC" SOY SAUCE

Woo had his first taste of kimchi pancakes when he was ten and immediately asked his uncle for cooking instructions—it was that good. The batter is versatile and can be used with different meats, seafood, and vegetables for endless iterations and experimentation. The "magic" soy sauce is a simplified version of the infused soy sauce that Woo's aunt makes in Seoul. Customize to your tastes and use anytime you'd use regular soy sauce, especially for marinades.

1. To make the "magic" soy sauce, place the onion, carrot, ginger, mushrooms, and peppercorns in a large pot with 4 cups (960 ml) water. Let rest at room temperature for at least 6 hours.

2. Add the soy sauce to the pot and boil over high heat for 30 minutes. Turn off the heat and let cool for 30 minutes.

3. Add the sugar, apple, pear, and lemon juice and bring back to a boil over high heat. Turn the heat to medium-low and simmer until reduced to about 1 quart (1 L), about 3 hours. Remove from the heat, add the kelp, and let cool. Strain to remove any remaining solids and store in a bottle or jar out of direct sunlight.

4. To make the kimchijeon, whisk the whole wheat flour, rice flour, and cold water in a bowl. Add 2 tablespoons of the oil to the batter and whisk again until integrated. Add the kimchi and, if using, the scallions, pork, and shishitos, along with the soy sauce, gochugaru, garlic powder, paprika, and salt and mix thoroughly.

5. Heat 2 tablespoons oil in an 8- to 12-inch (20 to 30 cm) skillet over high heat until it just begins smoking. Carefully pour in a scant 1 cup (roughly 150 g, depending on the ingredients used) of the batter. Cook until the bottom side turns golden brown, about 1 minute, and flip. Add 1 tablespoon of the oil along the edge of the pancake. Turn the heat to medium-high and cook until golden brown on the other side, about 90 seconds. Transfer to a cooling rack or paper towels and let drain for about 30 seconds. Repeat until all the batter is used, making about 5 pancakes.

6. Serve immediately with the "magic" soy sauce.

Makes 2 or 3 servings and 1 quart (1 L) soy sauce

"MAGIC" SOY SAUCE

1 sweet onion, sliced in half (include outer skins if clean)

1 carrot, sliced

Five 1-inch (2.5 cm) pieces peeled fresh ginger

2 dried shiitake mushrooms

1 tablespoon black peppercorns

1 quart (1 L) soy sauce

1 cup (200 g) granulated sugar

1 apple, peeled, cored, and sliced

1 Asian pear, peeled, cored, and diced

Juice of 1 lemon

One 2 x 4-inch (5 x 10 cm) piece dried kelp

KIMCHIJEON

⅔ cup (80 g) whole wheat flour

⅓ cup (40 g) rice flour

1 cup (240 ml) cold water

2 tablespoons canola oil, plus more for cooking

2 cups (300 g) sliced cabbage kimchi

⅓ cup (50 g) sliced scallions, optional

⅓ cup (65 g) cooked diced pork shoulder, optional

¼ cup (30 g) chopped shishito peppers, optional

1 tablespoon soy sauce

2 teaspoons gochugaru (Korean red chile powder)

2 teaspoons garlic powder

1 teaspoon paprika

1 teaspoon salt

KFC
Chicken
Bites

Juwon Song

KINI

(43) **SOUTH KOREA**

When Juwon was a kid in Busan, South Korea, his parents would usually work late, so after school, he and his younger sister would stay with his maternal grandmother, who would cook them delicious kimchi fried rice or chicken rice *dakgangjeong,* her specialty. She was an excellent cook and taught her own eldest daughter, Juwon's aunt, so well that she ran her own Korean restaurant in New York's bustling Koreatown using her mother's recipes. Juwon could never have imagined that he would someday join his pioneering aunt in New York and then go on to run his own Korean restaurant as a certified chef. As a teenager, he was helping his dad at his gas station after school. The future seemed uncertain.

Korea has a compulsory two-year military service, and when it was Juwon's turn to enter, at age twenty-one, he was assigned cooking duty. Although he made some friends in the kitchen, a hazing culture ruled, and being at the bottom of the hierarchy was exhausting for Juwon. There was no real "off-duty" time, even when work hours were officially over. At any time, if someone who ranked higher than you ordered you to do something, you had to obey. Cockroaches were placed on sleeping soldiers' faces or in their food as pranks, and people were just plain mean—all the time.

Juwon counted the days until his military service was over, reminding himself that his father must have had it much worse, doing his own much longer compulsory military service for three and a half years, back when there wasn't even enough food to go around, and the political situation was far less stable. At any rate, he could focus on the task at hand: preparing meals for thousands of soldiers, every day. He learned a lot, and ultimately credits those two trying years for making him stronger and giving him the courage to make the great leap across the Pacific.

At age twenty-three, he moved to New York looking for culinary programs to enroll in, while helping out at his aunt's restaurant. Just a few years later, after an internship with the prestigious nouveau Korean restaurant Danji, and with a degree in French culinary arts under his belt, he got a job as a chef de partie (or station chef) at Café Boulud.

In 2015, Juwon and his Korean American wife, Olivia Park, were strolling home in Long Island City one Saturday when they noticed a FOR LEASE sign in a little space that had previously been a Greek deli, just downstairs from them. They started dreaming up small fast-casual and takeout restaurant ideas, and soon those ideas became too attractive to let slide. With a little help from his parents, and a lot of support from his wife, Juwon opened Kini in 2016, hoping to make Korean food more accessible and fun for the young and mostly non-Korean professionals in the neighborhood.

As a huge baseball fan, Juwon dreams of seeing little Kini outposts by the stadiums. "Imagine if people had Korean fried chicken at baseball games, instead of hot dogs!"

DAKGANGJEONG
Fried Chicken

Juwong spent a lot of time trying to re-create the dakgangjeong his grandmother made, as he never got the recipe from her. The chicken is double-fried until super crispy and then tossed in a sweet and spicy sauce. It's delicious as a snack or as the focus of a meal. Juwong's version is less spicy than you would typically find in Korea, but it's easy to up the amount of gochugaru in the recipe if you're into the heat!

Makes 4 to 6 servings

FRIED CHICKEN

1 tablespoon sake

2 garlic cloves, grated

½ teaspoon grated peeled fresh ginger

½ teaspoon salt

½ teaspoon ground black pepper

1½ pounds (700 g) boneless chicken thighs, cut into bite-sized pieces

Vegetable oil, for frying

2⅓ cups (315 g) tempura flour

⅓ cup (40 g) Korean pancake mix*

3 tablespoons cold water

YANGNUM (KOREAN BBQ) SAUCE

1 cup (340 g) corn syrup or honey

¾ cup (150 g) granulated sugar

¼ cup (60 g) gochugaru (Korean red chile powder)

¼ cup (60 g) gochujang (Korean red chile paste)

¼ cup (60 g) ketchup

¼ cup (60 ml) soy sauce

3 tablespoons minced garlic

2 teaspoons minced peeled fresh ginger

Sesame seeds

*Substitute with all-purpose flour, more tempura flour, or potato starch if Korean pancake mix cannot be found.

1. To make the fried chicken, combine the sake, garlic, ginger, salt and pepper, in a large mixing bowl and add the chicken. Marinate in the refrigerator for at least 1 hour, but overnight is preferable.

2. Pour about 4 to 5 inches (10 to 13 cm) oil into a deep pot and heat over medium-high heat to about 325°F (165°C).

3. Combine ⅓ cup (45 g) tempura flour, the pancake mix, and the water in a bowl. Shake off or drain excess marinade from the chicken and coat with batter. Add the remaining 2 cups (270 g) tempura flour to a separate bowl or dish and coat the battered chicken for extra crispiness.

4. In batches, drop the chicken into the oil and fry until golden brown, 5 to 7 minutes. Be careful not to overcrowd the oil. Remove and place on a cooling rack or paper towels to drain.

5. Raise the oil temperature to 350°F (180°C). Fry all the chicken a second time until crispy and golden brown, 3 to 5 minutes. Remove and drain on the cooling rack or paper towels.

"Imagine if people had Korean fried chicken at baseball games, instead of hotdogs!"

6. To make the yangnum sauce, combine all the ingredients with 1 cup (240 ml) water in a medium saucepan and bring to a simmer over medium heat. Simmer to reduce and thicken, 4 to 5 minutes.

7. To serve, toss the fried chicken in the yangnum sauce and sprinkle with sesame seeds.

ACKNOWLEDGMENTS

John:

First and foremost, immeasurable thanks to all the past, present, and future vendors who make the Queens Night Market what it is. We are forever indebted to your passion, your dedication, your hard work, your talents, and the stories you share with all of us. The event certainly would not exist without you. And many thanks to their families, friends, and staff who support them.

Second, endless gratitude to the volunteers: Kyle Wong; Sharon Medina-Chavez; Rena Lee; Sarah Choi; Christine, Pascal and Olivia Guillotin; and Monty Stevens. The Queens Night Market would not exist without you, either. Thank you for sharing the vision, refining it, adding to it—and for the friendships forged over the countless Saturdays you've so graciously and generously donated to this project.

Thanks also to Charles Sturges, Merlin Pina-Sturges, Jeffrey Silber, and Ethan Frisch for your volunteer contributions. Thanks to Peter Burns for lifting tents with me for all these years. Thanks also to Felix Garcia, Mike McGuire, Sean Rooney, Maya Chavez, and Sebastian Chavez for sticking around through all the ups and downs.

Thank you to Greg Ho and Linda Sanchez, Yang Zhao, and Laure Athias, and Stéphane Harel—and, by proxy, my goddaughters Tessa and Tsipora—for your support, and for believing in me and the project. Thanks also to my parents (Lucy and David), my brothers (Paul and Solomon), and my friends (especially Marco and Wally) who encouraged me and acted as sounding boards over the years.

Thanks to all the DJs, musicians, and performing artists who have entertained us, challenged us, broadened our horizons, and brought so much energy to the Queens Night Market—and who did it *pro bono* for the first few years.

Thank you to all the New Yorkers, out-of-towners, and tourists who have come to support the idea, the project, and the vendors, helping us to build a community space that really reflects, represents, and celebrates NYC. Thanks to the New York Hall of Science, and to Dan Wempa and Jennifer Brunjes, for being such great and accommodating landlords.

Thanks to The Experiment for holding my hand throughout the process, for editing and focusing my rambling words, and ultimately for helping us share these vendors' stories. Thanks to Europa Content for approaching me in the first place, turning a first-time book proposal into something that would ultimately turn into this book. Thanks to John Taggart for all the wonderful photography documenting the food and people in this remarkable adventure.

And finally, thanks to my wife and coauthor, Storm, for everything.

Storm:

First, thank you to Columbia University's Oral History Master of Arts (OHMA) program for accepting me, teaching me, and indulging my natural tendency to overthink every little decision—while also making sure I actually got my big Queens Night Market Vendor Stories Oral History Project up and running. My OHMA professors Amy Starecheski, Bill McAllister, Zoë West, and Mary Marshall Clark have inspired me, challenged me, and encouraged me at various stages of the project—and so have some of my OHMA cohorts; Nora Waters even conducted an interview in Spanish for the project and helped edit Maximina Alvarado's chapter in this book.

Thank you, Doug Boyd and the Nunn Center for Oral History at the University of Kentucky, for offering the Queens Night Market Vendor Stories Oral History Project a permanent home, where these stories will educate and inspire many more than just those who read this book.

Thank you to all the Queens Night Market vendors who have taken the time to share their unique stories with me, sometimes even in their homes, despite busy schedules—and occasional technical hiccups, as I hone my one-woman film crew skills. . . . Filmmakers/QNM vendors Helena and Daniel (see page 153) even gave me an extra C-stand from their garage to add to my minimal, subway-ready equipment haul. . . . Thanks, guys!

Thanks to Charlie Nieland and BK Media Studio for helping me figure out studio recording logistics when home recording wasn't an option, and Deborah Wasserman: I would surely have many fewer oral histories recorded by now if you hadn't so generously loaned me use of your Woodside art studio as an interview location when I was in a pinch last August: *Muito obrigada!*

Thank you to my parents, William and Wendy Garner, for instilling in me—from the beginning—a deep curiosity about the whole world and all its people and cultures and languages and cuisines, for making me try all new foods at least *three times* before deciding if I like it, and for showing me, by example, how any chance encounter can become a life-changing conversation, especially when sharing stories over food.

Thank you to my cats, Attila and Spacebar, whose endless, fluffy lap-purrs are always a great comfort when one has to miss out on NYC fun with friends to stay home and write a book. . . .

Thank you to all our friends and family for forgiving our scarcity since the wedding. No, we didn't get lost on a long, luxuriant honeymoon, but we did put our heads together and drum up this book! We'll rejoin society soon—promise.

Thank you to The Experiment team. From our first conversation with Matthew, I knew our uncategorizable little book idea had found its home. Liana and Beth, you both just immediately *got* what we were up to—in every respect—and ran with it, honing your incredible skill-sets on our project as it developed. You patiently and exactly realized our dreams, beyond our imaginations, and I can't thank you enough.

John, love: We're good.

INDEX

ADDITIONAL PHOTO CREDITS

ABOUT THE AUTHORS

JOHN WANG was born and raised in Texas, but his love affair with night markets started during the childhood summers he spent visiting Taiwan. A graduate of Yale's law and business school (and triple-major from the University of Michigan), John quit his high-paying M&A attorney job at a premier law firm after paying off his student loans and, in 2015, pursued his dream of creating what came to be the Queens Night Market. Now in its sixth year, the popular event averages nearly fifteen thousand visitors on summer Saturdays—and has welcomed over one million visitors since its inception. Learn more about the Queens Night Market at queensnightmarket.com.

DC-born, Paris-raised, and based in New York City since working on her first La Mama, ETC theater production in 2006, **STORM GARNER** is a multi-disciplined artist—writer, filmmaker, designer, actor, musician—with a BA in nonfiction creative writing from Columbia University and current student in Columbia's oral history master's program. She created the video for the Queens Night Market's first Kickstarter campaign and the stories included in this book are derived from her long-form interviews with participating vendors for her thesis *The Queens Night Market Vendor Stories Oral History Project*, which will be publicly archived at the Louie B. Nunn Center for Oral History.

They married in March 2019.